UNDER MY HAT

Under My Hat

SALLY BERKOVIC

Dear Tamara,
hope you
enjoy the book!
Regards
[signature]

JOSEPH'S BOOKSTORE

Published by Joseph's Bookstore

TEMPLE FORTUNE • LONDON

First published in Great Britain in 1997
by Joseph's Bookstore, 2 Ashbourne Parade,
1257 Finchley Road, Temple Fortune,
LONDON NW11 OAD

A catalogue record for this title is available
from the British Library

ISBN 1 901611 00 0

Typeset by Antony Gray
Printed and bound in Great Britain by
MPG Books Ltd, Bodmin, Cornwall

*This book is dedicated to the
future of my cherished daughters,
Avigayil Chava Zehava and Elisheva Rivka,
and to the past of their beloved grandparents,
in whose blessed memory they were named,
Ted and Eva (Weiss) Berkovic and
Louis and Gertie (Segal) Fishburn*

Acknowledgements

My father used to say, 'What is mine is yours, what is yours is yours.' Only later did I learn that in the *Pirkei Avot*, Ethics of the Fathers, this is considered the voice of a pious person (Chapter 5, verse 13). Each person who helped me create this book also practised what my father said. They gave their support, counsel and knowledge, yet asked for nothing in return. All I can do is offer words of gratitude.

The world needs more *shadchanim*, more matchmakers. They are God's little elves, for without them, we do not meet the people who are destined to change our lives. Two *shadchanim* were central to this book. Sally Bassat Gillis kindly introduced me to my husband, and without him the story would be incomplete. Her intuition and persistence were impressive and it is a pleasure to thank her publicly.

Gail Sandler thoughtfully introduced me to Michael Joseph a year or so before I started to write this book. Without him, this book would have remained as scribbled notes in my daughters' nappy bag. He has been actively involved in the book at every stage, and always pushes me to stretch the limits of my own thinking.

When I told my childhood friends, now equally distibuted between Melbourne and Israel, that this book was a personal story, international phone calls, e-mails, faxes and letters were all concerned with one thing: 'Am I in it?' Now they will have to read the book to find out, but whatever they think I am saying about them, each one knows that their friendship, support, affection and humour has sustained me from afar.

My little brother Eugene, who suddenly grew up into an eminently sensible man, continues to be a beloved and caring presence in my life.

In Australia, Sam Lipski, the editor of the *Australian Jewish News*, gave me the motivation I needed to pursue my writing interests. He created the opportunity for me to go to New York, and after each article I sent him, he would fax me back a compliment. He was one of the first people to tell me that what I wrote made him laugh, and many of the issues discussed in this book were first explored in the regular column I write for his paper.

Wendy Weeks, now Senior Lecturer in Social Work at Melbourne University, originally employed me as a Senior Tutor in Social Work at Phillip Institute in 1987. From my first interview, she took an active interest in my intellectual development and respected my commitment to issues of Jewish identity and communal life. Fortuitously, she visited England just as I was struggling with the structure of this book. She sensitively read and commented on what I had written, thus helping me to consolidate and clarify what I was thinking.

In New York, Barbara Ribakove gave me two treasured years when she welcomed me into her apartment, her social activism and her community. She also conveniently came to England during an early draft of this book, and spent time reading the draft and making sensible and forthright comments, challenging my perception of some of my experiences in New York.

Renana Meyers became a buddy from the first time we met, and she generously gave me practical advice based on her experience in publishing. Her astute, intelligent reading of contemporary literature and her warmth and heartfelt enthusiasm for everything I do continues to be tremendously encouraging.

Susan Weidman Schneider, editor of *Lilith* magazine, introduced me to a parallel world of women writing about their Judaism and searching for spirituality in ways that I learnt to appreciate. I have the greatest respect for her judgement and boundless optimism which is a true gift to those around her.

When I came to London to meet my husband-to-be, my dear friend and former Jerusalem flatmate, Lisa Clayton, made arrangements for me to stay with her parents, Zena and David, who graciously welcomed me in for a couple of weeks. When they had to go away, and it looked like this romance thing would take a while longer than expected, Judy and Ronnie Usiskin offered me a place which I now regard as my other London home. Both families have continued to welcome Jonathan and me into their families, and Judy Usiskin, in particular, has become a sympathetic 'sounding board' on matters great and small, and a wonderful source of intelligent, motherly advice. She has devoted the last few years to the important work of Jewish Women's Aid, and I want to thank her for reading over the sections on domestic violence.

Sharon Lee, a brave woman who has pioneered women's prayer groups in England and co-founded the Jewish Women's Network, brought me into the coterie of dynamic women involved with important issues which are sometimes marginalised by the 'establishment'. Her generosity with her time, friendship and hospitality have helped me to understand the peculiarities of Anglo-Jewry.

I knew when I met Valerie Monchi that the heavens were smiling on me. She has become a great pal who gave me the confidence to pursue this book idea. Since we first met in a seedy felafel bar about a month after I came to London, we have spoken of most things under the sun. Her sharp intellect and philosophical bent often gives me a new way of looking at things and it has been a treat and pleasure to have her around.

Thanks also to Dr Adrienne Baker who read and commented on the section on Jewish divorce laws, Sandra Blackman who shared her impressive collection of newspaper clippings on *agunot* (Jewish women unable to obtain a Jewish divorce from their husbands), Nicky Goldman who shared her research on *bat mitzvah* ceremonies, Jeremy Schonfield who made carefully detailed comments on the book and Esra Kahn at Jews' College Library who kindly located several references. Eva Hoffman generously read the penultimate draft, and her constructive comments helped me complete the book.

Marilyn Branston and Sophie Levy at Joseph's Bookstore never lost their sense of humour when I pestered them. They were patient and helpful beyond the call of duty and each had an inspired moment: Marilyn suggested the title of the book and Sophie thought of the image for the book's cover.

I have been blessed with an uxorious husband, Jonathan Fishburn, whose tender concern for my happiness, intellectual integrity and scholarly interests, wicked sense of the absurd and unconditional support for everything I do are a constant source of delight.

The author and publisher wish to thank the following for permission to quote material:

Jonathan David Publishers, 68–22 Eliot Avenue, Middle Village, NY 11379, for *Jewish Way in Death and Mourning*; Greenwood Press, Connecticut, for *Henrietta Szold: Her Life and Letters*; Jewish Publication Society, Philadelphia, for Grossman and Haut: *Daughters of the King*; Victor Gollancz for Betty Friedan: *The Femine Mystique*: KTAV Publishing House, Hoboken, NJ 07030-7205 for Wolowelsky: *Women, Jewish Law and Modernity*; Schocken Books for Heschel: *On Being a Jewish Feminist* and Dawidowicz: *Golden Tradition*; and the Free Press for Sylvia Barack Fishman: *A Breath of Life*.

Glossary

agunah (pl. *agunot*)   a woman whose husband will not give her a Jewish divorce

akeret habayit   lit. cornerstone of the home. The term used to praise women who are devoted to their families.

aliyah   receiving an honour to say a blessing on the *Torah*. It also means to 'go up' and live in Israel.

ba'al teshuvah (f. *ba'alat teshuvah*, m. pl. *ba'alei teshuvah*, f. pl *ba'alot teshuvah*)   a person who chooses to become Orthodox, as opposed to someone who grew up in an Orthodox home

bar mitzvah   lit. son of commandment. At thirteen, a boy is required to fulfil his obligations; he usually reads a *Torah* portion to celebrate.

bat mitzvah   lit. daughter of commandment. At twelve, a girl is required to fulfil her obligations; she usually does not read a *Torah* portion to celebrate.

Beth Din   rabbinical court

bimah   raised platform in the synagogue from which the *Torah* is read aloud

birkat hagomel   thanksgiving prayer said after being in danger – for instance, after giving birth

bittel zman   a waste of time

bris/brit   circumcision, done eight days after a baby boy's birth

BT   abbreviation for *ba'al teshuvah*, see above

chagim   Jewish festivals

challah   bread eaten on Sabbath

Chanukah   eight-day 'festival of lights', celebrating the victory of the Maccabees over the Greeks more than two thousand years ago

Chassidism   a religious movement that began in eighteenth-century Eastern Europe, and originally placed less emphasis on formal *Talmud* study, focusing more on joyful prayer and piety. Each Chassidic group has its own *rebbe*, or spiritual guide, its folklore about the *rebbe* and particular customs. Nowadays *Chassidim* are regarded as part of the ultra-Orthodox community.

chuppah   bridal canopy

davenning   praying

dvar Torah   informal homiletical sermon reflecting on some aspect of the *Torah*

ervah   naked, erotic, illicit

frum   observant, religious

gabbai/gabbai'it   man/woman who organises the synagogue services

gemach   charitable fund for goods and money

get   Jewish divorce bill

goy   non-Jewish man

halachah/halachic   Jewish law, relating to legal decisions

hamotzi   the blessing said before eating bread

heimishe   slang for Orthodox

hevrah kadishah   burial society

Kabbalah   Jewish mysticism

Kaddish   mourner's prayer

kallah   bride

ketubah   wedding contract

Kiddush   blessing over the wine

kippah (pl. *kippot*)   skullcap

kollel   seminary for advanced *Talmud* study, usually for married men

kosher/kashrut   fulfils the requirement of dietary laws

mamzer (pl. *mamzerim*)   someone born of an adulterous relationship

Mazal Tov!   Good Luck!

mechitzah separation between men and women in the
  synagogue
Megillat Esther Scroll of Esther read on the holiday of *Purim*
menorah candelabra used on *Chanukah*
mensch a decent bloke
mikveh ritual bath
mincha afternoon prayers
minyan quorum of ten men (in non-Orthodox communities, a
  quorum is ten people)
mitzvah (pl. *mitzvot*) commandment
naches joy, pleasure
naarishkeit superficiality, an emphasis on material possessions
nebbish nerdy
niddah ritually unclean, usually referring to a menstruating
  woman
pas nisht 'It's just not done!'
Pesach Passover Festival
poskim/poskot male/female legal arbiters
Purim Festival of Lots, celebrating the saving of the Jews from
  their adversaries, as recounted in the Scroll of Esther
rebbetzen rabbi's wife
Rosh Hashanah Jewish New Year
Rosh Hodesh New Moon signalling the beginning of the new
  month
sandek he who holds the baby about to be circumcised
schleppers the people who do the 'dirty work'
seder meal eaten on Passover
Sefer Torah the scroll of the Bible
Shabbat Sabbath – Saturday
shalom zachor 'welcoming of a son' celebration, held on first
  Friday night after the birth of a baby boy
shaytel wig
shaytel macher wig maker

shidduch/shadchan   potential marriage partner/one who makes
   marriages

shiksa   non-Jewish woman

shivah   first seven days of mourning after a funeral

shloshim   first thirty days of mourning after a funeral

shtetl   small Eastern European town or village

shtiebl   a small informal synagogue

shul   synagogue

sitzfleish   patience

smichah   rabbinical ordination

taharat hamishpachah   laws relating to sexual conduct within
   marriage

tallit   prayer shawl

Talmud   oral law which expounds upon the *Torah*. It was
   compiled into thirty-six volumes and is the core-text of
   rabbinic Judaism. Contemporary legal decisions are based on
   precedents in the *Talmud*.

techinot   prayers composed mainly by women mostly in the
   seventeenth and eighteenth centuries

tefillin   phylacteries used during the morning prayers

Torah   Pentateuch, Five Books of Moses

trop   special musical cantillation for reading the *Torah*

yahrzeit   anniversary of a person's death

yeshivah   institution for study of Jewish texts

yizkor   memorial service for the deceased

Yom Kippur   Day of Atonement

yomtov   festival

zogerin   women prayer leader

Preface

You are asleep now. You insisted, as usual, that six books, Humpty-Dumpty and four odd socks accompanied you to bed. It is a small price to pay for the next ninety, noiseless minutes. Your father has taken your baby sister for a walk so that I can sit at my desk. This is my time. My time to think, to read, to write. Although I travel far in these ninety minutes, I always come back to the moment you were born. I was no one's daughter when they lifted you, all bloodied and shocked, out of my abdominal cavity, for both my parents had died. I was so used to being self-reliant that I had lost any capacity to feel like a dependent daughter. Now that I am learning to see the world through your eyes, I am thinking like a daughter again. You bring my mother back into the room.

She was born in 1937, the only child of my grandparents, Orthodox Jews from Bratislava in Slovakia. During World War II, my grandparents and my mother managed to hide in various places, and ended up in Australia in the late 1940s. A shadow of sadness always hung around my grandparents, but they never spoke about their experiences during the war, save for my grandmother's occasional outbursts about how terrible 'things' had been. My grandfather was a devout Jew who attended the synagogue regularly, though my grandmother refused to go, even on the Day of Atonement, the holiest day of the Jewish calendar. She kept a *kosher* home, and was quite happy to let my grandfather do as he pleased; but for her, the synagogue and public rituals were irrelevant. She claimed that as a child, she never went to the synagogue and never learnt to follow the service. When my mother grew up, she repeated the same mantra.

It was left to my father to take me to the synagogue and hide me under his flowing prayer-shawl. He came from an Orthodox family in a small farming village near the town of Michalovche, in

Slovakia. My father, who survived Auschwitz, always said he wanted to come to Australia after the war because it was 'the end of the world'. He also arrived in the late 1940s, and once there, neither my father nor my mother ever left Australia. Whenever I complained that the front-page news stories were mainly about sports, my father used to say, 'That's what I love about Australia. You should be grateful to live in a country that only cares about sport.'

My father never understood why I wanted to travel.

'What's to see? I've seen Europe, there's nothing to see.'

'But, dad,' I implored, 'it's fascinating. Different people, different cultures. There's more to life than Melbourne, you know.'

'I *know* better than you can imagine. Here, Melbourne, is life.'

Melbourne's Jewish community had such a high ratio of Holocaust survivors that I was seventeen years old before I became friendly with someone whose parents were actually Australian-born Jews. Our extended family consisted of my uncle, my father's brother, and his family, his cousin, other relatives by marriage, and their children, my contemporaries. We were indulged children, unceasingly loved and safe from physical harm.

The life I lead as an Orthodox Jewish woman is very different from that of my mother (your grandmother) and my grandmother (your great-grandmother). Although it looks somewhat similar – a *kosher* kitchen, Sabbath and holiday festivities, contact with relatives and friends in Israel and men departing for the synagogue – I have had experiences and opportunities which make it very different.

First, I have never suffered. I like to think I suffered – teenage existential angst, career dilemmas, boyfriend dramas (or lack thereof) and spiritual crises – but this was nothing compared to the wartime experiences of my mother and my father in Europe. My relationship to Judaism is one step removed from the traumatic complications of the Holocaust, so I have not suffered directly for being Jewish. Fifty years after the war, my uncle, who also survived Auschwitz, said to me in his beautiful dining-room adorned with original paintings and silver ornaments, 'When they treat you like vermin, you start to believe you really are vermin. In a way, that feeling never leaves you.'

It often seemed that my uncle's role was to articulate the thoughts my father shared but could not bring himself to voice. Yet I could never have imagined that my father really felt like vermin. Then I remembered that he would wear the same pair of shoes until the soles were literally falling off. I remembered that he would suffer years of back pain and complain so rarely that when he did we knew it was serious.

'Pain? What do you know about pain? This is not pain,' he gently chided me if I suggested he take a day off work. Off he went, to stand for another twelve hours making sandwiches for hungry workers.

'Hungry? What do they know about hunger?' he laughed to himself as he buttered white waspy bread for the ravenous men in their business suits jostling to be served first.

How did this make him feel about being a Jew? How did suffering for being a Jew affect his self-esteem and the messages he gave my brother and me about our heritage and faith? I never understood the possibility of a connection between suffering and self-esteem until I was an adult and so, as a child, my view of Judaism was uncomplicated and simply the source of many memorable happy occasions within the family. As my parents put my needs and those of my brother first, I thought being Jewish was essentially about being in a family where parents loved their children.

Second, I have had the opportunity to learn about Judaism. I can make informed decisions about my religious practices. I have teachers and role models I can turn to when I have questions and issues. I was privileged to spend time in Israel and America, studying with scholars whom I respect and acquiring some of the skills required to understand Judaism's primary texts and sources. I have so much more to learn, but it is comforting that I know whom to ask and where to go.

My mother did not have any opportunities for a Jewish education. Although our home was infused with a strong Jewish identity, and we celebrated the holidays, the strongest memory I have of my mother's Judaism is her lack of a Jewish education and her non-participation in the life of the synagogue. Perhaps that is why she always seemed uninterested in the minutiae of ritual. I only remember my mother in the synagogue at family *bar mitzvahs*, when her absence would have upset the family.

'I'm not going to *shul* on *Yom Kippur*,' my mother would announce every year. 'I don't know what's going on. I can't follow the service. Why do I need to sit there with all those women in fur coats talking about nothing? They don't know what's going on either.'

Although I always admired my mother's uncompromising lack of hypocrisy, sometimes I would have liked us to sit there, mother and daughter, together, in the synagogue. I guess that is why I like to take both of you to our synagogue. I want you to remember that your mother took you to the synagogue. We went together.

Third, your father is a rabbi. After high school, he studied for two years at Gateshead Yeshivah in England, and then spent four years at Mir Yeshivah in New York, where he obtained his *smichah*, rabbinical ordination. Your father is an unorthodox Orthodox rabbi; probably for that reason, he chose not to practise as a communal rabbi. He is ahead of his time in his own quiet way. He is a scholar who, except for cuddling his family, prefers the company of books to that of most other people. Your lives will be enhanced by his wisdom and his books.

The level of Jewish knowledge that you have in your home is so vastly different from that in mine when I was a child. My father had a Jewish education in his village, but this was interrupted. Although he remembered how to read Hebrew and could easily follow the prayer services, after the war he never formally studied Judaism again. He, too, except for cuddling his family, preferred the company of books to that of most other people. I remember him skimming the newspapers proficiently, and reading *Crime and Punishment*, when he had come to Australia without a word of English; my mind boggles to imagine how great a *Talmud* scholar he, and many others like him, might have become.

Finally, I feel as if I am much more in conflict than my mother or my grandmother were. At this age, I didn't expect to be. When I was about sixteen, I thought that by the time I was 'grown up' (defined at that point by marriage and children) I would have sorted out the answers to all those 'meaning of life' questions to do with faith and reason, good and evil, tradition and modernity. After all, I reasoned, I would be not be able to get married, raise children and perpetuate a lifestyle if I was not convinced that the sort of Judaism I had arrived at was the 'right' choice for me and the most satisfying way of leading my life.

Hence, it's a miracle I ever did marry. When I did, I was in my thirties and very much aware I still did not have the answers. Somehow, I had put together a rationale, a sort of party manifesto recognising that grown-up life is actually more about conflict than certainty, about tension more than resolution. Although there are religious people of various faiths who believe in absolutes, arguing that their religion is the absolute truth, I do not share this view about my Judaism. The luxury of a good university education, travelling, a circle of like-minded peers struggling with many of the same issues, and a varied career have forced me to engage actively with the modern world and in so doing to reject the possibility of being fundamentally certain about any dogma. I enjoy the intellectual freedom of the modern world and its permission to think independently and critically.

Yet, although I have more escape routes and alternatives to a traditional life than my mother could have imagined, I choose to stay in Orthodoxy. Why? It is what I inherited and it belongs to me. I am committed to the ennobling elements of the religion: a vast, rich literature, a dramatic history and strong collective memory, a serious concern for ethics and justice, a dignified framework for daily living and an overriding sense of community. I have been enriched by constructing a Jewish identity, developing a Jewish consciousness, and sharing codes and language with Jews around the world. I love the fact that I have turned up in a community and been welcomed to a Friday-night dinner with virtual strangers, and that after playing Jewish geography for fifteen minutes, have discovered mutual friends and possibly a family connection.

However, I am deeply troubled because most of the Orthodox world is failing to address the fundamental conflicts and contradictions in the modern Jewish woman's life: a life influenced by unparalleled access to the secular world and the impact of feminist thought and action. Unlike those in a minority of ultra-Orthodox communities, Orthodox people like me want our daughters to be players in the modern world. We encourage them to aspire to Oxbridge or Ivy League universities and graduate as professionals. Yet, when the Orthodox establishment does not provide the same opportunities for its girls to reach their intellectual and spiritual potential as its boys, the whole community colludes to tell its little girls that it is OK to expect less. We give our little girls permission to underachieve. This, from a bunch of overachievers obsessed with knowledge – Go figure!

Unless Orthodoxy can adapt to the changing realities of the modern woman's life, it will be insulting and irrelevant to both of you. While your father and I will endeavour to give both of you the best secular and Jewish education possible, the Orthodox establishment risks losing you and thousands of other young, intelligent and competent Jewish women. I can understand those women in England who grew up in Orthodox families and now belong to a Masorti (roughly equivalent to the American Conservative movement) or Reform synagogue. I can identify with the Orthodox women in America and Israel who could no longer live with the dissonance and have abandoned Orthodoxy. A few have become Conservative rabbis, but most of them have drifted away altogether from observant Judaism. It hurts to admit it, but if either of you move away from Orthodoxy as it currently exists in most of the world, I would understand.

Orthodox law is concerned with the nature of 'obligation', and men are obligated to perform certain rituals such as prayer and study. Although women are obliged to carry out a smaller number of rituals, they also have the option to choose to participate in rituals they are not obliged to perform. Over time, this choice has often been conveniently forgotten by some rabbinical leaders and the rules distorted to exclude women. Over time, women have been denied their inheritance. I want to reclaim your inheritance and I hope this book will help both of you understand what is possible within Jewish tradition, and how I have sought to bring a woman's understanding to the daily experience of being a committed Orthodox Jew.

Judaism gives me a moral anchor in the world which embodies my relationship to God and my relationship to humanity. Clearly, one can be a moral person without Judaism's prescriptions, but given that I inherited this code, it gives me a place to start. I think that personal relationships with God should remain just that, and I am uncomfortable with bringing God into the political arena, the classroom, the courtroom or any other public government space. Nevertheless, I would like to think that the values reflected in a just and compassionate society are those that are reflected in an individual's relationship with God.

There are many ethical and moral Jews who perform great deeds of kindness, yet they regard themselves as irreligious because they perform no rituals. I do not think of them that way: for me, those acts of kindness are religious rituals and mean they have made choices about which aspects of Judaism they are observing, just as the most ritualistic Jew makes a different sort of choice.

Other Jews who observe many traditional practices belong to the Reform, Conservative or Reconstructionist branches of Judaism. These terms are less than two hundred years old – Reform was established in early 1800s, Conservative in the late 1800s and Reconstructionist in the 1920s – and unfortunately, I think that these labels have been detrimental to the cohesion of the community. Although these labels reflect genuine theological differences and varying positions on the nature of *halachah*, Jewish law, I would like to see us in a post-denominational community, where doctrinaire theological positions have less importance than the actual acts of a Jewish life. I am more interested in Jews observing Judaism, because I believe that the very acts of observing Judaism will preserve our Jewish heritage. It is very difficult to pass on a feeling of being Jewish, or some sort of distilled message about the spirit of Judaism. Yet, how do we make the living words of the *Torah* meaningful in our times? It has to be about acts of *being* Jewish: the rituals, traditions and folklore; and the impact of *thinking* Jewish: communal responsibility, humanitarian compassion and turning the texts over and over. God does not have exclusive membership in any of these branches of Judaism, but rather we manifest God, and religious sensibilities, in all those aspects of being and thinking as a Jew.

This may sound a trifle Alice-in-Wonderlandish because recently world Jewry has been obsessed with defining the religious status of a Jew. There has been an emphasis on proving one's credentials and in demonstrating a belief in *Torah min Hashamayim*, the view that God revealed the *Torah* once on Mount Sinai, and that the *Torah* cannot be changed or adapted to suit modern sensibilities. This view is just too simple for me; fortunately, there are far greater scholars and theologians who have been struggling with the meaning of revelation for centuries.[1] I would like to sound more profound. I'd like to be able to say that I have developed a sophisticated theological response and a philosophical approach to the essential questions of the twentieth century. But I would be lying. I don't know why bad things happen to good people, and I don't trust anyone who claims to have an answer.

However, I do realise that any challenge to Orthodoxy raises the fundamental theological issue of revelation. Recently Dr Tamar Ross, senior lecturer in the philosophy department at Bar-Ilan University asked, 'What sort of God excludes women's voices and experiences?' I had to stop and think. Does a modern feminist critique of *Torah* undermine the traditional meaning of revelation? Dr Ross suggested a notion of successive revelations which does not seek to replace the traditional concept of *Torah min Hashamayim*.

I believe that the unfreezing of the simplistic dictation metaphor does not require a non-Orthodox framework ... There are on-going hearings of the voice at Sinai ... feminism is a new revelation and should be viewed not as a problem, but as an agenda to be incorporated into Jewish life.[2]

[1] See 'The Condition of Jewish Belief', a symposium compiled by the editors of *Commentary* magazine, American Jewish Committee, New York, 1966 (reprinted, Jason Aronson, Northvale, NJ, 1989), in which thirty-eight rabbis and theologians (all male) discuss the issues of revelation and belief in God.
[2] Ross, T., 'Women and Learning: New Visions', lecture presented at the International Conference on Feminism and Orthodoxy, 16 March 1997, New York City, USA

Clearly, these ideas merit a book of their own, but rabbis need not fear the Orthodox women who love the tradition so much that they are willing to confront the theological problems for Orthodox women with intellectual integrity, while still assiduously adhering to the *halachah*, Jewish law.

As a woman and a mother, I feel a responsibility to grapple with the tradition for the sake of my daughters. I stay within the Orthodox tradition because it is still the normative experience, and I believe that its essence most accurately reflects the teachings of Jewish law and lore. However, in the modern world, if I want my daughters to appreciate its smells, colours and textures, I have to find a place where elements of modern life such as equal opportunity, shared power in family structures and a critique of male authority can be combined with a commitment to improve and maximise women's participation in all aspects of Judaism within the boundaries of Jewish law. This will be a new place where women and men must grapple with the impact of modernity, feminism and gender relations on our self-perception as Orthodox people. It's a place where only the brave and the thick-skinned will travel. Do you want to come on the ride?

I am telling you about my struggles, but I believe they are the same as those of many other women caught between the pull of a powerful tradition and the tug of an inviting modern life. For me, they are the intellectual, emotional and religious struggles born of this extraordinary time of change in the lives of Jewish women. Some of this is reflected in recent scholarly books and the rise in Jewish women's studies courses.[3] As your mother, I wonder what impact these changes will have on your choices in the future. How will Jewish life be so different for you?

---

3 Brewer, J. Scherer, *Sex and the Modern Jewish Woman: An Annotated Bibliography*, Biblio Press, Fresh Meadows, 1986; Cantor, A., *The Jewish Woman 1900–1985: A Bibliography*, Biblio Press, New York, 1987; Hamelsdorf, O. and Adelsberg, S., *Jewish Women and Jewish Law Bibliography*, Biblio Press, Fresh Meadows, 1980; Masnik, A., *The Jewish Woman: An Annotated Selected Bibliography 1986–1993*, Biblio Press, New York, 1996. Each bibliography lists hundreds of scholarly books and articles about Jewish women. Baskin, J. and Tenenbaum, S. (eds), *Gender and Jewish Studies: A Curriculum Guide*, Biblio

So I am writing this book for both of you. My mother died when she was only forty-two and, as I approach that age, I am getting paranoid. I was nineteen at the time, so I have memories and a picture of her in my head. But now I realise how much I don't know about her life. I was too self-obsessed and fraught with angst to find out more about her. Suddenly, it was too late. I have only begun to comprehend what I am missing since I became a mother myself, almost three years ago.

This gap in my own personal history compelled me to write this book for both of you. If I can give you some of my history, I will be forced to remember as much as I can about my mother. If I tell you about myself, you will have a history. I don't want you to experience the same painful void as I have and I hope this book will help you understand me. One day, you might whisper between yourselves, 'Why does she make us brush our teeth . . . twice?' 'How can she just keep reading her newspaper while we are pulling each other's hair? Doesn't she notice?' 'What did daddy see in her?' 'What is she complaining about now?' 'Why doesn't she do something about it?' 'What is under mummy's hat?'

If you ask those questions, I hope you will find the answers in your memories of me, and in the following pages. I hope that anyone eavesdropping on this conversation with my daughters will find that some of the questions are relevant to their own lives. Perhaps we can find the solutions together.

Press, New York, 1994, lists thirty syllabi with a distinct emphasis on Jewish women's experiences which have been taught in American colleges. The Jewish Theological Seminary has recently introduced a Master of Arts degree in Jewish women's studies.

Chapter 1

'Mummy, where your mummy?' You are nearly three, my big little girl, and it is the first time you have asked me about my mother, your grandmother. I am not sure how to answer you, because neither you nor your little sister understand that you have no living grandparents.

In a strange twist to our romance, your father is also an adult orphan. We both lost one parent in our teens and the other in our early thirties. We met as orphans, and I think unconsciously that is why our mutual friend introduced us. We deeply empathised with each other's experience of loss, and shared a rootless sort of existence that freed us from any accountability to parental authority. Still, I am a little self-conscious and always imagine that people are saying, 'What a well-matched couple – their parents are dead.'

My mother died on a Friday night in May, 1980. The *Shabbat* candles were still burning when, during the meal, she stood up to get more rice from the pot. She fell down and died. As I phoned my cousin, a doctor who happened to live in the same street, my father was cradling her head, telling her that he loved her, telling her that it would be all right. When my cousin arrived, he tried to resuscitate her, urging me to call an ambulance and request an MCI. He said it wasn't looking good. It was not going to be all right. The ambulance came and the neighbours turned on their lights. But it was too late. I think about it every Friday night as I light my *Shabbat* candles, and I don't like rice served on Friday nights. She was forty-two. I was nineteen.

My father died on the last Sunday in June 1992. He was found slumped over the wheel of his car in someone's driveway. He was blocking their exit, and when they came outside, they found him. He had just been to see his cousin, and all we were able to assume was that while he was driving home, he had a pain in his chest and managed to pull over so as not to cause a serious accident. Considerate to the end. He died alone, and no one knows what his last words were. I never even found out the name of the people whose driveway he blocked. I don't really want to know.

After the police were notified of the death, they went to my father's house expecting to find a wife they would have to console. But there was no wife, there was no one. Even in death he had to suffer the indignity and embarrassment of being alone. The police told our neighbour who put them in touch with my brother and my uncle. I was living in New York at the time, and when my brother called me there at 9 a.m. on a lazy Sunday morning, I was planning last-minute details for my visit home to see my father after a year away. I was meant to be flying home in two days' time, but instead I calmly cancelled my social arrangements for the day and by five o'clock I was on a plane heading back to Melbourne. The funeral was delayed till I arrived on Tuesday morning. I will never forget that I missed my father by two days. He was sixty-five. I was thirty-one.

When I stood sobbing at my father's open grave, the years between my mother's death and my father's death compressed themselves into a single moment. It seems that between one event and the next time it happens, you find yourself at exactly the same spot. Those twelve years vanished – twelve years of old friends, new friends, study, work, achievements and travels – vanished. I felt I was still in the *shivah* week, the week of mourning, for my mother. It was one twelve-year *shivah* – I can still see the scene replaying – people who were at my mother's *shivah* reappeared as we mourned my father. A few elderly relatives had died, and there were some new friends I had made in those intervening years but, essentially, it was the same people, only with a few more wrinkles. Most of my friends still had two parents alive. Weren't they embarrassed to turn up to my home? Again.

When my father died I became an orphan. A word with such heavy connotations of loss. A tragic word. Part of me revels in the thought of being an orphan: you get so much pity, big pity, overwhelming pity, you can get high on pity. No one knows exactly what to say, and I am in control of the situation. (And all my friends know your mother likes to be in control.) But I don't really like being an orphan because it means something is terminally missing and I am always on a search.

Although my father's funeral is now a bit of a blur, one comment remains very clear. It was from a man who had known me since I was a child and should have known better. I was so stunned that I wrote it down in my diary. He came up to me and said: 'You know I really feel sorry for you. I have never seen anyone cry so hard – I didn't realise you were so emotional.'

It's always a surprise when you begin to realise that you see yourself in one way and people who you thought understood, people you believed shared your perceptions about the way you appear, betray you. You realise that they haven't a clue, and you are all alone.

As each of you were born, it was as if my parents had died all over again. That sense of being completely alone returned. My joy and excitement were buried by recurring images of their funerals. Some days I feel that motherhood is one long grieving process. I grieved as I watched with envy the boasting grandparents who came to the hospital laden with flowers, chocolates and expensive gifts for their just-born grandchildren. I listened with increasing jealousy as they made generous offers of babysitting, cooking and housecleaning. It didn't matter that both of you were beautiful and healthy, nor that your wonderful, devoted father could not do enough for me. These were mere consolation prizes. My self-pity was relentless. All I wanted was my mother to kiss me and my father to cuddle his granddaughters.

During those first unnerving weeks after giving birth, everyone else seemed to have it easier. Although I was reminded several times that I was lucky to have no overprotective or judgemental mother, or malicious and indifferent mother-in-law around to interfere, those same people had their mother drop in with a daily supply of meals, or their mother-in-law ready to take the baby for a walk in the park.

'So, when did your mother die?'

'Nearly fifteen years ago.'

'Mmm – not that I ever see my parents. My mum was meant to

come from America/Canada/South Africa/Israel' (delete as applicable) 'and visit when I had the baby, but she couldn't make it. She'll probably come in the summer.'

What was she implying? That dead equals a long aeroplane flight away? An expensive international phone bill? Is that what they teach at Jewish Finishing and Empathy School?

These are women who believe that it is worse for them than anyone else. They take the complexities of your life and turn it into an issue for them: they think they are identifying with your situation, but all they are doing is just being their usual self-centred selves. When a woman I know found out that my parents were not alive, she confessed to me that when she had children, almost thirty years before, her mother never came from South Africa to visit her in London. Sadly, the memory and pain is still so sharp that she wants to make the point that abandonment is even worse than death – they are there, they are alive, but they don't want to see you. I let her win the suffering game and didn't say anything.

When my mother died, I was a passive participant in the rituals. I was young, deferential, and relied on the authority of the presiding rabbis to handle spiritual matters. I trusted the received wisdom of my elders to guide me on the practicalities. My maternal grandparents were still alive and attention was equally divided between them (especially my grandmother), the desperate sadness of my father, who was a quiet, unassuming and gentle man, and the bewilderment of my brother and me. On reflection, I think that my brother was the most ignored – not deliberately, of course, but because there seems to be a pecking order of bereavement.

There is a very Jewish way to die. Funerals are held within twenty-four hours of the person's death, allowing the mourners to get on with their grieving work. (Only if a close relative has to travel from afar, or a person dies just before the Sabbath or a festival, may it be postponed.) The first week after the death is called the *shivah* week (after the word seven), and for seven days the home is open to all those who want to come and comfort the mourners. During this time, mourners rend an item of clothing, wear non-leather shoes, sit on low stools and cover their mirrors to discourage vanity. The front door is left open so that mourners do not have to open the door or get up to greet their visitors. There are traditional words one says to mourners, including the wish for a 'long life'. The first month is called the *shloshim* (the word *shloshim* means thirty – Hebrew is a very functional language!). During that time it is customary to refrain from shaving and listening to music, and people generally conduct themselves in a more subdued manner. The annual anniversary of a death is called a *yahrzeit* and it is customary to light a twenty-four-hour candle on that day.

At the heart of all these rituals is the recital of the *Kaddish*, the mourner's prayer. *Kaddish* is said at the funeral, in the synagogue and in the mourner's home. It is recited during the *shivah* week, and then daily during the three prayers in the morning, afternoon and evening for the first eleven months after the death of a parent. (*Kaddish* for a spouse, sibling or child is said for only thirty days.)

The *Kaddish* prayer is surprisingly not about death, but is a brief prayer which asks that God's name be 'blessed, praised, glorified, exalted, extolled, mighty, upraised and lauded'. In Orthodox settings, it can only be said when a *minyan*, a quorum of ten men, is present and they respond to the mourner with added praise of God's handiwork in this world. Women are not expected to say *Kaddish*, and in some communities women are effectively stopped from saying it, particularly in those places where women do not even go to the funeral. For Thena Kendall, this was the ultimate insult. At the cemetery for her father's funeral, she was told that she could not proceed to the grave:

> A solid mass of Orthodox gentleman blocked my way as they followed my father's coffin to his lasting resting place. However, I knew another route to the grave (which had been prepared next to my mother's) and managed to be standing alongside before the coffin was brought there. No one dared to tell me to leave. But with every clod that was thrown on to my father's coffin, another link that connected me to the Orthodox tradition was broken.[1]

[1] Kendall, T., 'Memories of an Orthodox Youth', p. 101, in Heschel, S., *On Being a Jewish Feminist*, Schocken Books, New York, 1983, 1995, pp. 96–104

When my mother died, I accepted these laws and customs unquestioningly. I was at the funeral, but I did not expect to say *Kaddish*, and did not understand why it was important. Secretly, I was relieved that *Kaddish* fell to my brother. To his credit he did it faithfully every day and I don't remember him complaining about the burden on his time or energy. As I felt I had a minor role in the unfolding drama, I never challenged the rabbi. After all, my grandparents had lost their only child and they deservedly got centre stage.

After my grandfather died in 1984, my grandmother became substantially weaker and more dependent on others. When my father died, she was almost ready to enter a nursing home. My brother was married and I was still single. So, the bereavement pecking order changed and now most of the attention focused on me. The fact that people felt sorry for me was both comforting and palpably irritating. It was bad enough that I had not seen my father for about a year, and people knew I was very close to him, but it was clear they felt sorrier for me because I was still not married. Ironically, my brother lost out again, this time because he was married with his own built-in support system.

When my father died, I was twelve years older, my cynicism was entrenched and my relationship to Judaism was different. For many years, I couldn't quite put my finger on the reasons why it seemed that my Jewish education felt homogenised and pasteur-ised. However, I began to realise that my Jewish education was ahistorical, taught as if the law had developed in a social vacuum. I never found this satisfactory, and as I began to appreciate the historical and social context of Jewish law, one of the things I learnt was that women can, in fact, say *Kaddish* and that many Orthodox women have said *Kaddish* in the past. Only social custom and a lack of education have led women to forgo the *Kaddish*.

Teachers had magically created a legal category of '*pas nisht*'. This can be translated as 'just not done', 'not appropriate', 'not fitting for Jewish women', 'nothing a Jewish woman has to bother about' or, perhaps most aptly, 'don't even think about asking the rabbi, or everyone will think you are crazy!' In practice, it means that while some action may be permitted and is fully sanctioned by

Jewish law, when it comes to women's participation, it is '*pas nisht*'.

Since I began to understand this premise of Jewish law, I have not been so intimidated by rabbinical dicta. Now I can recognise that there are various legitimate opinions which apply to different communities, but more significantly, I have become more ambivalent about my relationship to women's exclusion from public ritual. These intellectual developments were fostered while I was in New York, and occurred around the time my father died.

I discovered that the issue of a daughter saying *Kaddish* for her father first appears in the *halachic* (legal) literature in the seventeenth century in the work of Rabbi Yair Chaim Bacharach (1639–1702). He explained several reasons why legally it would be permitted but, in his final analysis, concluded that he would not allow a daughter to say *Kaddish* as it might change the accepted social custom of women not saying *Kaddish*. Clearly, it was a matter of public policy and not legal authority.[2]

However, other luminaries, including Rabbi Israel Meir Kagan (1838–1933), better known as the Chofetz Chaim, Rabbi Joseph B. Soloveitchik (1903–92), Rabbi Moshe Feinstein (1895–1986) and Rabbi Yosef Eliyahu Henkin, commented on the permissibility of a woman saying *Kaddish*, and cited anecdotal evidence of people they knew who said *Kaddish*.[3] These great *poskim*, legal authorities, made it clear in their responses that the woman must stay in the women's section in order to say *Kaddish*. Perhaps the location of the woman rather than her actual saying of the prayer was actually the contentious issue. This seems strange to me because all the Orthodox women I know who have wanted to say *Kaddish* expected to be in the women's section. Perhaps the public policy concern of the rabbis was that women wanting to say *Kaddish* might expect to say it in the men's section. This in turn, could lead to mixed seating, which in Orthodox settings is not possible.

2 Fink, R., 'The Recital of *Kaddish* by Women', *Journal of Halachah and Contemporary Society*, no. 31, Spring 1996, pp. 23–37
3 Wolowelsky, J., *Women, Jewish Law and Modernity: New Opportunities in a Post-Feminist Age*, KTAV, Hoboken, NJ, 1997, pp. 84–94, discusses these opinions and provides accounts of first-hand citings of women saying *Kaddish*.

In 1943, the *Jewish Chronicle* reported that at the memorial service for the Reverend Hyman Goodman his daughter said *Kaddish* for her father, and 'Dayan Harris M. Lazarus told the assembled company that he approved of this gracious act, it being both dutiful and logical.' The editorial of the *Jewish Chronicle* remarked :

> Would I be correct in inferring from this welcome statement that the *Beth Din*, of which Dayan Lazarus is such a valued member, sanctions the recital of the *Kaddish* by daughters, irrespective of whether there are sons, thus removing an injustice to Jewish women which has deprived them in the past of doing honour to departed parents? Perhaps such a sanction already exists, but if so I do not think it can be very widely known, otherwise I feel sure that greater advantage would be taken of it.[4]

Don't the rabbis of Orthodox synagogues know these esteemed rabbinical opinions and these publicised incidents? And if they do, why are they hiding them? Isn't that professional irresponsibility?

I thought about saying *Kaddish* on the plane home, arguing with myself and then debating the points. Even though I knew it was permissible for women to say *Kaddish*, that women must have the information to make an informed choice, and that God was waiting for the prayers of women, I was still unsure of myself. I was babbling to myself throughout the flight.

'What will everyone say?'

'I don't want to make a fuss.'

'It's Australia – what do they know about Orthodox women challenging the system?'

'I can't be bothered to take it up with the rabbi.'

'My father wouldn't expect it . . . well actually, he might quite like it.'

I realised that I barely knew the words. I'd seen them a thousand

4 *Jewish Chronicle*, 12 February 1943, cited in Goodkin, J. and Citron, J., *Women in the Jewish Community: Review and Recommendations*, Women in the Community, London, 1994, p. 74

times. I had a mental image of how they appeared on the page, but it was not a prayer that I grew up expecting to know how to say. I was expected to be silent. Women are taught to be quiet. I saw myself pick up the prayer book. I heard myself say the words. What sort of woman had I become?

During my father's *shivah* week, I said *Kaddish* in our home. During the following year, I went to the synagogue regularly to say *Kaddish*. I did not draw attention to myself, rather I said it quietly in the women's section, at the same time as the men. It was even more important for me when I returned to New York alone. Although I knew that my brother was saying *Kaddish* ten thousand miles away, I needed to say it for myself. When I think back about my reaction to my mother's death, I wanted others to believe that I was devout in the face of adversity. In those days, I thought being devout meant being silent, and I was quite prepared to sacrifice my spiritual, emotional and psychological needs to uphold a false notion of male leadership and honour. I was faking it. I wasn't devout then, I was just angry and conformist. Now I am devout because I found my voice in between the deaths of my parents.

Still, grief returns. It returns when people tell me that their mother has been on holiday for a week, and they are finding it really difficult to manage without her.

'I didn't realise how useful she is,' they laugh into the phone as I hold back my tears.

Grief makes fun of me when I see advertisements for mother and daughter competitions. I want to slash the photos of the people who win.

It returns every time people say, 'Oh it's so easy for you, you don't have to consider parents,' or, 'My in-laws are driving me crazy – they are forever wanting to come and see the baby.' Yes, they really say that.

I want to answer, 'Oh yes, it is easier for me because they are dead,' but, instead, I collude and I say, 'Yes, it must be irritating to feel invaded,' or, 'Yes, it's difficult to worry about ageing parents,' or, 'Yes, I have the freedom to decide to do things the way I want to.'

I mean who wants to make people with two healthy functioning parents feel bad?

It returns every Friday night as you both watch me light the candles which usher in the Sabbath. As I cover my eyes with my hands to say the special blessing, I peek through my fingers like a naughty schoolgirl to watch what you are doing. Can you imagine what it feels like to see Avigayil imitating me? And Elisheva squeaking with delight? Of course not, and I find myself wondering what my mother thought at that same moment when she lit her Sabbath candles when I was a child. After the blessing, I mutter a private prayer that I will survive from this Friday night to the next.

It returns when I go to *shul* for *yizkor*, the memorial prayer on the festivals. Usually, anyone who has both parents alive leaves the synagogue. As a child, I was meticulously shooed out of the *shul*. Now I wait with the other orphans until the *shul* is emptied of those with living parents. I stare at those who leave, the people-with-two-parents-alive, but they are too embarrassed to meet me eye-to-eye. I love making them feel uncomfortable. (You've got a nasty mother.)

Once, when I went to *shul* for the *yizkor* service, Elisheva was only a few weeks old. I left her in the pram at the back of the synagogue and hoped she would not be noticed. One of those people-with-two-parents-alive took Avigayil outside to play, and I just hoped Elisheva would stay sleeping. Of course, you didn't, and woke up crying just as the cantor was about to start the prayer. I had no choice but to pick you up and bring you into full view of everyone else. It was a strange moment because it is not the 'done' thing to have a baby present during these memorial prayers, nor did I actually want you to be present. At the same time, I had a gush of emotion, and it seemed right. Life moves on – the new is a reminder of the old and this renewal is what should be celebrated.

Twice a year, grief flickers at me for twenty-four hours. One candle for my mother, one for my father. On the anniversary of each of their deaths, I light a small, thick, white candle, that sits in a glass, on a piece of silver foil, near the kitchen sink. It is a Jewish candle, a symbol of the soul, and after it has finished burning, I throw the remains in the rubbish bin. But I do so tenderly, because I feel like I am throwing my parents in the bin.

Grief hovers when I remember that I missed the opportunity to say *Kaddish* for my mother, and recall the hesitation I felt before saying *Kaddish* for my father. Doesn't the grief and suffering of women count? Judaism unreservedly provides the structure for men to complete (as much as they can 'complete') their grieving, but for me, there was never that same sense of completion. I am sure that is why the birth of a boy is greeted with such relief – only a boy can be a *Kaddish'l*, the affectionate diminutive term for the son who will say *Kaddish*. Rabbi Joshua Hammerman, who performed the circumcision on his own son, recognised that 'with the birth of a *Kaddish'l*, the father hears the whisper that it is now all right to die'.[5] But where does that leave the mother? The desire for a boy is purely selfish because the son, and not the daughter, sister or wife will be guarantors of the *Kaddish*. Women rely on the goodwill of their husbands, brothers or sons to say *Kaddish* when one of their close relatives dies. Sometimes, women with no male relatives feel humiliated because they are forced to hire a man to say the prayers on their behalf. *Kaddish* can be bought at the right price.

Sociologically, *Kaddish* has an interesting effect on individuals and their families. Several men have told me that their return to Judaism was motivated by a sense of duty to say *Kaddish*. It is a common scenario: they grew up in nominally Orthodox homes, but ceased practising Jewish rituals as adults. However, when a parent died, they felt an obligation to say *Kaddish* to honour their deceased parent, and keep the living one happy. Through the process of daily attendance at the synagogue and emotional support from other people who had been through a year of saying *Kaddish*, these men felt a desire to reconnect to the community and observe Jewish rituals.

One woman recently told me that her family kept 'nothing – we didn't belong to a synagogue and we didn't even fast on *Yom Kippur*', but after her husband's mother died, he wanted to say *Kaddish* for her. He started bringing his children to the synagogue

5 Hammerman, J.,'Birth Rite', 'About Men' column *New York Times Magazine*, 13 March 1994, p. 30

on *Shabbat* mornings, he wanted to have a family *seder* on Passover and he became meticulous about fasting on *Yom Kippur*. Now, the whole family are staunch members of their local synagogue, and each member is actively involved in a religious life.

Conversely, several women have told me that they left their Orthodox synagogue when they were told that they could not say the *Kaddish* prayer after the death of a parent. At their moment of grief, their spiritual needs were ignored. Even though they found it difficult to leave the Orthodoxy of their youth, they felt so strongly about wanting to say *Kaddish* that they joined a Conservative or Reform synagogue where their need to mourn publicly was recognised. In these synagogues, they mourned not only for their parents, but it seems to me, also for the loss of their traditional upbringing which at a time of need, let them down.

You want to know why didn't I go to a Conservative or Reform *shul*? It's simple: I am used to an Orthodox service and I feel a tremendous loyalty to Orthodox tradition that is hard to walk away from. I want to say *Kaddish* the same way it has been said for centuries. Why is that so hard to understand? Why do people assume that I should be willing to compromise and go elsewhere: isn't there something a little awry that I feel the need to apologise for wanting to participate?

Why don't contemporary Orthodox rabbis understand that if they welcome the women into their synagogues to say *Kaddish*, that the women may also bring their families back to Judaism? Although a small number of Orthodox rabbis have supported women who want to say *Kaddish*, most Orthodox communities perpetuate the view that a woman saying *Kaddish* is making waves, or even worse being, 'a bit of a feminist'. The irony is that some women are more religious than their male siblings and are ready and willing to take on the obligation of *Kaddish* more seriously. Moreover, some men worry that a woman saying *Kaddish* would neglect her family. As Maurice Lamm explains, a son, rather than a daughter, has the obligation to say *Kaddish* for his parents because:

The sages in their infinite wisdom, deep human compassion,

and sharp insight into man realised only too well that the *Kaddish*, which must be recited at services before breakfast and at dinner time, could not be made compulsory for women – mothers and wives who must attend to their families. It was not prejudice, but down-to-earth practicality that insisted that daughters be exempt . . . The sages appreciated full well the equality of male and female in the realm of emotion and love, but saw the folly of legally requiring a woman, whose primary vocation is the home, to attend services morning and night.[6]

At the time of my mother's and my father's deaths, I was a single woman with no children – I had no family to attend to, no 'primary vocation' and no other responsibilities. How does the rabbi justify his position? Perhaps he, like many other men, is not fully aware how important it is to women to acknowledge their grief and participate in the rituals of mourning. Until recently, little public voice was given to the excluded woman's distress or her need for the catharsis of reciting *Kaddish* with a *minyan*. However, as women write about their experience, perhaps men will begin to comprehend the impact of their decisions to exclude women.

For example, Letty Cottin Pogrebin described the night she was rejected from the *minyan* that said *Kaddish* for her mother as

the turning point in my spiritual life . . . I could point to the *shivah* experience in my living room, say that my father sent me into the arms of feminism, and leave it at that . . . No woman who has suffered the anguish and insult of exclusion on top of the tragedy of her bereavement forgets that her humiliation was inflicted by Jewish men.[7]

In contrast, Sara Reuger took action:

Without even thinking, I joined the two men as we mumbled through the first choking *Kaddish* of the funeral service. After

6 Lamm, M., *The Jewish Way in Death and Mourning*, Jonathan David Publishing, New York, 1969, p. 166. Despite this selective comment, this is a popular and useful reference book.
7 Pogrebin, L., *Deborah, Golda and Me*, Crown, New York, 1992, p. 55

about three repetitions of the *Kaddish*, as we moved from the chapel toward the grave, the head of the *hevrah kadishah* suddenly realised that I was saying it aloud with the men. Before the next one, he ordered the men only to say it, repeating this order in Hebrew, then in Yiddish and finally in English. I looked straight through him and continued in an even louder voice. At the grave site, the same thing happened. He handed the shovel to my father to shovel some dirt into the grave, then gave it to my brother and then pointedly gave it to a male cousin. I ignored the man, bent down to scoop up some dirt with my hands, and threw it into the grave, as is required of all close relatives of the deceased, in keeping with the traditional attitude toward the reality of death. By now the man was livid, especially as he saw that he had no backing from any of my family.[8]

Other women have written about standing alone in the women's section secretly mumbling the *Kaddish*.[9] Are Orthodox women the new Marranos, the latest in a long line of crypto-Jews, forced to conceal their love of Judaism for fear of provoking the wrath of their feudal overlords?

In 1992, Chief Rabbi Dr Jonathan Sacks commissioned the Women's Review, a survey on the attitudes and practices of Anglo-Jewish women. Their frustration at being unable to say *Kaddish* echoes much of what has been written by others, but they also had practical suggestions. They requested assistance and guidance in saying *Kaddish* within accepted religious perameters. They suggested organising and publicising their own *Kaddish* support groups to accompany the female mourner, sit with her, rise with her and respond to her *Kaddish*. The *yahrzeit* was considered a 'non-event' by most women who receive a standard letter from their synagogue before a *yahrzeit*. This offers them the option of nominating a man to mark the event by proxy. Many women feel insulted by this

8 Reuger, S., '*Kaddish* from the Wrong Side of the *Mechitza*', p. 178 in Heschel, S., op. cit., pp. 177–81

9 Broner, E., *Mornings and Mourning: A* Kaddish *Journal*, Harper, San Francisco, 1994; Danis, N., 'Case No. 3, Sacred Fuse-Box Closet', *Lilith*, Vol. 21, no. 2, Summer 1996, p. 13

option. In particular, women strongly feel that a woman in a family of daughters should have a special entitlement.[10]

This was the view of Henrietta Szold, the brilliant scholar and founder of Hadassah Hospital. When I read her letter to her friend Haym Peretz, after he offered to say *Kaddish* for her mother, I knew I had found a voice for all grieving women.

New York, 16 September 1916

It is impossible for me to find words in which to tell you how deeply I was touched by your offer to say *Kaddish* for my dear mother. I cannot even thank you – it is something that goes beyond thanks. It is beautiful, what you have offered to do – I shall never forget it.

You will wonder, then, that I cannot accept your offer. Perhaps it would be best for me not to try to explain to you in writing, but to wait until I see you to tell you why it is so. I know well, and appreciate what you say about, the Jewish custom; and Jewish custom is very dear and sacred to me. And yet I cannot ask you to say *Kaddish* after my mother. The *Kaddish* means to me the survivor publicly and markedly manifests his wish and intention to assume the relation to the Jewish community which his parents had, and that so the chain of tradition remains unbroken from generation to generation, each adding his own link. You can do that for the generations of your family, I must do that for the generations of my family.

I believe that the elimination of women from such duties was never intended by our law and custom – women were freed from positive duties when they could not perform them, but not when

---

10 Goodkin, J. and Citron, J., op. cit., pp. 73–5. Consider the episode of Zelophchad's daughters (Numbers 27:1). He has no sons and, when he dies, the daughters want to ensure that they do not lose their inheritance. They petition Moses: 'Why should the name of our father be done away from his family, because he has no son?' (27:4) and he takes their case to God, who responds, 'The daughters of Zelophchad speak right . . . if a man die and have no son, then you shall cause his inheritance to pass to his daughter' (27:8). Can we apply this logic to the recital of *Kaddish*? (All translations from the Hebrew Bible are according to the *Jerusalem Bible*, Koren Publishers, Jerusalem, 1969.)

they could. It was never intended that, if they could perform them, their performance of them should not be considered as valuable and valid as when one of the male sex performed them. And of the *Kaddish* I feel sure that this is particularly true.

My mother had eight daughters, and no son; and yet never did I hear a word of regret pass the lips of either my mother or my father that one of us was not a son. When my father died, my mother would not permit others to take her daughter's place in saying the *Kaddish*, and so I am sure I am acting in her spirit when I am moved to decline your offer. But beautiful your offer remains nevertheless, and I repeat, I know full well that it is much more in consonance with the generally accepted Jewish tradition than is my or my family's conception. You understand me, don't you?

HENRIETTA SZOLD[11]

Recently, I watched a very moving television documentary about Anita Lasker Wallfisch[12] – a founder of the English Chamber Orchestra who survived the Holocaust as a cello-playing member of the Auschwitz Women's Orchestra. The documentary shows her in conversation with two other members of the Auschwitz Women's Orchestra as they reflect upon their experiences. One of the them asks Anita, 'Do you think that your children missed out by not having grandparents?'

'Of course,' she answers. 'That is why we are such good grandparents.'

I was struck by that comment. It would have given my parents such joy to be grandparents – I think especially my father, also a survivor of Auschwitz. Grief returns when I watch other two-year-olds being scooped up off the floor and lightly thrown into the air by their doting grandparents. You will never be lifted by anyone who loves like a grandparent does. Grief returns when people exclaim the sheer delight and joy of becoming a first-time

11 Lowenthal, M. (ed.), *Henrietta Szold: Her Life and Letters*, Greenwood Press, Connecticut, 1975, pp. 92–3
12 *The Works*, 24 October 1996, BBC2

grandparent. Thoughts like these make me appreciate how bereft you will feel when you understand that you have no living grandparents. You will see yourselves in the faces of faded photographs, but they will be the faces of distant strangers. You will ask questions that I cannot answer, for although I had a very good relationship with my parents, I now realise that there is so much about their lives that I did not bother to ask, and they did not bother to burden me with. I am sad that, just as the future grandchildren of today's war zones have had their memory scarred, their history changed, both of you will not only be denied your grandparents, but also their history. In this, you have taught me another level of empathy, and now I understand why I miss my parents. I never really empathised with their pain and their loss. It never occurred to me that my own father needed and missed his parents. It never registered that he yearned for a word of encouragement, or to be hugged by his own mother and father. He had safety, he had freedom, he had me. What more could he want?

The biblical command to honour one's parents has been bothering me for a while. The text says, 'Honour thy father and thy mother that thy days may be long ... '[13] Is God bribing us? Shouldn't a child love his or her parents unconditionally? What sort of love is borne of selfishness in order that one's life is lengthened? It is troubling, but I think I have one answer: we need a long life in order to have enough time to experience those things which will make us appreciate what our parents have done for us. When we continue to honour our parents after they die by naming a child in their honour, or acting in a way that emulates their virtues, we cling on to the hope of a longer life in order that their presence will stay in the world. *Kaddish* keeps them here a little longer.

I want to ask both you to be my *Kaddish'l*, but it is a tremendous burden. Why should I project my needs, my unfulfilled frustrations on to you? Because that is what mothers do. I worry that I will have an untimely death like my parents. Will you say *Kaddish* for me so that I can stay in the world a little longer? It is too painful to

13 Exodus 20:1

think of you suffering such a trauma, but you need to be prepared, and I wonder what you will do.

If you choose not to say the *Kaddish*, so be it. I will understand: mothers do that also. But, the real question is whether I can expect the community to have matured so that if either of you wants to say *Kaddish* other people will not intimidate you into thinking it is not a daughter's right? For surely, it will be your place to grieve, and what use is your religion, your history and culture, if you will not be able to draw strength from it in a time of such sadness and loss?

It has taken the birth of you two precious children to realise that I am not only grieving for the death of my parents, but I am grieving for my lack of empathy. I never appreciated how lonely and difficult it must have been to raise two demanding children. I never told them that I thought they did a wonderful job of parenting my brother and me. Although I was named after my paternal grandmother, and I can see facial similarities in our photographs, it never occurred to me how much it must have hurt my father to share those pictures with me. Each time he looked at me, he looked into a memory of his mother's face, and he understood what I was missing. I could never have imagined that loss. Now I can.

Chapter 2

I was deeply alone after my father died. Two months later, I left Melbourne again, having finally sorted through my parents' home and dispensed clothes and furniture to charity. Now it was time to get back to what I considered my 'real life' in New York. Little did I then understand that now, finally, I was ready to get married.

Until I was engaged, I was talked about in not-so-hushed tones as an 'older single'.

'I wish she wouldn't be so picky,' one friend whispered to a another.

'Such a pretty face – if she would lose a bit of weight, she could find a husband,' said well-meaning cousins.

'It's a problem, you know,' confirmed several voices, 'all these girls with their fancy education. It gives them ideas.'

And then the strangest thing happened: when I got married at the relatively old age of thirty-two and ten months (OK, OK, thirty-three if you'd rather, I just made the general point), I was suddenly transformed into a 'young newlywed'. And about a year later, when I had a baby, a relative said to me, with the best of intentions. 'Well now, Sally dear, you really have got something to show for yourself.'

Within eighteen months, I had been transformed into an easily recognisable package – wife, mother, dabbler in a part-time career and baker of cakes for synagogue functions. I was introduced to other newlyweds because naturally we would have something in common: things like washing detergent. As a young newlywed, my past was conveniently obliterated. In the past, I merely had my travels, my career achievements and my independence. Now, I have the symbols of a Jewish woman's success – a husband, a baby and a mortgage. I am far less threatening as a young newlywed. Now I have something to show for myself.

Everyone loves the story of how I met your father. As I was leaving Australia after my father's funeral to return to New York, a friend of mine asked if she could arrange for a friend of hers in England to write to me in New York. I thought the idea was so ridiculous that I said it would be fine. I did not think about it again. About two months later, a letter arrived from England. The handwriting and return address were unfamiliar. Casually I opened the letter, and burst out laughing. It was from the man who would be your father, and I was completely smitten. It was the endearing tone of self-irony that appealed to my own sense of the absurd. I reread his letter at least a dozen times – naturally looking to fault him, for he sounded too good to be true. I found no faults, and later that same day, I wrote him a six-page letter. Of course I didn't post it on the same day – that would seem too obvious or too desperate. I sent it the next day.

Although we quickly began writing regularly, I was too embarrassed to ask him for a photo as that smacked of superficiality (at least I was trying to hide that aspect of my personality). However, after his next letter, I had decided that if he was tall enough (height, girls, it's all in the height) I was going to marry him. After about three months of these letters, I decided to telephone. And three months later, I decided it was time for action. I came to London and stayed with friends who discreetly asked no questions. When the doorbell rang on the first evening we met, I opened the door to an adorable smile and a man who had tried to iron his shirt for the occasion. Three weeks after our first cup of coffee we announced our engagement.

Everyone was delighted: romance, they declared, is not dead after all. However, I found people's excitement and happiness a little embarrassing. Was I really so pathetic as a single person? Was I really such a threatening eyesore to the community? It was difficult to accept that people assumed I would be much happier and more fulfilled as a married woman. I am continually struck, and somewhat amused by the deference accorded to me as a married woman and mother: a respect I never experienced as one of the highly visible invisible army of single women.

So a year after my father's funeral, I was back in Australia for our wedding. It was a chance for Jonathan to have some idea of where I grew up and the people who were important to me. We had agreed to make our home in London, and I knew that after this big trip to Australia it was going to be a long time before we could afford to visit there again. It seemed that our wedding would be the perfect send-off, and we haven't been back since.

The bare essentials of a Jewish wedding are a *chuppah*, a wedding canopy, the *ketubah*, the wedding contract, the ring, an officiant, some blessings, some wine and two *kosher* (defined for this purpose as Sabbath-observing male) witnesses to the event. Most people add a meal with FLOP(S): flowers, liquor, orchestra, photography and in religious circles (S) – *shaytel*, a wig for the new bride (of which more later!)

Once the FLOPS were all organised, there was nothing left for me to do: just to be there and keep the make-up unsmudged. I became a passive participant in the most important event of my life. Would my friends recognise me? Where was their independent, stubborn and outspoken friend? Was that really her hiding behind the veil? Apparently so.

I respect the couples, and their co-operative rabbis, who are exploring ways and promoting innovations to help women feel more connected and integral to the wedding plot.[1] Initially, I also had my own requests: for example, our *chuppah* was on four poles held by four men. I asked if I could use four women to hold the poles, and the answer was no. In the wedding contract a woman is only described as the daughter of her father. I asked for my mother's name to be included so that I could be named as Sarah, the daughter of Eliyahu and Chava, not just Sarah, the daughter of Eliyahu, but again, the answer was no. Although I firmly believe these subtle changes are important symbols, I played the subservient role and caved in without much of a fight. I did not want to jeopardise the actual event and I reasoned that in the long run it wouldn't really matter.

1 Fishman, S., *A Breath of Life: Feminism in the American Jewish Community*, Free Press, New York, 1993, pp. 135–7; Greenberg, B., 'Feminism within Orthodoxy: A Revolution of Small Signs', *Lilith*, Summer 1992, p. 15

About an hour before we stood together underneath the *chuppah*, inside the synagogue, your father and a couple of rabbis gathered to confirm details of the wedding contract. I waited in the antechamber, receiving smiling friends and gasps of wonder that I had scrubbed up so well on the day.

Eventually, your father entered the antechamber, and in memory of the biblical story where Rebecca takes a veil and covers herself[2] just prior to her marriage to Isaac, he lifted a section of the veil that rested behind my shoulder and covered my face with it. The people of Israel are described as a girl who has no eyes, for they follow God with blind faith. So too, a wife's eyes are covered with a veil to indicate that she will also follow her husband with blind faith. At this point, I was blessed with Rebecca's blessing: ' . . . be thou the mother of thousands of tens of thousands, and let thy seed possess the gate of those which hate them.'[3]

What are they saying? Is this really happening to me, or is it an out-of-body experience?

Your father was led into the synagogue accompanied by the men, and I followed several minutes later. Once under the *chuppah*, I began to encircle him seven times, once for each day of creation, as a token that just as a man binds himself with the *tefillin* seven times in devotion to God, I would devote myself to my new husband. (Yeah, yeah, get a grip – is this the twentieth century or what?)

The circling is just a custom, and many women choose not to do it. In spite of modern sensibilities, it didn't bother me as I quite liked the sense of performance which a wedding provides, and the idea of being historically connected to customs from other times and places appeals to me.[4]

Then the rabbis took over: prayers, blessings, the reading aloud of the wedding contract, a speech. I stood immobile. Jonathan placed a simple gold band on the forefinger of my right

2 Genesis 24:65
3 Genesis 24:60
4 Lamm, M., *The Jewish Way in Love and Marriage*, Harper and Row, New York, 1980, explains many of the relevant customs and laws

hand and pronounced the words *harei, at mekudeshet li* – you are sanctified to me. He is marrying me, I will be his – the liturgy is not about reciprocity. We drank a few sips of wine and then, as a symbolic reminder of the destruction of the Temple, he broke a glass to thunderous applause of *Mazal Tov*. Good luck! I was going to need it.

So I started married life with a conventional wedding, six tablecloths and a range of hats. When a new Orthodox bride emerges on to the street the day after her wedding, the crowds are eager to see her. They have not rushed to the bedchamber to check the blood on the sheet,[5] rather everyone wants to be the first to assess how she is covering her hair. The big distinction is hat or *shaytel?* The rest, as they say, is commentary.

I have made an exhaustive study of the sociology of hair and I can reveal that a woman's place in the socio-religious schema of life is determined not by piety, devotion or good works, but rather by allegiance to the latest rabbinical rulings about the acceptable length of a horse-hair wig styled into a pony-tail.

Each option is coded – a fringe dangling out of a stylish beret is usually worn by a modern Orthodox woman with Zionistic leanings, while a woman who scorns the modern world and the State of Israel girds a kerchief tightly around her head. It is all part of 'the knowledge' that a young Orthodox girl acquires. For example, you can tell a Satmar Chassidic woman because she wears a little hat on top of her *shaytel*, lest, God forbid, anyone should think she has not covered her hair.

Orthodox yuppies come in two flavours. Adherents of one set walk around in berets teamed with long denim skirts and trainers; to the untutored eye, it probably seems a little odd to see grown women lugging several children about wearing running shoes, but for these women I think it is part of a deliberate pseudo-anti-materialistic identity they are trying to carve out. A typical member of the other set wears a £1,000 natural-hair wig and stylish

5 Reader, why have you bought into the anti-Semitic stereotype perpetuated by people who are not very nice? There is no basis for such a humiliating practice.

clothes with no pretence of hiding her materialistic identity. She often has a big piece of chewing gum in her mouth and drives a large people-carrier fitted with several children's seats.

In recent years, snoods have become very popular: these Jewish snoods comprise a net binding attached to a solid piece of material and are big enough to tuck in lots of long hair very comfortably – or make possible a fantasy about having long hair. There are, of course, some women who can't wait to get married to cover their hair because they can't stand the sight of their own hair, but this is not considered the purest of motives.

There is a popular story amongst *shaytel machers*, the women who sell wigs. It is the story of Kimhit, a pious woman with seven sons who all served in the office of the High Priest. 'The sages asked her, "What good deeds are there to your credit that you should be so honoured in your sons?" She replied, "The ceiling beams of my house have never seen the hair of my head or the skirt of my petticoat." '[6]

The *shaytel macher* is the backbone of the Orthodox community's cosmetic department, and is often burdened with a Yiddish name redolent of life in the *shtetl*: Gitty, Pesha, Fruma or Shprintza. Her own wig is often askew and fraying at the edges. Nevertheless, the *shaytel macher* is more than a hairdresser, and occupies a prominent social position in the community. With a deft hand, she can make even the dowdiest rabbi's wife look somewhat glamorous.

'I really enjoy it,' the *shaytel macher*, Fruma, said to me. I was sitting upstairs in her house, a couple of weeks before my wedding, staring at the *shaytels* on their Styrofoam heads, trying to decide how best to cover my hair. 'I mean the *shaytels* are important, but it's more than that. I really feel like I am helping somebody – some of these women come and they just want to talk for hours. And you wouldn't believe what I hear. I feel I'm a bit of a social worker like you.'

I swallowed my pride.

'I suppose the *shaytel macher* is to the Orthodox women what the

6 Babylonian Talmud, Yoma 47a

hairdresser is to the celebrities,' I suggested, and noting her smile, offered even more accolades. 'I mean, hair exposed, you become the confidante, spiritual mentor and nutritional adviser.'

'That's right,' she said, 'that's exactly right. Not many people understand.'

The practice of covering one's hair after marriage has a biblical source,[7] and rabbis of the *Talmud* considered a married woman's hair as *ervah*,[8] translated as naked-cum-erotic. The amount of hair which has to be covered is debated, and the form of covering is widely discussed. Therefore, hair has become a very sensitive topic amongst Orthodox women and is one of the laws that has caused unnecessary internal divisions.

Many women who observe the Sabbath, eat *kosher* food, go to the *mikveh* (the ritual bath used after menstruation) and have a very strong Jewish belief system do not cover their hair. Some women who cover their hair regard their hatless and wigless counterparts as not quite Orthodox enough. Recently, at a planning meeting to organise the *kosher* food (what else?) for a function, the tasks were meted out according to certain criteria. Only the women who covered their hair were allowed to bring a cake made in their kitchen – they were the only ones considered *kosher* enough – and the rest were asked to bring fruit or drinks. A friend, who does cover her hair, but is considerably more liberal on these issues, exclaimed, 'What, do we mix the batter with our *shaytels*?' The point was taken, but the ruling remained the same. No *shaytel*, no cake.

Unbeknown to her, Fruma helped me decide against a *shaytel*. It was just too serious, too grown up and too much of a commitment to the concept of covering one's hair. It was something *really* religious people did – it seemed a statement to the outside world – 'Hey, look at me, I'm *really* religious.' I also felt weird wearing somebody else's hair – I mean, did this woman abuse her children? Was she a KGB spy? What sort of hair was I dealing with?

---

[7] Numbers 5:11–31 recounts the story of the adulterous woman who has her hair 'unbound' as part of a ritual in which she must drink the 'bitter water' of the suspected adulteress to ascertain her guilt or innocence.
[8] Babylonian Talmud, Brachot 24a

Like many other ultra-Orthodox women who manage a little sideline from their loft, basement or converted garage,[9] Fruma supplemented her husband's meagre income with her small business. Fruma's friend Ruchie, sells housecoats. These matronly shapeless dressing-gown-cum-dresses that women wear around the house have become the uniform of the ultra-Orthodox woman. In Borough Park, an ultra-Orthodox enclave in New York, there are designer housecoats for *Shabbat* with elaborate and sequinned designs which cover the heavily varicose-veined women roaming the streets on Friday night. For women who have lost their shape after eight children, these housecoats are a lifesaver and I'll let you into a little secret: some of them wear nothing underneath save for knee-high stockings and shoes. These alternative shopping outlets are an important part of the social system because trying to buy modest blouses with long sleeves for the summer, thick enough tights or long enough skirts can be very difficult. Ruchie dreams of owning a place like the Salam Shopping Centre for Veiled Women in Cairo. It is a three-storey clothing store that only stocks Islamically correct outfits. [10]

When Fruma's two older boys left home to study in a *yeshivah*, she converted their loft bedroom into a salon. Fruma got her *shaytels* straight from the manufacturer (no middle-woman for her) and sold them to the women in her local community. Unlike some of the other *shaytel machers* who relied on just two or three designs, she kept up to date with the latest colours and fashions. Fruma was known for her pony-tails, plaits and detachable fringes. She also catered to the women with ginger-coloured hair because they found it so difficult to find the right colour *shaytel*, but they knew

---

9 Sugarman, M., 'My Wife the Breadwinner', *Jerusalem Report*, 20 February 1997, pp. 41–2. The article highlights the trend to teach entrepreneurial skills to ultra-Orthodox women planning to start their own small businesses and generally run them from their homes. See Kranzler, G., *Hasidic Williamsburg: A Contemporary American Hasidic Community*, Jason Aronson, Northvale, NJ, 1995, Chapter 7, 'The Women of Hasidic Williamsburg', for a sociological analysis of the role of women in Hasidic communal life.

10 Brooks, G., *Nine Parts of Desire: The Hidden World of Islamic Women*, Hamish Hamilton, London, 1995, p. 22

they could come to Fruma. Unlike the other-women-whom-Fruma-did-not-want-to-mention (for speaking ill of other people is worth thirty-three sins), she placed her customers under no obligation to buy. Even though she prided herself on her fashionable collection, she was always sure to remind her customers that one should not be too vain in the matter of covering one's hair.

The money that Fruma brings into the family (cash only, no questions asked; cheques or credit cards are of no value as Fruma has no bank account) will help support her children in their first years of marriage while they follow the time-worn tradition of young husbands learning in *yeshivah* and young wives bearing children. As long as the young men refuse to attend university, a place apparently rife with licentiousness and values that are foreign to a *Torah*-true lifestyle, the poverty cycle will be perpetuated.

While Fruma made me a cup of coffee (she prided herself on a comprehensive service), I picked up a recent issue of the *Jewish Woman's Outlook*, a publication sponsored by the Orthodox Union. It was littered with advertisements for wigs and fashionable clothes for the 'modest, discerning woman'.

JACQUELYN WIGS – *Viva, Celebrity, Sugar, Ciara*
Elegance and fashion you can be proud to wear. Because nothing compares to the beauty of a Jacquleyn. You'll never settle for less. You work hard enough and you deserve it. Make Jacquelyn a part of your life – you will enjoy every moment of it.

The advertisements showed glamorous women selling these wares – women whom the rabbis admonished for being too sexually alluring as they sought to emulate the Western, not Jewish, paradigms of beauty. It reminded me of the story of the Modesty Brigade in Bnei Brak, an Orthodox enclave near Tel Aviv. (In Saudi Arabia, the equivalent is called the Committee of the Ordering of the Good and the Forbidding of the Evil.)[11] They wanted the owner of a shop selling wigs to cover the wigs with scarves in order to hide the beautiful hair of the wigs. The shop owner refused,

11 Yamani, M. (ed.), *Feminism and Islam*, Ithaca Press, Reading, 1996, p. 267

claiming that she was selling wigs, not scarves. They reached a compromise: the wigs could stay without the scarves, if the painted eyes on the Styrofoam models could have glasses. (Even the Modesty Police know that men don't make passes at girls who wear glasses.) In recounting this story, one analysis suggests that 'to dim the (albeit non-existent) eyes of the female heads in that storefront would afford some measure of compensation for the erotic allure of all that feminine hair'.[12] This in turn reminded me of an advertisement in the *Jewish Tribune*, a newspaper catering for England's ultra-Orthodox community. The advertisement announced the opening of a new shopping complex, and in the ad all the sketchily drawn women characters wheeling their trolleys had their eyes (and most of their faces) blacked out.[13]

However, erotic allure doesn't seem to bother the women who revel in the idea of looking for a new image. Wigs come in different textures – human hair, horse hair, synthetic nylon or a combination. Wigs let you change the colour of your hair, and although wigs are meant to be a sign of modesty, it is clear that many of them make the women look more glamorous and, in fact, more attractive to men.

'Come, let's try on some *shaytels*,' Fruma was pushing me towards the mirror. Some have just arrived. I've got a lovely new style – Chantelle – it's a hundred per cent human hair.'

She also took out three of the popular blonde styles – the pony-tail with the fringe, the plaited pony-tail and the blonde bob cut. I have dark brown curly hair – who am I kidding?

I gathered up my shoulder length hair and wound it around the top of my head. She lifted Chantelle and cautiously put it on to my head. She pulled it down, and adjusted it.

'Now, doesn't that look wonderful. Your husband, God willing your wedding day will be blessed, will just love it!'

---

12 Levine, M. Myerowitz, 'The Gendered Grammar of Ancient Mediterranean Hair', pp. 76–130, in Eilberg-Schwartz, Howard and Doniger, Wendy (eds), *Off With Her Head: The Denial of Women's Identity in Myth, Religion and Culture*, University of California Press, Berkeley, 1995
13 *Jewish Tribune*, 23 November 1995

Oh no! Jonathan. I forgot about him. He would hate it. He is not the type to run his manly hands through a human-hair *shaytel* – the thought is too repulsive. If he is going to run his hands through anything, it should be my curly locks.

'Well, I am not so sure, it's not really me. You know what I mean?'

I never looked like one of the ultra-Orthodox unmarried girls you can spot in Jerusalem, New York and London. They share a secret code of dress. Their hair is already moulded into the latest wig styles, mimicking their mothers whose own natural hair has seen little daylight since their wedding day. Their skin is always blemish free, and their teeth are big, white and straight. Their ankles are slim, and they rarely have a ladder in their tights. Their gaunt lean bodies are victims of the paradoxical Orthodox beauty myth, in which young women, especially in those 'waiting years' between school and marriage, are expected to look extremely glamorous and immaculate whenever they leave the house.

However, at the same time they are expected to decry and denounce beauty as the epitome of *naarishkeit*, the antithesis of spiritual striving. At the age of eighteen, girls go '*shidduch* shopping' for new clothes in anticipation of the meetings they will have with a small range of suitable marriage partners. The mixed messages of disdain and delight in a young girl's emergence into womanhood are confusing. While clever young women are considered praiseworthy, they should not be seen to be too clever. Those girls seen to be too obsessed with their appearance are talked about disparagingly, yet they are given firm instructions to look their best at all times. Ultimately, women are admired and envied more for their beauty than their brains. Your father tells the story that when he was in *yeshivah*, it was common practice for matchmakers who wanted to extol the beauty of a potential marriage partner to say, 'Oh, she's very attractive. She looks just like a *shiksa*.' The fact that looking like a beautiful non-Jewish woman is considered the ultimate accolade must undermine the emotional confidence and spiritual aspirations of young women.

As I say, I always looked a little awkward in these circles. I have a gap between my two front teeth, and my ankles are particularly ugly. So, I settled for a range of hats and berets which I still try to wear as nonchalantly as possible. Just before I got married, I went to Borough Park, where the shops cater for every whim of the Orthodox family. There was a little shop staffed by a very pious woman who gave me a sob story about her children, her husband, her son without a job and sick grandchildren with inexplicable ailments. I liked her hats, and with each hat came another story, so that by the end of the morning, I bought about twenty hats in a completely irrational spending spree. I was in such a happy, carefree and generous mood those few weeks before I got married. This feeling has never repeated itself, and I have not bought any hats since. I have yet to wear all twenty.

I once attended a scholarly lecture, given by a woman who cited *Talmudic*, post-*Talmudic* and contemporary views on covering and not covering one's hair in certain situations. I was somewhat distracted by the lecturer's very fashionable hat. However, what I remember most were her concluding comments, and the responses of some of the hundred women who attended.

'I rang up a real estate agent in Jerusalem about renting an apartment,' she recounted. 'And the first thing he asked me was, "How do you cover your hair?"'

Everyone laughed because we all understood what she was really saying. In some perverse way, the external markers of a woman's religious behaviour, in particular her head covering, have come to identify her place in the Jewish world. I find it amusing and pathetic that the religious identity of a whole family is characterised by the way the woman covers her hair.

'How religious are they?'

'Well, the wife covers her hair.'

What does that really mean? You can safely assume that it is a *kosher* home, they keep *Shabbat* and she goes to the *mikveh*, but what does it really mean in terms of knowledge and belief? What does it really mean in terms of their behaviour to other people?

Another woman who teaches *Torah* confessed that to get a particular teaching job in a girls' school, she had to wear a head-covering that would cover all her hair. (She followed an alternative ruling that only part of one's head had to be covered.)

'I have a choice – cover my hair like they want and teach nine hundred young girls *Torah*, or stay at home.'

Others admitted to 'playing the game' in order to gain employment in certain jobs that mandated religious conformity as well as the necessary technical skills. Some women expressed a sense of comfort when they cover their hair: it highlights their 'differentness' from their work colleagues which maintains a separateness they need. For some, wearing a head-covering is a political strategy (my definition, not theirs) because it demonstrates to the rabbis that a woman is serious in her commitment to Orthodoxy. Hence, a woman who covers her hair *and* asks for more inclusion of women's needs in ritual life is more likely to be taken seriously. Geraldine Brooks makes a similar point about Muslim women activists. She suggests that the scholarly work of Fatima Mernissi in Morocco, which is well regarded in Western universities, is virtually ignored by the Islamic establishment because she doesn't wear a veil. In contrast, she says:

I found the brightest hope for positive change among the black *chadors* of devout Iranian women. Even the most narrow-minded fundamentalists can't criticize ... Their conspicuous adherence to religious rules gives them a high ground from which to make their case for women's rights.[14]

Recently, I have heard several rabbis appeal to women in the modern Orthodox community to cover their hair for the same reason that men wear a skull-cap: as a symbolic reminder of God. This is an interesting development because it does not ask women to be modest and demure: these rabbis are too astute to request this from modern professional women. Instead (somewhat dishonestly, I think), the rabbis appeal to women's spirituality and the opportunity to be like men. This is transformed into a much greater value than the original intent of modest behaviour. Ironically, I think these rabbis turn hair covering into a political strategy, because lurking underneath this idea of symbolically remembering God, is a much more pragmatic realisation that the

14 Brooks, G., op. cit., p. 233

majority of rabbinical leaders in a position to create change won't listen to a group of women with uncovered hair.

It seems that we all create sociological justifications that resonate with the values of the twentieth century in order to overcome our intuitive feeling that a particular legal requirement is anachronistic or insulting.

I have to admit that before I got married, I used to take a bit of a perverse interest in what a woman wore on top her head, and would catch myself judging someone accordingly. Since I got married, and began to understand the sub-text of head covering, I have been less concerned about what is on top of a woman's head, rather I have come to my senses and know that what is inside her head is much more important. We all know very intelligent, devout, pious women who perform great acts of kindness without wearing a wig, yet there is a certain arrogance amongst some wig-wearers that only they have inherited the mantle of religious correctness.

Now I catch myself reflecting on the scant attention the German guards in concentration camps paid to the sensibilities of women with regard to the covering of their hair. While the better known personal accounts of camp life have been written predominattly by male survivors of the Holocaust whose horrific experiences have been regarded as the norm, an increasing number of women's testimonies highlight the unique features of women's experiences in the camps.[15] I always gulp when I read about women's wigs and kerchiefs being torn off, and their heads shaved.[16] Who would dare to imagine what it was like, having meticulously and religiously concealed one's hair, only to be uncovered and shaved by a German camp attendant? I can't bear to

15 Horowitz, S., 'Memory and Testimony of Women Survivors of Nazi Geno-cide', in Baskin, J., *Women of the Word: Jewish Women and Jewish Writing*, Wayne State University, Detroit, 1994, pp. 258–82; Ringelheim, J., 'Women and the Holocaust: A Reconsideration of the Research', in Baskin, J., *Jewish Women in Historical Perspective*, Wayne State University, Detroit, 1991, pp. 243–64
16 Jackson, L., *Elli: Coming of Age in the Holocaust*, Times Books, New York, 1980, excerpted in Rittner, C. & Roth, J. (eds), *Different Voices: Women and the Holocaust*, Paragon, New York, 1993, pp. 73–83

think about it, but that is what comes to my mind when I listen to women comparing the human hair to horsehair ratio of their *shaytels*, or when I catch myself showing off my hats.

In one of those twists of modern life, the *shaytel* and veil have much in common. The Orthodox women with covered hair look outwardly more 'integrated' than the Muslim women clad in the *chador* wandering around Hendon, Golders Green or parts of Brooklyn. But somehow the Muslim women look much more pious. It always strikes me we live in such close proximity yet have nothing to do with each other. I wonder if different head coverings have the same nuanced meaning in the Muslim community? Are the women who cover their face considered more religious Muslims? Are the women with no veils liberal Muslims, rewriting their relationship to the Koran and questioning the traditions of their forefathers?

I'd like to know, but it's difficult to get close. It would be easy for us to lump them into one group, just as they might fail to differentiate between us Jewish women. Certainly, it is easier to deal with people if you minimise their existence and deny their emotional presence in your life. Occasionally, I fantasise about ramming my supermarket trolley into a Muslim woman's trolley just so that we could talk. I imagine the scene.

'I'm sorry, *so* sorry,' I say.

'It's fine,' she smiles. We admire each other's children.

'I like your hat,' she comments.

'Thanks. Your robe . . . ' I say swirling my hands to cover my body, 'is, um – um interesting.'

'Do not make the mistake of thinking that my veil is an oppressive instrument of the patriarchal society in which I live.'

'Me? I would never . . . '

'The veil liberates me from the dictates of the fashion industry, I do not suffer sexual harassment and I am respected. The veil represents the fact that I have not succumbed to Western ways.'[17]

---

17 Yamani, M. (ed.), op. cit. This collection of essays was first presented in a series of lectures on feminism and Islamic law, and highlights the different approaches to understanding the role of women in Islam. The number of parallels to Judaism convinces me that women across orthodoxies should be talking to each other.

That's a perfectly sound argument, I think to myself. My hat is also about differentiating myself from those around me, reminding myself that I can never really be a fully integrated member of the secular world around me.

'Would you like to come to Passover *seder*?' I respond.

'Look, I know the Holocaust really happened,' she says sincerely.

'And I can appreciate the anger of the Palestinians.'

'You should meet some of my friends.'

'And you mine. Let's start a dialogue group,' I suggest, envisioning the scene.

'Why not, it's good to talk,' she agrees. 'I'll ask my husband.'

'And me, mine.'

We meet next week by the cherry tomatoes. My children love them, as do hers, but they are expensive, and neither of us wants to be the first to put them in our trolley.

'He said it is forbidden to talk to the perpetrators of the Zionist state.'

'Oh. Mine said nothing and nodded his head. This means "are you crazy?" '

'Perhaps we could meet again,' she offers.

'Sure. Let's do lunch.'

It is obvious that your mother is no Kimhit. It is clear why I was sent daughters. It's not just these subversive fantasies: my roof has seen my hair, and sometimes I don't wear knickers under my skirt.

Chapter 3

One of the first *Talmudic* stories your father told me was the one about a man whose wife died.(You can imagine what this did for my paranoid obsession about an early death!) They had a baby who needed feeding, but this man did not have enough money to pay for a wet nurse. A miracle happened – his breasts started to produce milk and he was able to feed his son. A debate ensued. Rabbi Yosef said, 'How great is this man that such a miracle happened,' while Abaye claimed, 'On the contrary, how terrible it is that the order of nature had to change.'[1]

If your father had breasts, life would have been a lot easier. The moment that Avigayil, my first born, was delivered, I had a profound religious experience. I realised that feminist theologians who claim God is a woman are fundamentally mistaken – only a man would let this sort of thing happen to women. I understood what Bertha Pappenheim meant when she said, 'If there is to be justice in the world to come, women will be lawgivers, and men have to have babies.'[2]

I officially became a m–o–t–h–e–r (oh, how the enormous and grave responsibilities still rest uneasily on my flabby tummy) on 4 October 1994. A serious case of *Schadenfreude* broke out amongst my so-called friends who, laughing as they watched me desperately try to latch you on to my cracked nipples, made outrageous comments like, 'You are not the mothering type,' 'It's not in your nature,' 'You won't read the newspapers for six months' (a real insult as I am known to be a newspaper junkie), and 'You'd be hopeless without Jonathan.' The truth hurt.

[1] Babylonian Talmud, Shabbat 53b
[2] cited in Freeman, L., *The Story of Anna O.*, Paragon House, New York, 1972, p. 60

The 'Self-Hating Jew' is one who colludes with anti-Semitic stereotypes and denies his Jewish identity. There are days when I am the 'Self-Hating Mother' – I have bought into the negative perceptions of motherhood and it works against me. (I am the only woman I know who took out the books on post-natal depression before each of you was born.) There are days it eats away at my self-esteem and confidence. I plan aggressive acts of revenge on the Early Learning Centre or the Playgroup Association. And like the reformed self-hating Jew who overcompensates and becomes fiercely proud of his Jewish roots, there are days when I think motherhood is the greatest blessing and I can't imagine my life as fulfilled in any other way. I buy parenting magazines and take notes watching *Sesame Street*.

After we were told to be 'fruitful and multiply',[3] the rabbis recognised that obligating women to put themselves in a life-threatening situation was a non-starter. Hence the law evolved that men, not women, are obligated to have children, thus leaving a wife merely as the handmaid of her husband's religious duty. However, motherhood defines a Jewish woman, and as children we are taught to regard the barren biblical women who successfully beseeched God for children as our heroines: Rachel says to Jacob, 'Give me children or else I die' (Genesis 30:1), and Hannah talks of the 'bitterness of [her] soul' (1 Samuel 1:10).[4]

In modern terms, Sylvia Barack Fishman points out the conflict between feminist and Jewish attitudes toward the family:

> On the one hand, Jewish women have absorbed feminist goals more fully than have other ethnic groups: they are more highly educated, work in higher status professions, are sweepingly in favour of reproductive rights, and are more desirous of freedom and independence for their daughters than any other group. On the other hand, the vast majority of American Jewish women remain committed to the ideals of marriage and family.[5]

3 Genesis 1:28
4 Aschkenasy, N., *Eve's Journey: Feminine Images in Hebraic Literary Tradition*, Wayne State University Press, Detroit, 1986. See Chapter 3 which extensively discusses the representation of motherhood in the Bible.
5 Fishman, S., op. cit., p. 48

That's your mother she is talking about – even if she is a displaced Australian with her body in England, her heart in Israel and her head in New York.

Interestingly, educated married Orthodox women defy the suggestion that increasing education for women leads to decreasing birthrates. Many Orthodox and traditional Jewish women with university degrees and successful professional lives, also have four, five or even six children. They are the ones who, in the wake of the Holocaust, are ideologically committed to having large families. They are carrying on the tradition of their biblical foremothers who also sustained national goals by having children:

> As a small country surrounded by enemies, Israel was conscious of its vulnerable situation and needed to maintain its population . . . the Bible encouraged procreation by portraying the pursuit of children as a great goal and celebrated women for striving toward it.[6]

During my late twenties and early thirties, I watched with despair as my friends were transformed from confident professional career women into mothers with overdeveloped defence mechanisms which made them revile and patronise me. For some, I was a threat – independent, carefree and apparently unburdened with a sense of responsibility. For others, I was an object of pity – independent, carefree and apparently unburdened with a sense of responsibility.

I developed some simple rules for managing friends with young babies.

1. Give very little advance warning of a visit. That way they don't feel guilty if their place is a mess, and I get points for making the effort to drop in.
2. As soon as I arrive, I announce that I cannot stay very long.
3. Inquire about their spouse/partner. Feign interest if necessary.
4. Ask three pointed questions about the child's latest developmental milestones. I learnt the last rule the hard way when one very close friend accused me of a lack of interest in her children.

6 Frymer-Kensky, T., *In the Wake of the Goddesses: Women, Culture and the Biblical Transformation of Pagan Myth*, Fawcett Columbine, New York, 1992, p. 125

'You never ask me about the children!' she exclaimed.

'Oh,' I replied meekly.

'Even if you don't mean it, would it kill you to ask about them?'

I had no idea that I was meant to show an interest in her kids – to me, they were separate from her and I thought I was being so respectful by treating her as an individual woman, not as a mother.

Now that I have my own children, I understand why she was upset, but I do not share her outrage. Naturally, in a social context, children are often part of the chit-chat, but I am very impressed if someone talking to me on a professional matter does not feel compelled to end the conversation by cursorily asking about the children. When I occasionally get out of my pyjamas and leave both of you at home with your father to attend a lecture or workshop in the community, I am so annoyed when the first thing an acquaintance asks me is, 'How are the children?' or, 'Isn't Jonathan good to look after the children?' My respective responses are a curt, 'Fine' and an aggressive 'Actually, he is their father.'

Although every woman thinks that her birth experience is amongst the worst and most painful, I have empirical data to support my claim. But I don't like to show off; suffice to say that those who comfort me with the news that sex is better after a Caesarean, have no idea of the pain, agony and sheer hell of a Caesarean.

At Avigayil's birth, Jonathan was the only male in the room – all the doctors, midwives and other *schleppers* were all women – and I must say I preferred it that way – there was something very comforting about having all these women around. When Elisheva was born it was a repeat performance except for the wonderful male doctor who performed the surgery.

We never bothered with carry-cots for either of you – as we live in a complex of bookshelves surrounded by a house, each of you spent your first few weeks cosseted on the bottom shelf of an IKEA bookcase. I made some room between S and T – I decided we could do without every edition of Delia Smith and Martha Stewart, after all. There were going to be no dinner parties for the next thirty years.

On lazy Sunday mornings before I had children, I lay in bed

reading the paper, drinking coffee, pictured one of my friends changing nappies, and smiled smugly. I thought of my friends who had been up for hours, half dazed, scurrying to take out their breasts to placate crying babies. I watched mothers and toddlers in the park, and I saw right through them in the supermarkets. It is the same way people look straight through me now.

The shock of becoming a mother was extremely powerful, and now I understand why friends said that nothing could prepare me for the relentless emotional roller coaster. No wonder friends didn't tell me how terrible it really is – clearly they have suppressed those first few disorientating weeks in order to reproduce again. But it's not all bad news. While marriage brought rewards to compensate for the loss of freedoms in my single life, motherhood gave profound legitimacy to those former vices. Once again I had the freedom to hang out in my nightie all day – a custom that I practised for years, yet reluctantly rescinded upon marriage. A crumpled, milk-stained nightie became *de rigeur*, accessorised with a crumpled head of unwashed hair and unbrushed teeth.

Uncharacteristically, I tried to think positively. I reclaimed the freedom to be up at three in the morning, on my own, pottering around the flat. Although marriage demands a certain amount of time spent in bed, motherhood made me feel like I was single again. There I was, at three in the morning, talking on the phone to girlfriends like I used to – only this time they were in America or Australia, I was in London and there was a baby sucking and gulping away as if there would be no tomorrow. But tomorrow came, and even though night and day seemed inseparable, tomorrow brought the renewed challenge of quickly changing the nappy before you pished all over me.

I am glad we had girls: the birth of a son would have embarrassed me because then everyone and everyone's friends would know we had no parents. The fuss made over the arrival of a boy is in stark contrast to the non-event of the birth of a girl. First, there is the *shalom zachor*, the welcoming of the son, which is a traditional celebration held on the first Friday night after the birth. Friends usually come to the home of the new-born child, words of *Torah* are spoken, and bowls of chickpeas are eaten.

And then there is the circumcision. For us, there are no grandfathers alive to be the *sandek*, the man given the honour of holding the new-born baby during the circumcision. There are no grandmothers to lend a helping hand or offer words of much-needed advice. I did not want a crowd of people around me whispering in tones they thought I could not hear, 'Oh how sad! They don't have parents,' 'She's coping very well – all things considered,' and other demeaning forms of consolation. I know how much it would have hurt me – I know how much the absence of my parents would have made them present. I didn't need compassionate whispers to remind me and I was very relieved, perhaps selfishly, that I did not have to deal with any of it. Anyway, as no one hesitated to remind me, the sages say that, 'A baby girl is a good omen for the next child to be a boy.' [7]

When you were born girls, your father did what centuries of fathers have done: he went to the synagogue on the first Sabbath after your birth, said a blessing on the *Torah*, and announced your names. But I am the one who bears the scar on my bikini-line. I also wanted to acknowledge your arrival and, given the trauma and extreme pain I endured, I felt a need to bring the birthing experiences to a close. If I couldn't find something to help me within my own religious tradition, what use was it to me?

I knew that in the past, there were traditional ways of welcoming girls. For example, the *Holle Kreich* was established in Germany in the fifteenth century. On the first Sabbath after the birth the mother came to the synagogue, and children from the age of eight to ten were invited to the house for a party. They formed a circle around the cradle where the infant lay, and lifting the cradle three times they said, '*Holle, Holle*, what shall the child's name be?' and the child's name was called out. In some areas of Germany this happened to both boys and girls, but usually only girls.[8] In Poland, there was a *brisitzeh*, a little *bris*, but there was no circumcision. (While the physical act of circumcising a boy is a reminder of a spiritual covenant made between that child, God and the Jewish community, there has never been any intention in the Jewish community to circumcise girls. However, the idea of the same spiritual covenant between a baby girl, God and her community motivates this search for a meaningful way to celebrate a girl's birth.) In North Africa and Syria, a *zeved habat* – gift of a daughter – is celebrated and the mother recites the *birkat hagomel* thanksgiving prayer for recovery. After naming the baby, the rabbi prays that the parents derive much joy from her, and see her marry and become the mother of male babies.[9]

While most of these traditions have been lost, recently there has been increasing interest in ceremonies for baby girls within Orthodoxy. A public celebration for a baby daughter is not about imitating the circumcision rite, but is rather a way for parents to acknowledge the importance of their daughter's birth and welcome her into the community with the traditional words of blessing. In London, some Orthodox synagogues are coming up with new ways to celebrate the birth of a baby girl.[10] Families are creating new celebrations: in New York, a friend arranged a morning of study by women to honour the birth of her daughter. Guests were given *Talmudic* texts related to the education of children and my friend then gave a lecture about this to the women. This seems like a wonderful way to welcome a child into

9 Hill, H., '*Simchat Bat* Gives Fairer Start to Fairer Sex', *Jewish Chronicle*, 5 August 1994

10 In personal correspondence, Rabbi Dr Julian Jacobs at Ealing Synagogue, west London, in a letter dated 25 October 1996, explains what is done in his synagogue.

> After the Yom Tov service all the baby boys and girls and even some young children were brought up to the Ark by their parents (since the service was not a regular or statutory one the requirement to separate the sexes did not apply). The Ark was opened and some of the mothers read Psalms 127 and 128 in Hebrew and English (*Singers's prayer book*, old edition, pp. 247–8, new edition, pp. 467–8), as well as the Prayer of Thanksgiving for Women after Recovery from Childbirth (pp. 412–14, pp. 799–801). I then recited the priestly benediction and the benediction upon children (p. 167, p. 271) in Hebrew and English as well as the traditional blessing that they grow up to learn and keep the *Torah*, to marry and to perform good deeds.

the People of the Book. In Australia, some friends recently composed a service drawing on traditional blessings and sources to welcome their daughter into the covenantal community.

I wanted to create something that would reflect our lifestyle and the aspirations that your father and I share for both of you. I also wanted to create a ceremony that neither of you would be embarrassed about when you grew older. I had heard of ceremonies which involve dunking a baby girl into a mini-*mikveh*, but this did not appeal to me as it sounded too much like a mini-baptism.[11] In some communities the mother and father, cradling their new infant, are called up together to the *bimah* on a *Shabbat* morning and given the opportunity to recite the blessings over the *Torah*. Then they name their baby daughter in the presence of their friends and family who have come to honour the child's birth. Although the idea appealed to me, we do not belong to a community where men and women sit together or participate equally in the rituals of synagogue life.

I wanted a celebration with an intrinsically Jewish flavour, amid the camaraderie of women, reflecting a historical precedent. I found the content in the *techinot*, the prayers of supplication which became very popular amongst women and formed a separate, additional canon of liturgy in the seventeenth and eighteenth centuries.[12] *Techinot* were originally written by men and the first printed collection appeared in 1590. Later, as women wrote *techinot*, they created the classic *techinah* style: 'the uniquely diffuse and wordy, intimately tender, humbly feminine style'[13] which

11 Strassfield, S. and Strassfield, M., *The Second Jewish Catalogue*, Jewish Publication Society, Philadelphia, 1976, p. 37. Despite this, the *First*, *Second* and *Third Jewish Catalogue*s are excellent resources brimming with refreshing ideas.

12 See Weissler, C., 'Prayers in Yiddish and the Religious World of Ashkenazic Women', in Baskin, J. (ed.), *Jewish Women in Historical Perspective*, Wayne State University Press, 1991, pp. 159–81

13 Zinberg, I., *History of Jewish Literature, Volume 7: Old Yiddish Literature from its Origins to the Haskalah Period*, KTAV, New York, 1975, p. 251. He also claims that some *techinot* were written for men, but the overwhelming majority were for women. This twelve-volume English translation is an important resource for all aspects of Jewish literature.

usually focused on domestic concerns and family matters. They were said by women both at formal times, such as before lighting the Sabbath candles, and informally, whenever they were inspired to converse with God. [14] Over a hundred years ago, pious women, called *zogerin*, led other women in prayer in the women's section of synagogue. Many of the *zogerin* also wrote *techinot*, but they also showed the other women how to pray, when to stand up, when to sit down, and led participation in the women's section.[15] The *zogerin*, who were also represented in popular Yiddish fiction,[16] had special significance in representing illiterate women who asked them to intercede on their behalf in matters from the health of a child to the material success of a husband.[17]

In some instances men collated a series of psalms and other prayers and had them specially bound for their wives. One such collection was commissioned by an Italian, Guiseppe Cohen, for his wife in 1786. This collection in Italian and Hebrew was recently translated into English. It comprises about twenty different prayers

[14] For examples of *techinot* translated into English and an explanation of their origins, see Henry, S. and Taitz, E., *Written Out of History*, Biblio Press, New York, 1990, pp. 184–200, and Berger, S., '*Tehines*: A Brief Survey of Women's Prayers', in Grossman, S. and Haut R. (eds), *Daughters of the King: Women and the Synagogue*, Jewish Publication Society, Philadelphia, 1992, pp. 73–88. Tarnor, N., *A Book of Jewish Women's Prayers: Translations from the Yiddish*, Jason Aronson, Northvale, NJ, 1992, includes almost a hundred *techinot* and detailed notes about each one.
[15] Taitz, E., 'Women's Voices, Women's Prayers: Women in the European Synagogues of the Middle Ages', in Grossman, S. and Haut, R. (ed.), op. cit., pp. 59–72. Zinberg, I., op. cit., pp. 251
[16] For example, Brokhes, R., 'The *Zogerin*', in Forman, F. et al. (eds), *Found Treasures: Stories by Yiddish Women Writers*, Second Story Press, Toronto, 1994, pp. 85–90; see also Seidman,N., 'The Transsexual Imagination', in *A Marriage Made in Heaven: The Sexual Politics of Hebrew and Yiddish*, University of California Press, Berkeley, 1997, Chapter 2, esp. pp. 62–4, for a gendered analysis of the role of Yiddish in women's religious literature.
[17] Waxman, M., *A History of Jewish Literature, Volume 2: From the Twelfth Century to the Middle of the Eighteenth Century*, Bloch Publishing, New York, 1933, pp. 641–3, and Niger, S., 'Yiddish Literature and the Female Reader', in Baskin, J. (ed.), *Women of the Word: Jewish Women and Jewish Writing*, op. cit., pp. 70–90

covering a variety of life-cycle events. [18] And so the idea came to me – to recite some of those same prayers that women in the eighteenth century recited and name Avigayil in the company of women. I chose one from Guiseppe Cohen's collection and a couple of others written by Sarah Bat Tovim, who composed many *techinot*.[19] I decided that the most appropriate forum would be a women's prayer service being held in December, 1994 about two months after Avigayil was born, at Yakar, an independent Orthodox synagogue in London. [20]

When Elisheva was born, I also wanted to celebrate her birth. Again I chose the setting of a women's prayer group and was offered the opportunity to give a *dvar Torah* in Elisheva's honour. I started by quoting the story of Joshua Ben Hannaniah, whose mother took him in his cradle to the house of study every day so that his ears would become attuned to the words of the *Torah*.[21] I introduced my brief talk by suggesting that I was just carrying on this tradition by bringing my daughter in her cradle to a house of study and prayer, so that her ears might also become attuned to the words of the *Torah* and the calming melodies of communal prayer.

After both services, many women said to me, 'Oh I wish I had done something like that for my daughter.'

It is so hard to respond to such a comment and I stood there thinking, 'Well, why didn't you?' But I know the answer. Most of us in the Orthodox world live in communities where a little innovation is considered a radical revolution. Yet, I believe Orthodoxy can only be enhanced by these innovations which allow

18 Cardin, Rabbi N. (ed & trans.), *Out of the Depths I Call to You: A Book of Prayers for the Married Jewish Woman*, Jason Aronson, Northvale, NJ, 1992
19 Zinberg, I., op. cit., see p. 253 for comments about the rewriting of women's *techinot* by men who were part of the Enlightenment, and particularly Joshua Mezah who made up *techinot* under the name of Sarah Bat Tovim, having believed she never existed.
20 I said prayers taken from Cardin, N., op. cit., and Klirs, T. (compiled and introduced by), *The Merit of Our Mothers: A Bilingual Anthology of Jewish Women's Prayers*, Hebrew Union College Press, Cincinnati, 1992. The issue of women's prayer groups is discussed later in this book.
21 Palestinian Talmud, Yevamot 1:6, 3a

women to express themselves within the parameters of the *halachah* and to engage with tradition. I am very happy that I chose some way to recognise your births. If you ever ask me what I did to celebrate your arrival into our lives, I will be pleased to tell you. After all, your births transformed our lives and sharing our joy was the least we could have done. Ironically, creating opportunities to celebrate your births allowed me to feel more connected in the religious process than if either of you had been a boy. Occasionally, it occurs to me to feel sorry for the mothers of boys.

Now, I am meant to be creating a bank of dreamy childhood memories for you. The sort of stuff to halt assimilation: Friday nights with the white tablecloth, ornate silver candlesticks with flickering candles to usher in the Sabbath Queen, fresh *challah* bread, piping hot chicken soup, delicious chopped liver, a sumptuous meal and mouth-watering deserts, all accompanied by your cuddly father dispensing kindly advice and me, your serene, graceful mother, who despite having slaved in the kitchen for days, has managed to arrange you around the table, all organised and talking about your week's activities.

Sorry kids, it's not going to happen in your lifetime. You'll have to go to one of my perfect friends for that. I've got lots of them. Four kids, nice husband, big house, obliging grandparents. Your mother is not serene – I come to the *Shabbat* table full of rage – the cooking, the cleaning, the over-priced chicken and the burnt mushrooms – am I the only one who resents domestic chores and feels like she doesn't cope? Of course not, and it has nothing to do with Orthodoxy – the gendered division of labour has long been a *bête noir* of the feminist movement; however, its impact on Orthodox women's lives is now being discussed more openly. As more Orthodox women gain better qualifications and enter the workforce, is it still reasonable to expect them to carry the burden of domestic responsibilities? How does the shifting nature of Orthodox women's lives impact on the traditional expectations of Orthodox men? If you are lucky, you will get a SNOG – a sensitive-new-Orthodox-guy, and domestic life will be different by the time you both have your own homes. But at the moment, despite endless discussions between your father and me about

breaking down the gender stereotypes and sharing the cleaning of
the toilet bowl, I always end up worrying about those last-minute
Friday-night details. At least he feels remorseful and promises that
on retirement he will cook the chicken, but, in the interim, it is
down to me.

Then I get upset because I know I am the one at home because
I chose a career which is poorly paid and hardly worth returning to
once childcare, tights and petrol are paid for. Then I realise that
when Jewish women make career decisions, they are encouraged to
do so as potential mothers. While other women have birth control,
Jewish women have career control. Dentistry is good, medicine is
bad, accounting is good, law is bad. Something that can be fitted
around the yet-to-be-born children, and yet-to-be-ensnared
husband is lauded as careful planning. Teaching in a Jewish school
is obviously the best choice for Jewish women: holidays, short days
and reduced school fees for one's own children. And as teaching
doesn't usually threaten the financial power-base of their
husbands, it is a profession that continues to keep women
financially dependent on their husbands. It is all part of the
conspiracy to keep women busy till they have children and then,
kapow, they are left to stay at home with their children. Once I
start thinking like this, I am just too worked up to relax, and I sit at
the Friday-night table sulking like a four-year-old child. Is that the
sort of model mother you really want? Then I get upset that I have
no parents. I have no business sulking because now I am the 'elder'
of the family, someone whom others will turn to. Will you turn to
me? Whom will I turn to? The task is too great, the responsibility
too daunting and the rejection too familiar. If you want your
deposit back, I will understand.

But there is one thing I hope you will thank me for. On the first
Friday night after we were married, your father said the *Kiddush*
over the wine. When it came time to say the blessing over the
bread, he nodded his head in my direction and said, 'Go on, you
do it.'

My voice still quavers when I say the blessing, and my hand still
trembles when I cut the soft *challah*. It is as if I don't believe that I
deserve the right to participate. But the beauty of it is that you

think it is normal. You expect me to do it, but you will soon find out that is not the way it happens in the majority of Orthodox families where the man, the 'head of the household', is in charge of the religious rituals. There are a small number of women who say the blessing over the bread, but I know people whisper about us behind our backs. I am sure that some of your father's friends think he is a wimp. I know they don't like me. The genial smile on one man's face literally switches off when I appear at his front door to visit his wife. I am considered deviant and a bad influence, but I know that what I do is a hundred-per-cent *kosher*.

A woman is as obligated as a man to say the *hamotzi*, the blessing over bread. Therefore, she can say it for him.[22] Wolowelsky regards it as 'concrete expression of the current perception of the modern religious woman as co-equal head of the household'.[23] Daughters seeing their mothers participate in more than doling out the soup, and sons watching their fathers share authority will change the expectations about relationships. Are we afraid of these changes?

I have been in homes where single, divorced and widowed women deferred to their male guests, requesting them to say the *Kiddush*, when in fact the women are the heads of their households.

Years ago, a girlfriend and I travelling together ended up spending a *Shabbat* in Williamsburg, a New York enclave of Satmar Chassidim, with a lovely young woman and her five little children (don't ask why, it's a long story). This is an ultra-Orthodox community regulated by strict adherence to Jewish law, where secular literature, newspapers and television are virtually banned. Tragically, her husband died in his late twenties, and her family were helping to support them. She kept a copy of the *Jewish Press* in

22 Babylonian Talmud, Shabbat 117b. Ramban (Nachmanides) quotes Rabbenu Tam who says that 'women are obligated to have three meals (on *Shabbat*) because they were also included in the miracle of the manna and are obligated to break bread on two loaves for this reason'. We can extrapolate that if women and men are equally obligated, one can do it on behalf of the other. Technically, the woman can also recite the *Kiddush* for a man, as they are also equally obligated in this commandment.
23 Wolowelsky, J., op. cit., p. 34

the cabinet under the kitchen sink, lest any of her neighbours caught her with a copy. Even though it is an Orthodox newspaper and widely read in the religious neighbourhoods of New York, it is generally not considered *kosher* enough in the strict Satmar community. She kept asking both of us all sorts of questions about the outside world. At the time, I was about twenty-six, but when she asked me how old I was, I lied and said twenty-two. (I was just too embarrassed to be twenty-six and unmarried.) Even then, she thought that was terribly old not to be married, and expressed grave concern at my marital status, proudly telling me her third child was born when she was twenty-two.

When it came to say the Friday-night blessing over the wine, I assumed that, in the absence of a male, she would recite it. But no, we had to wait about an hour until one of her brothers-in-law came to her cramped apartment, crawling with over-tired and over-hungry children, in order to say the blessings so that we could eat our meal. At the time I stored it in my bag of amazing religious moments and thought of it as incredibly sad. Now, of course, I think it is outrageous. I don't want either of you to end up hiding the newspaper under the sink or waiting for a man to rescue you from a religious black hole.

I often think back to that woman in Williamsburg. Can I presume that the women in her community did not want any changes? It is not so straightforward. I am lucky: I married your father when I was older and knew enough to expect to establish a home of shared authority with someone very open to women's concerns.

Unconsciously, I think I also delayed getting serious about finding a husband because it wasn't clear to me exactly how religious I wanted to be. I mean, it was always obvious that I wanted to marry someone who observed *Shabbat* and shared the same values, but I feared marrying someone who would be oppressive. I worried about marrying a religious man who was dogmatic and unyielding in his attitudes because I figured that was going to have repercussions for me as a woman. I think it is an unarticulated worry that many older religious single women have: they have tasted the fruits of the modern world, yet they are committed to the traditions of the past, and they want a husband who can appreciate this dichotomy in their lives.

Many of the women who marry at eighteen may never change their expectations, but what happens to a woman who, in a state of heightened consciousness ten years later, decides she wants more participation in Jewish ritual? What can she do? It's not so easy to leave everything behind, and I can understand why it is too painful for some women in the ultra-Orthodox community actually to grapple with these issues. The reality is that for many ultra-Orthodox women, large families and the burdens of childcare, poverty and a lack of employable skills are more immediate concerns.

This has led to what I regard as a perverse relationship between some professional Orthodox women who use birth control and their ultra-Orthodox sisters. For example, although motherhood is the most highly valued career path and the community prides itself on the women who orchestrate their large families, strange inconsistencies in childcare arrangements mean that many women from the ultra-Orthodox community are running makeshift crèches for the relatively well-off children of professional women. The professional women think they are doing the carers a favour by providing them with employment, while the carers often regard these 'modern' women as irresponsible mothers more interested in their careers than their children. At some level, each group of women despises the other. Are the women with large families jealous of the women with careers, or is it the other way around?

Some of the professional women do not have to rely on the ultra-Orthodox community as they have the financial resources to employ a nanny (live-in or live-out, full-time, expensive, qualified), or an au-pair (live-in, five-hours-a-day, grateful-to-be-in-England-far-from-Eastern-Europe, keen to improve her English, relatively cheap), or a child minder, or an occasional babysitter who comes to the house. Many of these young middle-class women spend long days, connected to each other by cordless telephones, languishing like prisoners in their large houses. I was sick of hearing them compete for the title 'husband with the longest working hours', 'most unhelpful mother-in-law' and 'most unreliable hired help'. Yet, in north-west London, where the 'help' is relied on for so many essential functions, some women are locked into a symbiotic relationship with their 'girl', whom they unwittingly value more than their husbands.

I am perfectly aware that I am part of an educated, privileged, élite middle-class stratum of Jewish women who have the time, the resources and the intellectual freedom to be disturbed by their position in Orthodoxy. Because the secular world offers me basically the same white-middle-class opportunities as other women, ultra-Orthodox women view me with suspicion. Yet, it is amazing to me that we don't see more of what unites us as Orthodox women: it is no coincidence that the religious squabbling and communal in-fighting is mainly orchestrated by men and often about issues which impact on women's lives. Should we leave it to the men to decide our fate because each group of women is busy distancing itself from another with a mixture of pity and scorn?

Additionally, many of the ultra-Orthodox women are teachers and secretaries working in communal institutions to support their growing families. Their husbands are learning in a *kollel*, a *yeshivah* for married men, and receive a small stipend, or earn small incomes at menial jobs. New Labour would be proud of these women who have understood the basic requirement for the transition of feminist rhetoric into feminist practice – working mothers need affordable, culturally sensitive and reliable child-care. This has spawned an even wider range of clandestine cash-only nurseries and play groups, usually in the converted garages or basements of other ultra-Orthodox women. One could leave a toddler there knowing she'd drink special *kosher* milk, but not always so confident that the house would pass local council regulations. Some of these arrangements remind me of what Susan Cheever noted about nannies. She comments about women from poorer countries who take on nanny jobs to raise money to send back to their own children:

> We've decided to let other women take care of our children so that we can give those children a better life. The truth is that we are more like our nannies than we realise – strung out between

the old ways and the new, between the demands of money and the demands of love. They have chosen to give their children less mothering so that they can make more money, and so have we.[24]

At first, I strongly resisted help with the children. After all, I reasoned that, as an older mother, I should be thrilled to have the opportunity to spend time with my children, and I balked at the idea of having someone else look after them. I thought I should try mother-and-toddler groups. I went to one at the local synagogue and came home in tears. I didn't know any of the songs, and all the other mothers were talking about their mothers coming around to help. I tried baby-gym but I was too unfit to keep up with the music. I even went to some people's houses for morning coffee, but I felt so incredibly alone that I gobbled up one chocolate digestive after another.

'In Australia,' I complained to Jonathan, 'I could visit my real friends.'

That made him feel really bad, and I felt great. Until I felt really bad again. Although Jonathan kept urging me to have someone look after Avigayil, I conveniently couldn't find anyone, and then when I did, I argued it was too much of a luxury. (I majored in martyrology.) Once I won ten pounds on the lottery, and I decided that an afternoon of childcare would be a good idea. Then I had to face the awful truth that I didn't really know what to do. At the time I was dabbling in a book business, dabbling in some teaching, and dabbling in some freelance writing. Dabble, dabble, dabble . . . I had become a dabbler.

24 Cheever, S., *New Yorker*, 6 March 1995

Chapter 4

I never used to be a dabbler. I used to be dynamite. I started my professional life as a social worker, driven by passion to change the world. Before that, I thought I would be a judge. 'Justice, thou shalt pursue justice.'[1] The idea of presiding over a courtroom in long black robes, ensuring that good would triumph over evil, had great appeal. Where did I get this preposterous idea?

From watching my mother? She arrived in Australia as a ten-year-old refugee after the war. Her mother immediately launched herself into the work of most immigrants – repetitive factory work, sewing on buttons and ironing. After a brief spell at school, my mother went with my grandparents to Healsville, home to Melbourne's famous wildlife sanctuary, and helped in their small grocery store. She did that sort of work till she died – first with her parents, and then with my father in a series of small food shops. My childhood memories centre on the milk bar, the sandwich bar and the coffee shop, in which my parents worked long hours and many years so that my brother and I would never have to slice a tomato for someone else.

When I turned thirty, I was gallivanting around the world, dabbling with purpose while squandering all that I had saved during a few years of emotionally stressful work. When my mother was thirty, she was slaving away every day from 6 a.m. to 9 p.m. to help support her family. Now, I get teary thinking about the contrast in our lives. I never really appreciated how difficult things were for her, although I console myself that she was very happy with her family.

I am not sure where I got the idea of becoming a judge. I did not have any role models as none of my closest friends had professional

[1] Deuteronomy 16:20

parents. They were also mainly immigrants doing immigrant work. Perhaps that is why I instinctively felt that the world was an unfair place – hadn't these people had a hard enough life already? Neither of my parents laughed when I said I wanted to be a judge, and neither felt it was not a woman's job. (However, they did think my very first career plan, to be an air hostess, had less merit.) They were more the sort of 'well don't talk about it, just do it' sort of parents, and given I was only ten years old at the time, they had the foresight to wait and see if I had the requisite smarts. Several years later, when I secured a place in the law school at Melbourne University, everyone was very happy, especially me – Supreme Court here I come. But then the folly of youth interfered.

I took a year off between matriculation and university and spent it in Israel, working on a kibbutz and studying in Jerusalem. That's when it all started to go wrong. I decided I wanted to help people. At the time, I did not understand that my desire to help stemmed from being the child of Holocaust survivors. I felt that I had to do something meaningful, something that impacted on the lives of others less fortunate, something noble, something that would allow me to suffer a little and identify with my parents. I realised this much later, without any therapy I hasten to add.

'What a load of rubbish,' I can hear my father saying. 'Just get a job that makes lots of money so that you won't have to struggle like we did.'

But after a minor battle, they quickly realised there was little they could do to stop me (it seems that they were counting on a daughter-judge after all) and I qualified with a Bachelor of Social Work degree from Melbourne University in 1982. At least my brother realised that my parents had the right idea, and he completed a law/commerce degree at Melbourne University a few years later.

My first job was in a hospital in a working-class area of Melbourne. I was the social worker responsible for geriatric and ante-natal wards. I was so proud of my windowless size-six shoebox of an office, in the most decrepit part of the building. My diary was filled with appointments and I felt extremely important. One day when my car was being repaired, my father came to the hospital to pick me up. I was looking forward to his visit so I could show him my real job. The poor man was horrified and dumb struck.

'That my daughter should have worked in such a dump,' he said for several years after, whenever we drove past that hospital.

Now I understand that it was precisely because he had suffered so much that he wanted to spare me any hardship. I, of course, revelled in hardship and trying to sort out other people's lives. I was only at the hospital for about a year, and then moved on to a series of jobs with increasingly spacious surroundings and even a window, but he refused to visit, arguing that he could not bear to see me in another shoebox.

I shifted between jobs in and out of the Jewish community. Part of me felt I should work with Jewish families, especially in the religious community. I knew I understood the boundaries defining the ultra-Orthodox world better than many other social workers. After all, I too observed the Sabbath, ate only *kosher* food and had a certain empathy with their moral code. But, when I started my career, I did not want to get pigeon-holed as an 'ethnic' worker, much less a Jewish 'ethnic' worker – somehow, it didn't seem credible enough. I had a sense that I needed to 'prove' myself in a deprived housing estate dealing with child abuse and domestic violence.

After I 'proved' myself, I saw that working in the religious Jewish community is fraught with its own idiosyncratic conflicts. Although Jews are very prominent in the world of counselling, psychoanalysis and therapy, the Orthodox community is very wary of all such professionals. Asking for help acknowledges that the internal structure of the community is not strong enough to militate against these problems. The values underpinning therapy are perceived as antithetical to the religious values of the community. In other words, therapy is not '*Torah*-true'. (Unless it has the approbation of a respected group of rabbis and is trusted to counsel clients without inferring any criticism of an Orthodox way of life. For example advertisements displayed in the *Jewish Observer*, a showcase magazine of the ultra-Orthodox community, indicate that there are some services considered acceptable: ' "I wish I could speak to a *frum* therapist on the phone without giving my name!" You can! Just call the Yitti Leibel Helpline.') [2]

However, more significantly, '*shidduch* anxiety' gets in the way. This fear that any hint of a blemish in the family will ruin a potential *shidduch*, marriage arrangement, leads to a disproportionate fear of the stigma of any psychiatric illness in the Orthodox world. It also impedes the establishment of preventive mental health programmes.

When I first started working at Jewish social services, the staff were so keen to get the Orthodox clients through their front door, that they suspended the usual expectations of client appointments, punctuality, and good manners. The staff treated them with kid gloves because it was well known that one good word about a particular social worker would bring in more families, and equally powerful, one bad word about any of the social workers, and no one from the community would come near the agency. This deference towards the ultra-Orthodox was ironically matched by a certain repugnance and negativity in their attitude towards them. Some social workers secretly maligned them for having so many children and putting their spiritual needs before filling their children's lunch boxes with nutritional food.

So, when I visited religious families I considered myself sensitive to their needs, able to handle denial, yet ready to help work through the psychological and emotional stresses about which they would be forthcoming once they realised I was just like them. But when I arrived, I was regularly asked to do the ironing. That was considered helpful. Talking about one's feelings was not helpful. As so much of a woman's life was consumed with concern for feeding her family, organising the children, nurturing their husbands, caring for their ageing parents and doing good deeds throughout the community, there was little time left for the highly undervalued act of self-reflection.

As for the men, they are even more likely to think that too much introspection is a self-indulgent diversion from a man's true path of study and the fulfilment of God's commands. I realised that the

2 *Jewish Observer*, April 1997. This service has been regularly advertised for many years.

most effective way to reach these families was to provide the
practical support they requested, and use this as a means of
exploring other issues. Although I never did the ironing (but
contemplated the act so that I could submit an article to a
professional journal. I had a working title: 'An Iron in the Fire:
The Therapeutic Value of Ironing and Housework in the Social-
Worker–Client Relationship'), I tried to ensure that the families
knew about cheap, practical help.

Anyway, what did I really understand about the intricacies of
family life, especially raising children? As an arrogant, child free
social worker, I couldn't really understand what these women did
all day. I mean, how difficult could it be to look after children?
Guess who's had the last laugh.

What did I really understand about someone like Mrs S? When
her seventh child was born with Down's Syndrome, she accepted
him as a special gift – a sign from God that she and her husband
were chosen for a purpose. As much as the body is a mirror of the
soul, a disabled child is the mirror of an incomplete soul – a soul
that has been entrusted to special parents to develop and nurture
to its fullest potential.

'We believe,' she said to me, clearly excluding me from her
community of believers, 'that according to tradition, Adam fore-
saw that King David would die at birth and lent him seventy years
of his life.[3] My little boy is the incomplete soul of someone else.
He was brought into this world and our family to finish the work of
someone else's life. God does not test us beyond our capacity.'
(That's what they told me when my mother died, but I have to say
that God tested me beyond my capacity.)

What could I say to someone so devout? Although religious
faith always helps people to overcome and rationalise tragedies, I
am convinced that there is a lot of repressed anger – a natural
cynicism does not let me believe that people could be so passive
and unconditionally acquiescent. Don't they stare back at God,
angrily cursing their burden? No one really knows, for their
collective public face is of stoic belief, taking comfort that they are

3 Numbers Rabbah 14:12

'chosen' to bear the burden. The greater adversity, the greater the proof that God loves you. But I share the view of Tevye in *Fiddler on the Roof*: 'Couldn't God love me a little less?'

Mrs S's denial frustrated me immensely. As long as the word 'doubt' existed in my mind, I would see the world standing on premises contrary to those that defined the reality of Mrs S and her community. She was not going to trust me, and I resented the fact that the rabbis did not encourage her community to heed the professional advice of trained experts. Sometimes, it seems that some rabbis have a vested interest in maintaining their own community in poverty of mind and matter.

As for Mr S, I often thought of him, and of many of the husbands in the community, as a two-bit actor in a second-rate play with a small non-speaking role. He was completely emasculated and stunted by an inability to express his needs. He was a victim of the '*Torah* Trap' – that pressure to enter the *yeshivah* world straight after high school with little regard for the aptitude or interests of the student. Full-time study of the *Talmud* does not suit everyone, but the men who realise that they do not have the *sitzfleisch*, the patience and stamina, to study further have had little opportunity to gain commercial or professional qualifications. They are trapped. If they are lucky, they can go into their father's business, or marry well and go into their father-in-law's business. If they are unlucky they are stranded, and rely on the limited number of jobs available within the community – at the butcher's, the baker's, the laundromat or the mini-cab office. But there are not enough of these to go around, and all of them are lowly paid jobs, not providing enough to support a large family. Hence the humiliating and degrading turn to various charities for help. While a woman can rationalise that the help is really for her children and the good of her family, it is much harder for a man to accept charity.

However, one of the great things about the Orthodox community is the network of informal supports: for instance, there are *gemachs* or loan societies for maternity clothes and baby equipment and meals are made for women with new babies so that during the first couple of weeks they don't have to worry. Inevitably, this means that there is also an abundance of informal advice.

'I am not sure if you realise, but since Mrs B's baby was born' (for Mrs B has been advising) 'there has been a lot of research done, and we now know that there is a very important connection between the amount of early intervention and the progress a child will make. These first few months and years have a tremendous impact on your baby's development. Do you understand?'

'Of course.'

It was the same vacant stare with which Mrs S usually responds. Was it a question, an affirmation or just an appeasement?

'I'd like to arrange an appointment for our special-needs teacher to come and visit. Would you agree to that?'

This would be a start and the only thing that had any remote hope of being accepted. Any talk of the impact of this baby on the family dynamics was a long way off.

'Fine.'

'I'll ask her to phone you in the next day or two. Her name is Sharon.'

'Is she a *heimishe* girl?'

I sighed, knowing that the fact Sharon was not Orthodox would discredit her professional qualifications and years of experience.

'No, but she is very experienced, and she does understand.'

There was the usual shrug of suspicion.

'Oh, there is something very important that I wanted to ask you.'

'Yes?' I answered brimming with expectation. Maybe Mrs S was about to share a feeling or two.

'Can you send someone over to do the cleaning for Passover – I haven't had a chance to do anything.'

I sighed heavily.

'I'll see what I can do.'

Usually, I couldn't do very much, and often I was sorry that I didn't study law. I am also sorry that I didn't do medicine, or become a *Talmud* scholar. I would have liked the status of the first two, or the respect of the third. Then I would be taken seriously. Have you noticed the way people ask doctors their opinion on foreign policy, as if they know everything? I would like people to regard me as having authority: OK, so I am not perfect.

Instead, I get to say things like, 'You know, it's hard, I have a couple of kids, they're little. I used to be really interesting' (snigger, snigger). 'Now I do a bit of writing when they're asleep, you know, I do a bit of social work, I get a babysitter sometimes, I do a little teaching, nothing really high-powered. I'm a bit of a dabbler really.' I get to practise my defence mechanisms and justify my whole existence. That is what became of your mother, an ambitious modern Orthodox woman.

Chapter 5

The problem is that I harbour a delusionary belief that if I was single I would be *somebody*. Especially after I get a letter from a friend who hunts Nazis. Then, when your father starts getting romantic, I feel a little guilty.

'Think how many nice things we could have done together if we had met fifteen years ago,' he says sweetly.

'You're right, you're right,' I say, because I don't want to hurt his feelings. 'Are you crazy?' I am thinking to myself.

Yet he has a point because if we had married fifteen years ago, you could both get yourselves dressed by now, and I'd have my self-esteem back. But the truth is, I had little interest in getting married when I was twenty-one and would probably have regretted it. I would still be wondering if I was destined for something great. (Now it is clear that I wasn't, nevertheless . . .) It seemed to me that for some of my friends, who did get married at twenty-one, it was one of two legitimate ways that they could leave their families (going to live in Israel was the other). Many seemed in love with the idea of having their own home, playing with the new appliances they received as wedding gifts, and the elevated social status that came from being A Married Woman. I didn't need any of that.

After my mother died, I was in charge of the domestic routine in our home, and the last thing I aspired to have was my own twin-tub washing machine. My brother, on the other hand, got married at the age of twenty-four to a young woman he had been dating for nearly four years. He was lucky to find a woman who enjoyed the rituals of domestic life and would reproduce the sort of routine and stable family environment he lost when our mother died.

Between you and me, I know what your father is really worried about. He worries in the rabbinic sense, for it is written: 'A daughter is a deceptive treasure to her father. Because of anxiety on her account, he cannot sleep at night . . . after she is grown up, *lest she fail to marry* . . . [1]

I say, get a decent education, independent earnings and travel the world. Don't waste your time with boyfriends until you are in your late twenties, and then, in your early thirties, you could settle down and have some kids. Be like me. He says, then it could be too late and, statistically, he is probably right. If you want a Jewish husband, it is only going to get harder because more Jewish men are marrying 'out' than Jewish women. Yet, would it be so terrible to be single? (At this point any of my single friends reading this book will be furious, rounding on me accusingly with, 'Oh, it's easy for you to talk Miss-Oh-How-Quickly-We-Forget-Would-You-Really-Swap-Your-Life-For-Mine?')

But there's more – and *after she is married, lest she have no children.*[2] That is what really concerns him.

'A woman is not just a baby-making machine!' I scream, as if I was at a political rally in the 1970s.

'Calm down. Aren't you happy with a couple of kids.'

'Yeah.'

'Well, don't you want them to be happy?'

'Yeah.'

'Then it would be nice for them to have children.'

'Oh, don't be so simple. Children don't make everyone happy.'

'Fine. Just stop accusing me of wanting them to conform. You're the one who just wants them to conform to some sort of outdated feminist agenda – to be the radical you weren't.'

Then I storm out of the room, but I'm back a few minutes later.

'They could just stay single and have children. It's the 1990s you know.'

He rolls his eyes, but its true. Obviously, you can choose to be a single birth-mother. On a practical level, this has serious *halachic* difficulties because it would be a violation of the prohibition against premarital sex. (Don't tell the other kids at play group that I have been putting these ideas into your head, or you will be

[1] Babylonian Talmud Sanhedrin 100b
[2] ibid.

expelled, and no one will let me bake cakes for synagogue functions, hat or no hat.)

I have many single Orthodox acquaintances in their late thirties and early forties who are grappling with this issue at the moment. I'll let you into a secret: what separates modern Orthodox people from the ultra-Orthodox is not obscure theological differences or the brand of *kosher* meat they eat, rather it is the fact that many modern, professional Orthodox single people in their thirties are sleeping around. I say, the women could put that to good use and have a baby. Or they could avoid the whole sex thing, and get artificially inseminated with the same outcome. I have been saying this for years, but just as I was completing this book, I was fascinated to read an article about the 'world's first *kosher* in-vitro fertilisation clinic' which recently opened in Manhattan. Then I was amazed to read that one of the ethical issues raised at a seminar to discuss the implications of in-vitro fertilisation for Orthodox people was 'whether single Orthodox women who choose not to marry may be inseminated'.[3] This is mind-blowing stuff for the Orthodox world even to contemplate, let alone actively provide a service for. Your mother is a prophet!

Amongst many non-Orthodox Jewish women this is already happening: the New York chapter of Single Women by Choice is mainly Jewish professional women.[4] I have a thirty-eight-year-old friend with several degrees who has just had a baby girl with artificial insemination by a close male friend. Although she conceded that she would have preferred to be in a stable marriage, she heard that biological clock ticking. I know my friend, and I am sure her baby will be better loved and cared for, emotionally and physically, than some children in two-parent families. Although I do believe that a child benefits from a happy, functioning (stress on the happy and functioning) two-parent family, not everyone can

3 Jolkovsky, B., 'A *Hechsher* That's Hard to Conceive: Fertilization Clinics, Orthodox-Supervised Semen Samples come to NY', *Forward*, 12 June 1997, p. 2
4 Fishman, S., op. cit., p. 57; Loeb-Kreuzer, T., 'Jewish Single Mothers by Choice; *Lilith*, Vol. 21, no. 1, Spring 1996, pp. 24–31

find that suitable partner. It doesn't mean they have to stop being Orthodox: in fact, the communal structures which Orthodoxy provides are even more important for a single mother. It also does not preclude the option that a single mother might eventually marry and establish a more 'traditional' family structure.

Adoption presents a much less problematical alternative. In recent years, the paucity of Jewish babies available for adoption has led Jewish people to adopt non-Jewish babies and convert them to Judaism. Many rabbis complain that non-Orthodox families adopting children are not providing a religious environment. But if rabbis would encourage single Orthodox women to adopt babies, then they would see the child grow up in an environment structured around the Sabbath, the Jewish holidays, the dietary laws and a Jewish education. In general, ignoring this growing number of single professional women is indicative of the Orthodox community's inability to address contemporary patterns of social behaviour. Rather than blame the women for making a proactive choice to raise children alone, we should be thanking them for helping to solve the decline in Jewish births which is troubling demographers and communal planners.

There is one small group of Orthodox women who are completely marginalised: single women, with or without children, who are in a lesbian relationship. I was told by a reliable journalist of a Jerusalem-based group of gay Orthodox women who meet regularly for support, and it seems an underground group of women calling themselves Orthodykes also exists.[5]

We might feel uncomfortable about single Orthodox mothers and we might not like much of what we know exists, but, ironically, the Orthodox community can offer the structure and communal facilities to welcome single mothers and their children. I know there is an emphasis on traditional two-parent-Volvo-in-the-garage-families, but Orthodox rabbis and lay leaders have to

---

[5] Alpert, R., *Like Bread on the* Seder *Plate: Jewish Lesbians and the Transformation of Tradition*, Columbia University Press, New York, 1997, p. 180, n4. I had also heard about this group from people who knew people.

broaden their definitions of family life and seriously confront these alternatives. Otherwise, women will find another place where their concerns are validated and appreciated. And you might need to look for that place too.

What if you don't have children? There are many great role models – like Nettie Adler (1868–1950), daughter of the former Chief Rabbi of England, who devoted her life to communal service and education[6] or Rebecca Gratz (1781–1869), who founded the Hebrew Sunday School of Philadelphia in 1838 and was among the founders of several other important charitable institutions. She was an internationally respected advocate of women's rights, who 'gained respectability of the growing number of Jewish women who remained single in order to preserve their independence'.[7]

I have my triumvirate of favourite single women: Bertha Pappenheim, Sara Schenirer and Henrietta Szold. I have thought so much about them that they have become, as it were, familiar friends.

Bertha Pappenheim was born in Vienna in 1859 into an Orthodox family, and is better known as Anna O, the patient whom Josef Breuer treated and discussed with Freud. The stress and emotional demands of nursing her father during his terminal illness led to the onset of severe hysterical symptoms (as they were termed in Freud's era). Her body was paralysed, her hearing and sight impaired and she mumbled incoherently in what sounded like several different languages. Bertha's mother called in Dr Breuer, who experimented with a 'talking cure', the precursor of psychoanalysis. He tried to encourage Anna O to reveal what was really troubling her and to 'talk away' her physical symptoms. Breuer treated her between 1880 and 1882 and confided in his

6 Alderman, G., *Modern British Jewry*, Clarendon Press, Oxford, 1992, pp. 200–1. Alderman mentions that her father forbade her to marry Isaac Friedner, and although she always remained Orthodox, she took on social causes her father did not always endorse.

7 Kuzmack, Linda, *Woman's Cause: The Jewish Women's Movement in England and the United States, 1881–1933*, Ohio State University, Columbus, Ohio, 1990, p. 22. Kuzmack brings to life a range of single (and married) women actively involved in social causes.

younger protégé, Sigmund Freud, who used this information to develop his nascent ideas about psychoanalysis. In 1888, Anna O moved with her widowed mother from Vienna to Frankfurt, her mother's birthplace.

The identity of Anna O remained a secret for more than fifty years, until in 1953 Ernest Jones revealed her identity in his biography, *The Life and Work of Sigmund Freud*. Bertha Pappenheim was the founder of the influential Judischer Frauenbund (JFB – League of German Jewish Women) and dedicated her later life to the abolishment of white slavery and the rampant Jewish prostitution which was such a dominant social problem for world Jewry in the late 1800s and early 1900s.

During the 1890s, Bertha took an increasing interest in the emerging suffragette movement, and decried the inability of Jewish women to participate fully in religious life or pursue educational opportunities. Bertha Pappenheim was deeply disturbed by the news that Jews were active in the white slave traffic. Young girls were being sent abroad, often unwittingly by their parents who believed their daughters would face a better future away from the poverty and pogroms that gripped Eastern Europe. They arrived clueless in countries such as Turkey, Greece and South America where well-organised gangs of pimps preyed on vulnerable women who eventually submitted to prostitution. Pappenheim knew that the Protestant and Catholic women in Germany organised welfare federations and supported feminist causes. She was convinced that the Jewish community needed a similar women's organisation and, in 1904, she founded the JFB. It later became accepted as a member of the German Federation of Women's Organisation, and eventually enrolled nearly a quarter of all German-Jewish women.

In 1907, Pappenheim founded Isenburg, a home which became the first place on the continent where 'endangered and morally sick' Jewish girls and unmarried mothers with illegitimate children could find acceptance and care. She challenged the prejudices of the Jewish establishment, and was adamant that no Jewish child should be lost to the community.

She was also a scholar and avid writer. After reading Mary

Wollstonecraft's *A Vindication of the Rights of Women*, she translated
it into German in 1899 (under a gender-ambivalent name, P.
Berthold). In 1910, she translated the *Memoirs of the Glückel of
Hameln* from Yiddish to German, and later, in 1929, she translated
the *Maasse Buch*, a book of ethical tales, and the *Tsena Urena*, a
Yiddish version of the Bible.[8] These were two significant works
written particularly for women, of which the latter has been the
recent subject of substantial academic scholarship. However, her
best known work is *Sisyphus Arbeit* ('Sisyphus Work'), published
under her real name, which documents the extent of Jewish
prostitution she uncovered in her travels during 1911 and 1912.[9]
Amongst other diary entries, she notes a visit to a hospital for
venereal disease in Budapest where all the patients were prostitutes
and one third of them were Jewish. In Alexandria, Greek and Jewish
prostitutes dominated the market, while in one Rumanian port four
of the seven brothels were owned by Jews. In Constantinople, she
recorded that almost all of the traffickers, and approximately ninety
per cent of the prostitutes were Jewish. One rabbi in Constantinople
admitted that there was a synagogue were the prostitutes donated
money so that their pimps could receive the honour of saying a
blessing on the *Torah*.[10]

8 Pappenheim, B., *Maasse Buch*, J. Kauffmann Verlag, Frankfurt am Main,
1929
9 Pappenheim, B., *Sisyphus Arbeit*, Paul E. Linder Verlag, Leipzig, 1924
10 For more information about Pappenheim and Jewish involvement in the
white slave trade, see Bristow, Edward, *Prostitution and Prejudice: The Jewish
Fight against White Slavery, 1870–1939*, Oxford University Press, Oxford,
1982. See also Edinger, D., *Bertha Pappenheim: Freud's Anna O.*, Congregation
Solel, Chicago, 1986 (this is cited by all works on Bertha Pappenheim as an
important source); Freeman, Lucy, *The Story of Anna O.*, Paragon House,
New York, 1972; Kaplan, Marion, *The Jewish Feminist Movement in Germany:
The Campaigns of the Judischer Frauenbund, 1904–1938*, Greenwood Press,
Connecticut, 1979; and 'The Rebel as Lacemaker: Bertha Pappenheim and
the Problem of Jewish Feminism', Chapter 6, in Shepherd, N., *A Price Below
Rubies: Jewish Women as Rebels and Radicals*, Weidenfeld & Nicolson, London,
1993, pp. 208–242. For a 'factionalised' account of Anna O's treatment, see
Yalom, I., *When Nietzsche Wept: A Novel of Obsession*, Harper Collins, New
York, 1992.

The JFB established outposts at railroad depots and ports where volunteers met unaccompanied girls – often competing with traffickers who procured destitute girls as they disembarked. JFB volunteers waited for these young girls, wearing yellow armbands with the motto HELP BY WOMEN FOR WOMEN, with offers of food, financial aid, counselling and information. The JFB was hampered by many rabbinical leaders who refused to acknowledge the extent of the problem (although some were actively sympathetic), and the Jewish press who were reluctant to cover the issue extensively for fear of aggravating the growing anti-Semitism in Germany.

She was invited by American Jews to lecture on white slavery, and she came to London to represent German-Jewish women at the Jewish International Conference on the Suppression of the Traffic in Girls and Women in April 1910.[11] (In fact, England was the first country to support an organised Jewish effort to stem the growth of prostitution and white slavery among Jews – the Jewish Association for the Protection of Girls, Women and Children was founded in London in 1885 by Lady Constance Battersea, a Rothschild who married a Gentile.)

Inspired by Pappenheim's writings and research, the JFB considered prostitution partly as a result of the low status of women in the Jewish religion. It was not enough, they argued, to be revered as mothers and wives, Jewish women must be appreciated as individuals, and given adequate education to enable them to become independent. The JFB went as far as to suggest that the sexist bias of Jewish divorce laws contributed to the white slavery problem.

This is what I am passing on to my daughters: the painful acknowledgement that Jewish divorce laws, developed within a religion that characterises its members as 'merciful, modest and benevolent',[12] are filled with structural inequities biased against women.

---

[11] See the 'Official Report of the Jewish International Conference on the Suppression of the Traffic in Girls and Women', held on 5, 6, 7 April 1910, for transcripts of speeches by several international campaigners, including Pappenheim, and also reports of activists who travelled to visit areas with a high number of Jewish prostitutes and brothels.
[12] Babylonian Talmud, Yevamot 79a

The biblical source of Jewish divorce is clear: 'When a man hath taken a wife, and married her, and it come to pass that she find no favour in his eyes, because he hath found some uncleanness in her: then let him write her a bill of divorcement, and give it in her hand, and send her out of his house.[13]

The *Talmud* devotes several tractates to the legal status of women, including *niddah* (rules of sexual relations and menstruation), *kiddushin* (marriage), *ketubot* (the marriage contract) and *gittin* (the procedures for giving and receiving a *get*, a Jewish bill of divorce).

Divorce is a unilateral act in Judaism, and one of the key requirements of a Jewish divorce is that the man must give his wife a *get* voluntarily.[14] Technically, the term *agunah* means a chained woman and it applies to a woman whose husband is missing: he may have disappeared on a trip or been killed in war, but there are no witnesses to his death. Since he is unable to free his wife from the marriage, she remains an *agunah*, unable to remarry.

During Pappenheim's activist years, pogroms, wars and economic insecurity separated a great number of husbands from their wives, leaving many women as *agunot*. Pappenheim was concerned that these abandoned women fell prey to traffickers who offered a rosy future or phoney divorces; she estimated that there were about twenty thousand *agunot* in Eastern Europe in 1929.[15]

The issue of the *agunah* is not new and has been represented in literature by writers such as Shmuel Yosef Agnon, Isaac Bashevis Singer and, more recently, Mayer Krich.[16] The latter author in

13 Deuteronomy 24:1
14 See Riskin, S., *Women and Jewish Divorce: The Rebellious Wife, the* Agunah *and the Right of Women to Initiate Divorce in Jewish Law: A* Halakhic *Solution*, KTAV, Hoboken, NJ, 1989, for a good overview and more detailed explanation of these issues. See Strassfield, S. and Strassfield, M., op. cit., pp. 113–18, for a blow-by-blow description of the procedure of receiving a *get*, which involves a set script between the rabbi, the husband, a couple of male witnesses and the scribe of the document. After the document is written, the wife must accept it in a prescribed manner, agreeing that she accepts it willingly.
15 Kaplan, M., op. cit., p. 117
16 All excerpted in Porter, J. (ed.), *Women in Chains: A Sourcebook of the* Agunah, Jason Aronson, Northvale, NJ, 1995, pp. 73–83

particular, illustrates how the term *agunah* nowadays includes a woman whose husband refuses to give her the *get* voluntarily, and makes demands such as financial compensation or custody of the children as a prerequisite to granting the *get*. These men know perfectly well that the *get* should be given voluntarily, but it is their final spiteful act of revenge and power. However, even more shameful is the anecdotal evidence of some *agunot* who claim that some rabbis have encouraged them to 'pay up and get it over with'.

Although some rabbis have been putting forward proposals to modify the laws, the vast majority of *agunot* are held to ransom by a system which handicaps them with a religious disability. Without a *get* a woman cannot remarry in an Orthodox synagogue, and if she proceeds to have a sexual relationship with another man, she is branded an adulterous woman. Any children from this relationship are considered *mamzerim* (usually inadequately translated as 'bastards'). According to Orthodox law, a *mamzer* is unable to marry another Jewish person unless that person is also a *mamzer*. The consequences are grave.

I know one person whose mother was civilly divorced from her first husband, but he never gave her a *get*. Although they were married in an Orthodox synagogue, she was never a particularly religious woman, and after her negative experience of divorce, severed her ties with the Orthodox community. She decided not to pay her husband's price for a *get*, and made a new life for herself.

A few years later, she remarried in a Reform synagogue and had a couple of children. According to Orthodox law, these children are *mamzerim*, but because Reform Judaism has eliminated this category of personal status, it never became an issue in their community. When my friend was in his early twenties, he decided he wanted to be an Orthodox Jew, and discovered that his status effectively barred him from marrying all other Jews except other *mamzerim*. As Judaism is matrilineal, he could marry a non-Jewish person, and his children would be free of this spiritual stigma. But if the *mamzer* is a woman, her disgrace is passed on to the next ten generations.

So we have a bizarre situation in which Orthodox Judaism ironically appears to encourage men to intermarry while women are left with no resolution to this problem. Aged forty, my friend is still single, although in moments of dark humour, he plans to set up a *mamzer* dating service. Rabbis seem unable to solve this tragedy, although in individual cases they try to find a loophole (a favourite Jewish pastime) that would make the parent's original marriage invalid, thus abolishing the need for a *get* and invalidating the status of *mamzer*.[17]

It is difficult to determine exactly the number of *agunot*, not least because it is difficult to determine exactly how many Jewish couples get divorced as many couples just rely on the procedure of the civil court and never bother to inform the religious equivalent of the civil Registrar of Births, Deaths and Marriages, nor subsequently bother to go through the procedures of obtaining a *get*. One thing is known: increasing numbers of Jewish couples are divorcing and it is happening in every section of the community. This reflects the national trend, and even the Orthodox community, which has traditionally prided itself on a relatively low divorce rate, has, at various times, acknowledged the extent of the problem. For example, in the 1960s, there was concern about the relatively increasing divorce rate in the ultra-Orthodox community of Stamford Hill, and the rabbinate of the Union of Orthodox Hebrew Congregations contemplated proclaiming a public fast day.[18]

In London, the *Beth Din*, religious court, deals with about two hundred and thirty *get* applications a year, but according to the Women's Review, there are over two hundred unresolved cases on their files 'and the numbers appear to be escalating rapidly'.[19] In Israel, the Israel Women's Network estimates about ten thousand *agunot* in Israel, and American advocates for *agunot* have suggested

---

17 Sometimes, when a Jewish couple divorce, they are unaware that a religious divorce is necessary and would be happy to co-operate with the procedures. Kayama is an organisation in New York which tries to raise public awareness about the need for a Jewish divorce to avoid unintended births of *mamzerim*.
18 Cited in Rabinowicz, H., *A World Apart: The Story of the Chasidim in Britain*, Vallentine Mitchell, London, 1997, p. 222. In Judaism, a fast day is a symbol of national mourning or a call for a day of prayer and introspection on the community's 'sins'.
19 Goodkin, J. and Citron, J., op. cit., p. 80

thousands of *agunot* in America.[20] Does it really matter how many? One is too many! The point is that the divorce laws leave women around the world in a powerless position, and the vast majority of rabbis have been reluctant to initiate any creative application of the *halachah* in order to alleviate the woman's suffering.

Instead, some communities have bypassed the *halachic* system and sought help from the civil courts to address the problem of *agunot*. This usually requires the civil court to demand a *get* as a prerequisite for a civil divorce, or the enforcement of a prenuptial agreement that states that, in the event of marital breakdown, a husband will give his wife a *get*. Examples of civil remedies are the *Get* Law of 1983 and 1992 in New York[21] and the 1990 Bill C-61 in Canada. The latter stipulates that 'initiators of civil divorce suits must ensure that all potential obstacles to a partner's religious remarriage are removed'. It sets procedures in place to assure this and grants judges the power to use sanctions against a recalcitrant husband.[22]

In South Africa, President Nelson Mandela signed the Divorce Amendment Act, 1996 (amending the Divorce Act, 1979), which in effect, means that a civil court will not grant a civil divorce until all barriers to a religious divorce are removed.[23]

In Israel, where there is no civil divorce, the rabbis have a complete monopoly. Many women have commented that it is very daunting, especially at such an emotional and difficult time, to attend the religious court and to find oneself the only woman in the room. In the last few years, women have been trained as *to'enot*, pleaders to act as advocates on behalf of women appearing before rabbinical courts. This development is also a reflection of increased

---

[20] See Grossman, N., 'Breaking the Chains of Jewish Divorce Law', *Lilith*, Summer 1993, pp. 8–12, for a comprehensive global overview, and a list of organisations in various countries able to help *agunot*.
[21] see Part V in Porter, J., op. cit., pp. 123–84, for essays regarding the *Get* Law. However, as this book was being completed, the future of the *Get* Law in New York was under threat: see Kessler, E. 'NY's *Get* Law Facing Constitutional Challenge', *Forward*, 15 August 1997, p. 1.
[22] See *Lilith*, Fall 1992, pp. 3–4, for more background.
[23] Harris, Chief Rabbi C., 'Getting the Getbill', in *Jewish Tradition:National Publication of the Union of Orthodox Synagogues of South Africa*, Passover 1997, pp. 7–8

educational opportunities for women to study the *Talmud* and be accepted as authorities in their relevant speciality.

The growth of women's advocacy organisations prepared to challenge the rabbinical courts and agitate for legal reform has helped to bring the issue to public consciousness. The JFB in the early 1900s demanded a general rabbinical convocation which would modernise marriage and divorce laws.[24] In 1922, the Council for the Amelioration of the Legal Position of the Jewess was founded by Lizzie Hands in London. According to its constitution, it was established 'in the interests of those Orthodox Jewesses, throughout the world, who are labouring under serious disabilities in respect to divorce, legal impediments to marriage and other matters'.[25] Among its many activities, it appealed to rabbis for changes to Jewish law, ultimately to no avail.

In the 1990s women lobbyists (with occasional support from men) have protested outside synagogues, chained themselves to each other, disrupted public meetings, picketed the homes of recalcitrant husbands, published the names of recalcitrant husbands and used the non-Jewish media to publicise their concern and highlight the problem to the general community. The year 1993 was declared Year of the *Agunah*, and the International Coalition for *Agunah* Rights was launched to co-ordinate international lobbying efforts. *Agunot* themselves have spoken at demonstrations and have been interviewed by the media. [26] Often these women are condemned by the male leadership as disrespectful and causing public embarrassment in front of the non-Jewish media. (These same men know that Jewish law is being abused as a political tool and they, too,

24 Kaplan, M., op. cit., p. 137
25 See the Lizzie Hands Collection at Jews' College Library, London, which has copies of the minutes of the meetings of the Council and correspondence with rabbis and other Jewish women's organisations about this issue. Thanks to Mr Esra Kahn for pointing this out to me.
26 Bunting, M. & Freedland, J., 'The Trials and Tribulations in a Marriage of Inconvenience', *Guardian*, 21 January 1995; interview with Gloria Proops who recently received her *get* after waiting for twenty years; Gledhill, R., 'Jewish Women stage protest over male grip on divorce law', *The Times*, 21 October 1995; Rocker, S., 'Women are to protest outside Chief's office', *Jewish Chronicle*, 20 October 1995

are embarrassed.) These women are accused of being 'rabble-rousers,' unable to understand how difficult it is to change the law. Yet I am always left wondering why these women are never lauded for bothering to care about the status of an *agunah*. It seems to me that these women should be congratulated, not condemned: the rabbis should appreciate that women care enough about the personal religious status of future generations to want to ensure that religious divorces are not jeopardised by men exploiting the vulnerable position of women. When some women are forced out of Orthodoxy because they don't want to remain loveless, isn't it time to ask not what women must do for Orthodoxy, but rather what Orthodoxy must do for women?

In Britain, the *Get* and *Agunah* Working Party, established as part of the Women's Review, was chaired by Dr Adrienne Baker. In their extensive 1994 report, the working party made twelve recommendations, most significantly urging support of the pre-nuptial agreement (PNA) announced by the Chief Rabbi, Dr Jonathan Sacks, in October 1993.[27] The essence of a PNA is that, in the event of a marital breakdown, the couple agree to a religious divorce. Other recommendations included a Jewish Family Mediation Service and training for rabbis on issues of marital conflict. However, this 1993 PNA was not the first time such a solution was suggested as a previous attempt by Dayan (Judge) Berel Berkovits to introduce a pre-nuptial agreement in the early 1980s was rejected.[28]

However, by the end of 1995, more than twelve months after women activists had put forward their recommendations, they were frustrated by the inaction on the part of the Chief Rabbi's office to implement the PNA. With the support of individual *agunot*, and the Jewish Women's Network, a grass-roots organisation of women drawn from across the religious spectrum which campaigns for change, a nationwide *Agunot* Campaign was launched. A simultaneous five-city protest against the recalcitrant rabbinate who had stalled on the implementation of the October 1993 pre-nuptial agreement was arranged for 17 December 1995.

27 Goodkin, J. and Citron, J., op. cit., pp. 93–4
28 The *Jewish Chronicle*, 15 December 1995, provides more extensive details.

(A few months earlier, in March 1995, a National Day for *Agunah*
Rights was organised in North America, and several rallies took
place in cities across the USA and Canada.)[29]

Additionally, in a significant complementary initiative to the
PNA, the former Chief Rabbi, Lord Jakobovits, was lobbying for a
change to England's new Family Law Bill, to ensure that a civil
divorce would not be granted without a *get*. [30] As far back as 1985,
he had convened a meeting of rabbis, judges and academics to
explore possibilities in changing the civil law. If any of these
proposals help the situation of *agunot*, great, but at the same time,
I think it is an appalling indictment on the religious system that we
appeal to the secular courts to do 'our dirty work'.

Then, in a strange confluence of events, two days before the
scheduled protest, the front page of the 15 December 1995 issue of
the *Jewish Chronicle* announced that 'Rabbis agree on radical
divorce reform package'. It was reported that a PNA had been
agreed upon by five different rabbinical courts and that it would be
available from February 1996. The PNA includes stipulations that
couples agree to attend a *Beth Din* (rabbinical court) if there are
problems in the marriage. If the *Beth Din*'s recommendations (e.g.
mediation, counselling) do not reconcile the couple, they must
then agree to abide by the requirements of a religious divorce.
Nevertheless, the organisers of the *Agunah* Campaign decided to
forge ahead with their demonstration and billed it as a celebration
of their lobbying efforts to produce change.

(No one will ever know the real motivations of the *dayanim* to
agree to act on the PNA at that point. However, a cynical observer
could suggest that the *dayanim* are supreme strategists who were
motivated largely by political reasons – not just to appease the
women, but to avoid further embarrassment in the non-Jewish
media, and to appear to be as serious as Lord Jakobovits in finding
a resolution).

I was there. It was Avigayil's first act of social protest. Not bad

---

29 Reported in *Lilith*, Summer 1995, p. 7
30 Jakobovits, Rabbi I., 'The Tortuous Path to Relief for *Agunot*', *Jewish
Chronicle*, 26 July 1996

for a one-year-old. We were offered a safety pin with a small chain attached – a symbol of the *agunah*, the chained woman. She smiled when I pinned it on her. Smart kid. Did she know that I was doing it for her protection in the years to come?

At our demonstration-cum-celebration outside one of the rabbinical courts, the mood was cautiously optimistic. When one of the *dayanim* came out, he asked if there were any *agunot* in the crowd. A young woman, no older than thirty, stepped forward and followed him inside. When she emerged, twenty minutes later, everyone was curious to know what he had said.

'He said he wants to help, he said he would do anything to help.' She had heard it all before. 'Everyone wants to help, but that's not the point. I don't need the help – my husband needs help – he needs psychiatric help.'

No divorce is straightforward and there is never one correct interpretation of events. But, as a *get* is meant to be granted voluntarily by the husband, should we expect men with diagnosed psychiatric problems to take responsibility for such a rational, voluntary act? It seems that in such cases, rabbis should have at their disposal some way of annulling a marriage without requiring a *get*.[31]

Another woman who has been an *agunah* for six years has just found out that her ex-husband (they have a civil divorce) has recently remarried in a Reform synagogue. She is very disappointed that the Reform rabbi agreed to perform the wedding, and thinks it would have been a perfect opportunity for the rabbi to say that he would not perform the ceremony unless her ex-husband gave her a *get*. For this reason alone, the sporadic dialogue between Orthodox and Reform communities needs to continue and be encouraged. A centralised body that deals with conversion, marriage and divorce laws has been discussed at various times but has

---

[31] It should be noted that part of the divorce requirements state that a woman must accept the *get* willingly. There have been a small number of cases where women did not want to be divorced and were not prepared to accept a *get*. In these instances, the rabbis rely on a loophole called *heter meah rabbanim*, the permission of a hundred rabbis. If a hundred rabbis sign a petition agreeing that this woman must accept the *get*, she is considered to be a divorced woman, even if it goes against her will.

yet to be agreed upon, due to the complexities of demanding that all groups defer to Orthodox standards and that the Orthodox establishment formally recognises the other denominations. Nevertheless, for the sake of the religious status of future generations, some resolution is imperative or we really will be Two Peoples, if not Three, Four or Five.

I was amused, but also disturbed to read that the Chief Rabbi reportedly argued that the 'vigils had, if anything, been counter-productive, and could have led to the rabbis refusing to support the PNA and the sanctions package because they did not want to be seen to bow to any pressure'.[32]

But the Chief Rabbi and his omnipotent bevy of theocrats would be in good company if they, like the rabbis of the *Talmud* and their medieval successors, were to respond creatively to public pressure and changing political, social and economic realities. It has happened before: the Bible explicitly says you will not charge interest[33] but over time an arrangement called *heter iska* was developed which allowed the charging of interest. Similarly, we are told that during Passover, we may not possess any leavened goods, or any dishes that have been touched by leavened goods.[34] So the rabbis worked out a system to allow us to sell our leavened products and dishes to a non-Jew for the week of Passover.

Specifically in relation to *agunot* there have been some changes. For example, the law states that the husband has to pay for the scribe who writes the *get*. However, after some time this changed, and the *Talmud* explains that the rabbis gave the wife the duty to pay for the *get*, so that her divorce would not be unduly delayed. (Some men were leaving their wives stranded as *agunot* if they left town without paying for the *get*).[35] Although this may have been a

---

32 *Jewish Chronicle* 15 December 1995, p. 33
33 Exodus 22:25
34 Exodus 13:6–7
35 Berkovits, E., *Jewish Women in Time and Torah*, KTAV, Hoboken, NJ, 1990, pp. 101–2, explains this in more detail, and gives the *Talmudic* sources. See also Berkovits, E., *Not in Heaven: The Nature and Function of Halakha*, KTAV, New York, 1983, pp. 32–45 and 100–6, for explanations and suggestions of ways to amend the marriage and divorce laws.

financial hardship for the wife, it was done with her best interests in mind. There are other examples of change, and no doubt there was debate, argument and perhaps even some public demonstrations, but the point is that when there was a need to adapt biblical law to the realities of modern life and human sensibilities, the rabbis were sometimes able to find a way.[36]

In our time, consider the tremendous energy and compassionate concern spent on questions of Jewish law and medical technology, particularly in the area of infertility treatments. Look at the ingenuity employed on working out ways to use an elevator on *Shabbat* (even though the use of electricity is prohibited) so that tourism in Israeli hotels is not affected. When we want Jewish law to work for us, and not against us, we find the means. Or as Blu Greenberg summed up in her dictum which has become the battle-cry for change: 'If there was a rabbinic will, there was a *halachic* way.'[37]

We have given the rabbis a mandate to respond more compassionately to the issue of *agunot*, yet they claim that they do not have the authority to change the laws. They humbly suggest that they are not 'great enough'. If that is the case, why do we continue to invest our hopes in their sage counsel? Is God waiting for us to come to our senses? 'Don't they *get* it?' God is laughing at us. Perhaps this is another of God's challenges to us, and God is waiting to see if we really are a compassionate and just people. Is it time for the community to invest its growing number of women scholars with the authority to free a wife from an intolerable situation? Is that what God is waiting for too?

In tandem with the PNA, the Women's Review recommended that a recalcitrant husband be refused synagogue honours, burial rights and other communal privileges, such as positions of authority. In 1997 (not bad, given Jewish historical precedents), the United Synagogue announced a list of six communal sanctions to

36 For a fuller discussion and explanation of these laws, see Elon, M., *The Principles of Jewish Law*, Keter Publishing, Jerusalem, 1975, pp. 275–87.
37 Greenberg, B., *On Women and Judaism*, Jewish Publication Society, Philadelphia, 1981, p. 44

deal with recalcitrant spouses, and four of the categories –
religious entitlements, synagogue membership, burial rights and
synagogue rights and privileges – deal with the denial of certain
privileges if a man withholds a *get*. The fifth category, 'rabbis and
ministers', indicates that a rabbi at his discretion may withhold his
duty to perform a religious rite for the man, and the sixth category,
'public announcement', gives permission for a *Beth Din* to publicise the fact this man has withheld a *get*.[38]

While we wait to see how successfully these sanctions will be
implemented, Dr Baker has pointed out that, in defiance of them,
an obstinate husband may choose spitefully to dig his heels in even
more, thus further abusing the religious law which allows him to
deny his wife a *get*. Rabbis are therefore reluctant to apply the
sanctions, which puts them in an extraordinary bind.[39]

Currently, the PNA is offered as an option to couples about to
be married, but there is anecdotal evidence that when it is
mentioned, it is offered half-heartedly with no explanation of its
meaning or the consequences of divorce. Sometimes it is not
mentioned at all. Before I got married, I was not offered a PNA as
the option was not available in Australia. Now I realise that I
should have arranged a pre-nuptial agreement with your father. I
know it doesn't sound very romantic: it almost sounds pessimistic,
as if I was already planning how the spoils would be divided should
we get divorced (he can have the double buggy, I'll take the
dishwasher). But it is specifically because I would submit myself to
the authority of the rabbinical courts and not remarry until I had
a proper *get* that a PNA is important. Until a PNA can be accepted
as part of the norm, it will not be respected. I should have written
a PNA to encourage other women to do so, and help normalise
the experience. I would like to have played a small part in

38 The *Jewish Press*, a Brooklyn-based newspaper largely read by the Orthodox
community, has a weekly column which exposes the names of recalcitrant
husbands. This newspaper took up the cause of *agunot* after Naomi Klass, the
daughter of the publisher of the paper, was unable to receive a get from her
husband.

39 Thanks to Adrienne Baker, who pointed this out to me in written
correspondence.

historical and religious change so that things might be a little different for you two girls. That would have been much more significant (albeit less aesthetic) than lobbying for women to hold the poles of my *chuppah*. While some of the minor changes to involve women in their weddings may give women a sense of greater participation, they are cosmetic changes designed to assuage the bride and the adulation which an accommodating rabbi receives is misplaced.

A few decorative changes to the wedding ceremony on the happiest day of a woman's life will make no difference if, in a few years, the marriage falls apart and her husband refuses to grant her a *get*. As long as the divorce laws directly discriminate against women, they damage the integrity of the whole community. So, unless the PNA is made mandatory, it will always be regarded as a stigmatised agreement which only unromantic, ultra-wary couples enter.

I think that women who balk at the idea are doing their future daughters and granddaughters a disservice, while men who shy away should not be trusted. If my husband-to-be was someone not prepared to be part of a process to reform inequities facing women, including his own future daughters and granddaughters, then I would have seriously to question my own judgement in marrying him. The plight of the *agunah* is not a 'women's issue' to be conveniently sidelined and perceived as a hobby-horse of angry feminists. It is a communal issue that must be owned by all Jews. We should be equally shamed by what it does to the moral fibre of our community.

When the International Council of Jewish Women was founded in 1899, it became involved in the social welfare of women and children, challenging the establishment to address some of the inequities faced by women in Jewish law.[40] Similarly, when the Union of Jewish Women in Great Britain was founded in 1902 it was billed as an 'all-embracing sisterhood', and took on campaigns

[40] Las, N., *Jewish Women in a Changing World: A History of the International Council of Jewish Women, 1899–1995*, The Avraham Harman Institute of Contemporary Jewry, Jerusalem, 1996

to improve the opportunities for women in religious life and lobby for improved social conditions. In 1922, the Council for the Amelioration of the Legal Position of the Jewess dedicated itself to the specific issue of *agunot*. Why are we fighting many of the same wars all these years later? While there have been changes in Jewish women's lives, largely due to the influence of secularism and feminism, where are the changes due to a compassionate and contemporary understanding of religion? Where has life for Jewish women improved because the rabbis love the *halachah*, rather than fear the *halachah*?

I know that Orthodoxy is not a democracy, but it is painful to accept that the power and authority of the rabbis is entrenched in a divinely sanctioned non-democratic hierarchy which does not respond to lobbying by women activists who care so much about our heritage and religion. I could walk away and it might make my life simpler. But I, like so many other women, care too much about our children, and the future religious status of our children. Ultimately, I am the quintessential good and responsible Jewish girl who doesn't want to do anything that might jeopardise my children's ability to be counted in the community. My reward? Accusations of trouble making and tampering with God's laws.

While I can hope that you both have loving husbands, I pray that if, unfortunately, you need to divorce, it will be as dignified as possible – but all the hope and prayer in the world doesn't change the fact that until the rabbis show some courage, you are both *agunot*-in-waiting.

Back to Bertha – she not only campaigned on behalf of *agunot*, she also fought against Youth *Aliyah*,[41] a scheme which shipped children from Germany to Palestine in the 1930s. She would have clashed with Henrietta Szold, a pioneer of Youth *Aliyah* and a staunch Zionist. Szold was born in Baltimore in 1860, one of eight daughters of Rabbi Benjamin and Sophie Szold. She never

---

[41] Youth *Aliyah* was actually founded by Recha Freier. See Greenberg, M., *There is Hope for Children: Youth Aliyah, Henrietta Szold and Hadassah*, Hadassah Organization, New York, 1986, for more background about Youth *Aliyah* projects during and after World War II.

married,[42] and she never had children. As a child at Hebrew
School, I had heard about her as the founder of Hadassah Hospital
and saviour of thousands of children. I never heard that she was a
brilliant scholar, journalist, editor at the Jewish Publication
Society, translator of Louis Ginzberg's works and, in 1903, the first
woman allowed to attend classes at the Jewish Theological
Seminary (on the condition that she did not seek rabbinic
ordination).[43] She went to live in Israel at the age of sixty and
became a member of the Palestine Zionist Executive, a forerunner
to the Israeli parliament after the establishment of the State of
Israel in 1948. I had to discover this myself after I stumbled across
her moving letter about *Kaddish* following her mother's death.
That letter made me curious, and when I looked for more
information, I realised that there is extensive documentation about
her life. Why did my teachers choose not to tell me the whole
story? Did they know themselves?

Can you imagine Pappenheim and Szold in the same room?
Two highly articulate, scholarly women immersed in social activism, deeply connected to Jewish tradition and committed to the
welfare of women and young children. Yet they were ideologically
opposed to each other on the issue of Zionism. While Szold
embraced it as the means to save Jewish children and give Jews an
independent homeland, Pappenheim rejected Zionism partly
because she was concerned that the majority of its secular leaders
did not respect the religious customs and traditions of Judaism. As
a German patriot, she never imagined how bad the situation would
become. She was also angry that the Zionist movement paid scant
attention to the issue of white slavery, and she disapproved of what
she regarded as the subordinate position of women in the Zionist

---

42 Although it is well known that the 'love of her life' was the scholar Louis
Ginzberg, and that she was heartbroken after he announced his engage-
ment to Adele Katzenstein. See Shargel, D., *Lost Love: The Untold Story of
Henrietta Szold from her Journal and Letters*, Jewish Publication Society, Phila-
delphia, 1997, for the most recent and exhaustive exposé of the depths of
Szold's unrequited love.
43 Fineman, I., *A Woman of Valour: The Life of Henrietta Szold*, Simon and
Schuster, New York, 1961, p. 113

movement. She was concerned that their childcare policies on the *kibbutz* were anti-family and negated the importance of mother-hood. She regarded Youth *Aliyah* merely as a Zionist plan to populate the land of Israel.[44] Her death in May 1936 spared her the truth of the Nazi danger, and the knowledge that Isenburg, the project she held dearest, was partially destroyed on Kristallnacht in November 1938 and closed permanently in 1942. The young women were sent to the concentration camp in Theresienstadt, and the remains of Isenburg were used by Hitler youth.[45]

On the other hand, Bertha Pappenheim was particularly inter-ested in and supportive of, the Beth Jacob network of schools for girls in Poland. They were founded, in 1917, by Sara Schenirer, another extraordinary single woman[46] who also never had her own children. (Are you noticing a theme?) Her radical and brave plan to provide a Jewish education for Orthodox girls initially met with tremendous opposition. But the numbers say it all: in 1917 there was one school with twenty-five students. By 1937, there were two hundred and fifty schools with almost thirty-seven thousand students. She explains it better than I could:

> I was born in Cracow in 1883. My father did his utmost to bring up his children in the ways of *Torah* and Judaism. When I was six, I was nicknamed Miss Hasida (pious one). In school, religion was my best subject, though I was good in all subjects and received some distinction each time I was promoted. I was also good at sewing.
>
> It gave me great pleasure to spend the Sabbath reading the *Tsena Urena* [a Yiddish translation of the Bible], reviewing the

44 Kaplan, M., op. cit., pp. 48–9
45 Kaplan, M., op. cit., p. 136
46 See Zolty, S., *And All Your Children Shall be Learned: Women and the Study of Torah in Jewish Law and History*, Jason Aronson, Northvale, NJ, 1993, p. 281; in a footnote which cites Weissman's dissertation on the Beth Jacob movement, Zolty discusses the discrepancy in Schenirer's marital status. Although Schenirer wrote in her diary that she got engaged when she was twenty-eight, there is no further mention of a wedding or husband. One obituary notice claims that she was divorced 'from the husband of her youth'.

portion of the week and the *haftorah*. My sister and her friends used to spend the Sabbath singing and dancing. I went off into a corner, immersed in the portion of the week. They used to say that I was so absorbed in my religious books, that I would never have noticed if the house was being robbed. It hurt me even then to see my Jewish sisters transgress the spirit of the ancient Jewish people and disregard Judaism ... As I grew older, the income at home was small and I had to find work. I became a seamstress. I worked all day; in the evening however I worked on myself. I bought a Bible with a Yiddish translation and studied every evening. My pleasure was boundless.

On one Friday evening a cousin invited me to attend a meeting of the organisation called Ruth. I was shocked to see with my own eyes one of the officers lighting candles on the Sabbath. I had known that this group had no records in piety, but I never imagined they would have publicly violated the Sabbath. The lecture of the evening, distorted and impious, was heard by girls whose fathers were that moment studying *Gemara* and their mothers were reading the *Tsena Urena*. There it first occurred to me: if only these girls would be in the right environment, things would be different ...

After the great war broke out in 1914 we left Cracow for Vienna ... my landlady told me of a nearby Orthodox synagogue. I went there on the Sabbath during *Hanukah*. The rabbi Dr Flesch delivered an inspiring sermon about Judith, calling on the daughters of Israel in our time to follow in her footsteps. As I listened I thought: if only the Jewish women and girls of Cracow could hear him and learn who we were and how great is our heritage. But I realised that unfortunately our daughters knew little of our splendid past, a lack of knowledge that estranged them from their people and their tradition. Then I dreamed of great deeds, but Providence decreed a long time would pass before something practical came of these thoughts.

Listening to Dr Flesch's sermons, I kept thinking how to bring his message to the Jewish women of Poland. As time passed, my plan became concrete. How would Cracow respond to my plan to establish a school in which Jewish girls could be educated in an Orthodox environment. I knew they would ask, 'Now, in the twentieth century? Do you want Jewish girls to return to the past?' But an inner voice kept calling me: 'It is your responsibility to submit your plan to establish an Orthodox school. This is the only way to rescue for Judaism the new generation.' I decided that when I returned to Cracow, I would convene a meeting of girls and women and submit my proposal. I went back to Cracow in the summer in 1917 and invited a small group of observant women to listen to my plan. They approved. I was afraid that if adults were excited about my idea, the younger generation would laugh at it . . . I knew how hard the road I had marked out for myself would be, but I did not give up.

. . . The days turned into weeks; my plan began to take shape. The girls' organisations I had founded began to grow; yet I feared it would not bring the results I hoped for. Was it possible to influence grown girls who had ideas of their own? I decided to move in another direction. One must begin with little children. A young shoot bends more easily. Orthodox schools should be organised in which girls could be educated in the spirit of the ancient Jewish people. The idea preoccupied me. I wrote to my brother asking advice. At first he cautioned that I would become involved in disputes with the Jewish parties already operating their own school systems. But he suggested that I come to Marienbad, where we would visit the Belzer Rebbe and ask his advice. Though I could ill afford the trip, my joy was so great that I went. My brother took me to the *rebbe*, to whom he submitted a note explaining: 'My sister would like to guide and teach Jewish girls in the ways of Judaism and *Torah*.' The *rebbe* gave me his blessing and his wishes for my success. It was as though new energy poured into me.

In 1917, I finally had my own school. Who could understand how I felt with twenty-five beaming little faces before me? Once I had sewn clothing for many of them. Now I was giving them spiritual raiment. The school expanded from day to day. Soon I had forty pupils. The children were choice material; they had not yet tasted sin. They learned that man does not live by bread alone and that everything comes from God's mouth. They came to know that only by serving God sincerely could they live truly happy lives. [47]

Towards the end of 1935, Pappenheim visited the Beth Jacob school in Cracow to help develop its curriculum. When they were initially established, they were open to a much more varied student population and, according to Freeman, Pappenheim wanted to expand the teaching seminary which prepared teachers for Beth Jacob schools to include training in nursing and social work, as she intended to send some of the young women in her care to Beth Jacob to further their education.[48]

Nowadays the Beth Jacob schools in the USA, Israel and England are the exclusive domain of the right-wing branch of ultra-Orthodoxy (partly because there is now a much wider range of schools, so parents 'self-select' according to their religious level). While the girls may not always be prepared for a university education, they are certainly given functional skills to gain some employment (usually as teachers, secretaries or healthcare assist-ants) because they will often be the breadwinner in a family where the husband will continue to learn on a full-time basis.

However, unlike Bertha Pappenheim, who is virtually ignored by the Orthodox community, Sarah Schenirer is revered and would be beatified if Jews did that sort of thing. Sarah Schenirer was no intellectual (or if she was, that information has been conveniently censored by Orthodox historical myth-making). She was safe. She never sought to undermine the centrality of the family unit, nor change the essentially domestic role of women as the primary caregivers in Jewish children's lives. Actually, neither did Bertha Pappenheim, and they both clearly understood that women must be both educated and actively involved in communal work themselves or they will be lost to the whole community.

Unlike the single women activists of the past, single Jewish women of the 1990s are generally not investing their energies in

---

[47] Excerpted in Dawidowicz, L. (ed.), *The Golden Tradition: Jewish Life and Thought in Eastern Europe*, Schocken Books, New York, 1967, pp. 206–9
[48] Freeman, L., op. cit., p. 159

the Jewish community. Susan Weidman Schneider, a prominent
writer on Jewish women, suggests that

> because women were traditionally closed out of much of public
> religious life, community involvement through philanthropy
> became an alternative route to participation and empowerment
> in the Jewish community. Jewish women's organisations have
> been, in the past, the *shul* for women. Philanthropy was not only
> a road to participation and (relative) power in the Jewish
> community, but also one of the few sanctioned ways of express-
> ing publicly the religious or spiritual malaise.[49]

Nowadays, philanthropy will not give young women a spiritual
fix, and those who cannot find religious fulfilment in Judaism find
it elsewhere.

Cantor argues that historically in a community where 'men
were responsible for the mind, and women for the body'[50] much
communal work was divided along gender lines. Men were
involved in setting up educational facilities and championing
political causes (particularly in the Zionist movement), while
women established health and social services to meet the physical
needs of women and children. Nevertheless, a hundred years ago it
seems the community was more tolerant and accepting of the
dynamic contribution of these single women. In turn, they
strengthened their Jewish identity by a commitment to a Jewish
cause.

Nowadays, the young women who are prepared to work in the
Jewish community expect power-sharing with men and working
relationships that respect a woman's strength and intellect. Maybe
that is why many young Jewish women can be found in a range of
important non-Jewish welfare causes representing minority

---

49 Schneider, S. Weidman, 'Jewish Women's Philanthropy – Part 1: Women's
Giving to Jewish Organizations', *Lilith*, Winter 1992, p. 9. See also 'Part 2:
Feminist Philanthropy: Women Changing the World with their Dollars',
Lilith, Fall 1993, for more information on how women decide what to fund.
50 Cantor, A., *Jewish Women, Jewish Men: The Legacy of Patriarchy in Jewish
Life*, Harper, San Francisco, 1995, p. 318. Chapter 13 is an insightful and
iconoclastic analysis of women's volunteer organisations.

groups and oppressed people in society. There, a single Jewish woman doesn't have to apologise for her lifestyle choice.

While I have done my share of guilt-ridden, middle-class female volunteering in Jewish organisations, it always annoys me that the majority of the senior social-work management positions and titular heads of these organisations are men. Glossy newsletters and advertising campaigns are full of rich men who support the organisation, shaking the hands of the male heads of organisations. Where are the pictures of the women in the front-line working with the families and children? Where is the credit due to the radicalism, nerve and foresight which inspired the volunteers who founded many of the Jewish social services?

When a revered teacher or *Talmud* scholar enters the room, we are obliged to stand in their honour.[51] Why don't we stand for a great woman who has contributed her life's work to the welfare of others, a woman who lives by the law to 'love thy neighbour as thyself'?[52] Do we value study more than kindness? Why do we ascribe status only to an achievement that the majority of women are unable to attain because they have been denied access to the full range of Jewish texts and legal sources?

I would have stood up for Bertha Pappenheim, Henrietta Szold and Sarah Schenirer. Then I would have liked to invite them over for tea.

'Are you sorry you didn't have children?' I would have asked, indifferent to their feelings.

'Of course I missed being a mother,' Bertha might have replied, 'but I also think that women who have to miss the happiness of real

51 Aviva Zornberg, a highly respected *Torah* teacher, and one of the few Orthodox women who gives lectures to mixed audiences, recounts that 'one Conservative rabbi on the verge of retirement – he would stand up when I came into the room. It's right, according to Jewish law, if a teacher comes in, you get up, it's *kavod letorah*, honour to the *Torah*, it's not personal' – quoted in Ochs, V., *Words on Fire: One Woman's Journey into the Sacred*, Harcourt Brace Jovanovich, San Diego, 1990, p. 124. This is a very accessible and insightful account of Vanessa Och's year in Israel studying *Torah* with a range of women scholars in a variety of institutions.
52 Leviticus 19:18

personal motherhood may have an opportunity for spiritual motherhood, if they go the quiet way of helping children and adolescents whose actual mother may have failed.'[53]

'In fact,' I would pompously reassure her, 'our sages say "he who brings up the child is called father, not he who merely begot him",[54] but I'm sure they meant mothers as well.'

'Of course, that is right,' I hear Sarah chime in. 'I called them my daughters to my dying day.[55] One of my teachers even described me as the "black-clad figure of a little mother walking along with a swarm of girls round her".[56] When they collected my diaries and letters after my death, they entitled them *Mother in Israel*.'[57]

'They called me the "Mother of the Yishuv",' Henrietta would have reminded us, 'and I did get a stamp, after all.'[58]

'Me too!' Bertha again. 'I guess that's what happens to old maids who do good works – we get our face on a stamp.'[59]

'I should have had children,' Henrietta would have been wistful. 'Many children. I would exchange everything for one child of my own.'[60]

53 Kaplan, M., op. cit., p. 40
54 Exodus Rabbah 46:5
55 See Schenirer's ethical will, reprinted in Rubin, D., *Daughters of Destiny: Women Who Revolutionized Jewish Life and Torah Education*, Mesorah Publications, New York, 1988; see Weissman, D., 'Bais Yaakov: A Historical Model for Jewish Feminists', in Koltun, E. (ed.), *The Jewish Woman*, Schocken Books, New York, 1976, pp. 139–48 for a sociological analysis of the way the Beth Jacob movement ascribed the status of 'mother' to Sarah Schenirer and engendered total allegiance to her. In today's parlance, it would be about 'cult of the personality'.
56 cited in Grunfeld-Rosenbaum, J., 'Sara Schenirer', in Jung, L. (ed.), *Jewish Leaders, 1750–1940*, Boys Town Jerusalem Publishers, 1964, p. 408
57 *Em B'Yisrael* is the Hebrew title of her collection of letters. This translates as *Mother in Israel*.
58 Marcus, J., *The American Jewish Woman, 1654–1980*, KTAV, New York, 1981, p. 94. Yishuv refers to pre-1948 Jewry living in Israel. She was in fact honoured with her likeness on a five-pound note in 1975, as well as a stamp!
59 In 1954, the West Bonn Government issued a stamp in honour of Bertha Pappenheim, as one in the series Helpers of Humanity.
60 cited in Wagenknecht, E., *Daughters of the Covenant: Portraits of Six Jewish Women*, University of Massachusetts Press, Amherst, 1983, p. 167

That really depresses me. After everything she did, literally saving the lives of thousands of children and building a network of health and social services that helped hundreds of thousands, she still felt that a child of her own would have been more satisfying. Is it terrible to admit that there are days when I look at my daughters and feel guilty that I would rather be a hero and save thousands of defenceless children than wrestle with them to change a nappy or sing 'I'm a little teapot' for the hundredth time?

'Tell me, Bertha, how did you challenge the rabbinical establishment on the issue of *agunot*? How did you recognise that this increased the vulnerability of women and raised the likelihood that they would turn to prostitution.'

'Well, Sal . . . ' and I fill in the rest. Somehow she seems to have recognised that Jewish women are simultaneously cast into the contradictory roles of, to borrow a phrase, 'Damned Whores and God's Police'.[61] Orthodox women are God's Police, obligated to uphold a strict moral code, yet it seems we have only to cross a very thin line to become a Damned Whore. How does an Orthodox Jewish mother keep her daughters on the right side of the line?

Bertha Pappenheim's psychoanalytic biographers have explained her interest in prostitution as a great act of sublimation. Little is known of any romantic or sexual relationships and it has been argued that her conflicts as a young woman arose from a wish to possess her father or become a prostitute, or both. She resolved this conflict by working on behalf of prostitutes. Was it so simple? Her biographers did not seem to understand the dynamics of Orthodox Jewry, and largely failed to acknowledge the importance of her commitment to Orthodoxy, despite her disappointment with the rabbinical establishment.[62] She bothered to translate

---

61 Summers A., *Damned Whores and God's Police*, Penguin, London, 1975 (by an Australian writer, not the founder of the lingerie chain!)
62 See Boyarin, D., *Unheroic Conduct: The Rise of Heterosexuality and the Invention of the Jewish Man*, California University Press, Berkeley, 1997, p. 317. I came across this book during the final stages of writing this book, and was thrilled to find someone who felt as passionate about Bertha Pappenheim as I do. Boyarin aims to 'reclaim Bertha Pappenheim as a devout, feminist, radical, Jew' (p. 326), and, like me, considers Bertha as his role model/hero.

Jewish texts into a language accessible to women because she wanted them to know and to love their literature, and at Isenburg she made sure that *Shabbat* and *kashrut* were observed.[63] Yet the Orthodox establishment has hardly noticed her. Why? Could it be because she, of all the Orthodox single women who took on social causes, identified with perhaps the most difficult issue to resolve: 'the woman who stands outside of the family, the single woman, the woman who is not attached within a sexual relationship, [who] represents women's unharnessed sexuality'? [64]

There is a level at which being Orthodox in the modern world is psychologically compelling because it sets up almost impossible contradictions. I enjoy being on the margin and this feeling of straddling two worlds and being forced to reconcile 'real life' with a tradition that has endured for three thousand years is very challenging. It is not for everybody: some people are equally compelled by the certainty of dogma while others balk at the suggestion of having their lives ruled by Jewish law. In the meantime, can you tell me how an Orthodox mother even starts to think about her daughters as single women with all this unharnessed sexuality?

The whole book is a challenging read, but in particular his analysis of her treatment as Anna O and subsequent re-emergence as Bertha the social activist is fascinating, original thinking about this topic.
63 Kaplan, M., op. cit., p. 136
64 Eichenbaum, L. & Orbach, S., *Outside In, Inside Out: Women's Psychology: A Feminist Psychoanalytic Approach*, Penguin, 1982, p. 39

Chapter 6

But I am being unfair. You can be great and married. You can be a great wife. However, that requires finding a husband, which can be harder than being a great wife. I was sick of hearing stories like the one about my friend who was to be introduced to an eligible bachelor rabbi. When they spoke on the telephone, he suggested that she introduce herself on Saturday morning after the prayer service at his synagogue. If upon inspection it seemed worthwhile to date, he would pursue it further. He rationalised it as an efficient use of his time. When she told me, I was appalled by this crass plan, but it is a sign of how desperate a woman can be to try anything that my friend agreed to go along with it. She is now married, but he is still single.

While I lived in New York, I witnessed the thousands of yuppie Orthodox men and women who over-populate the streets of the Upper West Side of Manhattan after synagogue services on the Sabbath morning. The synagogue is the hottest dating scene, where the only rule is 'remember the girl's phone number', as you cannot write on the Sabbath. The women look seductive – the collars of their shirts are lacy and demure, the soothing pink or coral lipstick is designed to lasso the man's interest, and as they nod their tilted heads at appropriate ten-second intervals, they can make that man feel special and desired. Many women dress in clothes designed to infantilise them – bright colours, short skirts and garish make-up. Some say it is the New York look, but I think it is about acting in a childish mode, dressing in ways that will emphasise their willingness to be dominated and treated like a child. (Of course, that is what I'd say, because I never scored a date that way and they all did.)

The road to marriage is paved with disastrous dates, and when occasionally I was set up on blind dates, I didn't want to play the waiting game, feigning desperation and aspiration to be knee-deep in crappy nappies. It left me feeling dishonest and unable to share the dilemmas of a Jewish woman who wants the best of both worlds. I was warned not to say too much, for fear of scaring them off.

'Look at him with a new perspective, think about him differently,' I was told, as if I was the one who had to do all the compromising. I felt like a walking, talking time-womb and resented having to compete with younger women. I was reaching my use-by date, constantly being told by those in authority that my life was on hold until I found a husband.

It was time to call in the professionals. I would have to submit to a *shadchan*. *Shadchan* is such a pejorative word for an age-old figure – really, everyone's a *shadchan* – it is really just someone who provides an introduction to someone. At least that is how I rationalised the descent into paid help.

'Don't forget to take your passport,' my friend reminded me.

'Passport?'

'Haven't you heard? They want to see your passport to check your age before they will set you up. Apparently all the thirty-year-olds are claiming to be twenty-seven because the guys have got their pick.'

'This is crazy – maybe I shouldn't go.'

'Go, go – it'll be fine – you are giving the women of the world hope and fortitude.'

Until this point, I had had a pathetic love life. Essentially, I was a mate to many men, an intellectual mistress who would listen to their woes while fully cognisant that they lusted for others more attractive. This dismal situation allowed me successfully to develop my career and strengthen my defence mechanisms against accusations of making myself unmarriageable. Now having realised that someone was not going to pick me out of a crowded synagogue lobby, I would have to take action.

'So, come in, Sally,' Mrs F greeted me with a crooked smile. 'Please let me take your coat. Come into the lounge and meet my husband.'

The Fs' reputation as a *shadchan* team was very positive because they both saw the prospective client. They considered themselves more effective in making a match because each one came to the idea with a different perspective – the husband being able to suggest (or project) how a woman would be seen by her potential dates, and Mrs F able to evaluate how a male client would be seen by the women.

'Hello. Please,' he pointed towards a chair.

I took a seat and desperately conscious of my body language made a concentrated effort to deny my natural state and tried to sit as if I was relaxed. I sat back in the chair and put my palms in my lap. Don't make wild hand gestures, calm down, keep your knees crossed, I muttered to myself.

'If you don't mind, can you tell me how you heard about us?'

'From someone else who used you a while ago – Susan.'

'Ah yes, what a lovely girl. Let's hope she finds the right one soon. So, let me see – we need to take down a few details first of all. How do you spell your last name?'

'B–e–r–k–o–v–i–c.'

'Where were you born?'

'Melbourne.'

'And your parents . . . '

'They are Czech – they went to Australia after the war . . . survivors.'

'Ah. Where were your parents married?'

'In Melbourne.'

'Do you have a copy of the their *ketubah*, their wedding certificate?'

'I can get one.'

'Good. You do understand – it's for our records. We have to make sure that anyone we introduce to another Jewish person is fully Jewish himself or herself.'

'Yes, of course, I understand.'

'And how old are you?'

'Thirty-one,' I said without flinching. True, I had (unconsciously?) made this appointment two weeks prior to my thirty-second birthday.

'Do you have some form of identification – a driver's licence, or passport perhaps?'

'I have a passport.' I pulled it out of my handbag and passed it to Mrs F . . .

'Excellent – I'm sorry to ask for such details, but you wouldn't believe some of the people we have coming to see us. And it is better to get the awkward questions out of the way – don't you agree?'

'Of course,' said I quietly. How could I not agree?

'Now tell me a little about yourself.' This was a coded invitation to measure myself against Mrs F's expectations.

'Well, I grew up in Melbourne, I went to a non-Jewish school, Jewish youth groups, university. I've worked as a social worker and a freelance journa . . . '

'I see.'

No, you don't see, you stupid woman, I thought to myself. You haven't got a bloody clue.

'Now, what sort of boy are you looking for?'

I was trapped. If I say 'a religious boy', it appears that this is at the expense of his personality and makes me out to be more pious than I really am; if I say 'a nice guy', then it could seem that his religious observance is less important than it should be (should, should, why should I care what it sounds like?) If I say, 'I don't know what I want,' I sound like a wimp. And then I remembered, my rehearsed answer that I had always imagined using but had never had the opportunity. There was no time like the present.

'That's a really difficult one to answer – I suppose that ideally I am looking for someone with whom I can find a real rapport – someone who understands me, someone with whom I share interests and ideas, someone with common values.' I thought this was sounding quite constructive and intelligent.

'Yes, of course you do,' Mrs F replied distantly. 'And does he have to be a professional? What income bracket were you thinking of?'

She is not listening to a word I am saying, thought I to myself.

'Oh, I'm not fussed.'

They both stared at me completely bewildered.

'Oh, I suppose I would prefer someone with a university education.'

'Yes, I am sure you would. And what about his own property?'

It was so brutal, so unrelenting – did this flesh broker have no feelings?

'No, that's not necessary. I mean, it would be nice but it's not essential. I really am more interested in how cultured he is – you know, the books he reads, where he stands on political issues. Someone I can really talk to.'

'How much talking do you plan on doing?' laughed Mr F. 'Talk, talk, that's all the girls want – you know, talk is only good the first six months.'

'OK, I think we are getting the picture,' said Mrs F patronisingly. She really wanted to wag her finger at me and say, 'You know what you need – a boy who makes a decent *parnassa*,[1] can give you children and make you settle down.'

No doubt Mr F wanted to say, 'Marilyn Monroe you're not. You think it makes such a difference which boy you marry? Be grateful someone will support you and give you children.'

'So tell us, what do you think you can offer a young man?' asked Mrs F.

'I think I would make a good partner – I think I could nurture someone and give them the security of a relationship that would enable them to grow and develop their own personality.'

The Fs' looked at each other and nodded that patronising nod. It was time for the death-knell question.

'What about your career?'

'What do you mean?'

'Well, how do you see it in relation to your responsibilities as a wife and mother?'

'Until we have children, I don't see any conflict. We would both work and I suppose I would assume that my husband would share the shopping, the cooking and cleaning. When there are children – '

'Please God, there should be many,' Mrs F hastened to interpose.

'When there are children, I suppose we would need to look into that – I imagine that I will want to be at home looking after the

---

[1] regular income and good earning potential

children when they are very young, but I imagine that I would like to fit in some part-time work – it's really hard to predict all of that.'

'Yes, yes of course it is – but you are not one of those women who feel that they would put their career before their children.'

'I suppose not.' I was trying to sound convincing but was failing miserably. 'No, of course not.'

'Do you wear trousers?'

'No.'

'Good.'

'And do you intend covering your hair?'

I should have been prepared for this one, but I never know how to answer it properly.

'Um. I guess it would depend on the man.' I knew this was not the right answer, but it was the honest one – in my circles. The answers to these questions are not always black and white. (Where it is clear cut that the woman will abide by all the rules, there is no dilemma, but sometimes the situation is more complex. Pragmatically, I know that if I want to maximise the number of men I am introduced to, I must appear to be as flexible as possible.)

'What do you mean?' asked Mrs F.

'Well, if it was really important to him, then I would.'

'So you do not want to yourself?'

'Yes I do, but not if he objected to it.' I was sounding muddled.

'How tall are you?'

'Five-seven, I guess.'

'Will you go out with a boy a little shorter? I think I might have someone, but he's maybe five-five, five-six.'

'I suppose so, but I prefer tall.'

'But if he talks good?' Mr F was enjoying my meltdown.

'If you think he would be good to meet, that's fine.' I was humiliated. Did it matter what I said?

'And acne?'

'Excuse me?'

'Acne. Will you marry someone with terrible acne. I have someone on the books – a special boy, but he's had no luck because of his acne.'

'Fine, fine – I'll try anything.' I realised I was in the hands of really sensitive professionals. 'I really should get going.'

'We will try our best. If you will indulge me a moment longer, I like to tell all our clients this little story.'

Did I have a choice?

'A Roman noblewoman asked Reb Yose, "How many days did God take to create the world?"

' "Six days," Reb Yose answered.

' "And what has He been doing since then?" she asked.

'Reb Yose answered, "God has been busy making matches – the daughter of so-and-so to the son of so-and-so."

'The noblewoman was amused. "If that is all He does, I can do the same thing. I have all these manservants and maidservants! In no time at all, I can match them up."

' "Matchmaking might be a trivial thing in your eyes," responded Reb Yose, "but for the Holy One, it is as awesome an act as splitting the Red Sea."

'As soon as Reb Yose left the noblewoman, she took a thousand manservants and a thousand maidservants, lined them up row upon row, facing one another, and said, "This man shall marry that woman, and this woman shall be married to that man," and in this way she matched them all up in a single night. In the morning, the ones thus matched came to the lady, one with his head bloodied, one with her eye bruised, one with his shoulder dislocated, and another with his leg broken. "What happened to you?" she asked. One replied, "I don't want that woman," and another replied, "I don't want that man."

'The noblewoman promptly sent for Reb Yose.

'She said to him, "Master, your *Torah* is completely right, excellent and worthy of praise. All you said is exactly so." '[2]

'Is that not a beautiful story?' his wife could not wait to say. 'My husband likes to tell it to all who come to see us.'

'Sweet,' I mumbled.

'So you see Sally, matchmaking is not an easy business – if it is difficult for God, how much more so for mere Moshe F. All the

2 Genesis Rabbah 68:4

same, I have a couple of men in mind who I think might be appropriate – let me call them and find out if they are involved with anyone at the moment. I will ring you in the next few days. Are there any other questions?'

'I am a bit unclear about your charges – what is your fee?'

'We ask you to pay $36 to register (a nice twist, twice the Hebrew symbolic amount '18' for the value of life), which covers administrative costs. There is no fee until your partner is found, and once you have found your mate, we charge you $180. We see it as a small sum really for lasting happiness and it makes us able to go on. If, out of gratitude, you would like to make a donation, that will always be welcome.'

I wanted to ask if there was a money-back guarantee but I stopped myself.

A few days later, I got a call.

'Sally, I'm telling you, this boy is a real *mensch*. All day, he's working – a big law firm – and he studies every night. His mother, *nebbish*, is not a well woman – all she wants from her son is a bit of *naches*. And oy, is he good-looking? So special.' (Translation and cultural reinterpretation: This guy works all hours, his mother is on anti-depressants and is desperate for grandchildren. And he's as ugly as sin. I soon realised that the word 'special' was the most overused word in the *shadchan's* vocabulary.)

It was arranged – he could fit me in between meetings for a lunchtime date. I watched the entrance for a sign of his arrival. 'Where is he? It's already 1.30 p.m. I can't believe I am waiting in this restaurant for a guy and I don't even know what he looks like. We had agreed to meet at a popular Israeli restaurant. I definitely preferred coffee to a meal for the first date, although my friends laughed at me.

'Are you crazy, let him pay – he probably earns a fortune – it's the only decent meal you'll get all week!'

That was probably true – after all, what did young single women eat besides cottage cheese, Ryvita and tuna? Or pasta on a good night? Even though I offered to pay, *shidduch* protocol demanded that the male pay on the first date. I once calculated that a man with twenty dates a year, at an average cost of $50 an evening, would spend $1,000 on women he only ever met once. When neither was interested in the other, it was just a waste of money. But if the male was interested, even the most basic meal engendered a certain amount of gratitude, and women sometimes felt that they had to go out a second time even though they had no interest at all in the person. Coffee was less obligatory, and it also meant that if the date went terribly wrong it could be over in an hour. All these rules and unwritten codes of behaviour drove me mad.

Sometimes I thought it would be easier to be like the ultra-Orthodox where parents negotiated matches for their children. The young couple meet only a couple of times before the wedding ceremony. Romance was ridiculed as a concession to modernity. There was no room for romance in a holy relationship between husband and wife that would build a solid, respectable and Orthodox home, faithful to tradition and filled with children, scholars and guests. There were none of these agonising dating rituals.

'Could this be him?' I thought to myself. The signs were promising. No briefcase – he plans to go back to work; no book – so he doesn't plan to read with his meal; a *kippah* on his head – so he's Orthodox; glasses – a typical feature; and most importantly – he was alone. Tall enough, I thought to myself, but a bit on the scrawny side (oh well, what can you expect with a guy living alone?). As I started to rise from my chair to motion that I was the one, I caught his glance and noticed that he blushed. I liked that in a man. But then, just before he reached my table, he took a sharp turn to the right and went straight to the table at the other end of the restaurant. Clearly, this was not a first date for him – a petite blond woman greeted him effusively. To avoid further embarrassment, I rose to my feet and proceeded to go to the bathroom. Seeing this act of gallantry, he smiled to himself.

Several minutes later I returned and saw another man hovering at the entrance to the restaurant. The signs were there again – no briefcase, no book and he was alone. But he also had the look. A certain look of arrogance that told me he was doing me a favour by squeezing me into his busy schedule. A look that said dating was all beneath him, but he did it to help the plight of the Jewish woman.

He did a quick check around the restaurant, and realised that I was the only woman alone at a table. He looked experienced enough at these encounters to work it out. And he did. He approached me.

'Sally?'

'Hello,' I motioned to stand up and then sat down again.

'Hi, I'm Avi. How ya' doin?' (Damn, you're not that blonde astrophysicist with the perfect figure who is dying to have my kids)

'Hi. Fine, thanks.' (All right, so I'm not the blonde astrophysicist, but you think you're such a catch?)

'Have a seat.'

'Thanks.' He took his coat off.

'Did you have trouble finding the place?' I asked politely. (Pathetic, Berkovic you are PATHETIC.)

'Oh no, I've been here before.' (A thousand times with boring dates like you, honey.)

What is this *schtick* with Jewish men and Aryan blondes? Have they learnt nothing in three thousand years?

'Mmm.'

'Would you like to order?'

'Sure. I'll have humus and pitta.' (That's what women have – we don't think we deserve a man's meal.)

'I'll take the chicken shish kebab.'

(Of course you will, you're a man who likes to play with his skewer).

'And could we have a jug of water,' I asked.

'Are you sure you don't want juice?' he asked magnanimously.

'No water is fine, unless you want juice.'

'No water is fine.'

Next . . . next . . . right, right. Checklist, point 4. Work.

'How's your day at work so far?'

'A real bummer. We lost out on this really big deal with a Japanese bank. Some other firm offered them a better deal. And my boss called me in about all the *yomtov* days I want off work. The guy's a Jew but he's embarrassed about it – he takes off first day *Rosh Hashanah* and *Yom Kippur*, but the rest, it's as if it doesn't exist for him. I take them all off – another eleven to twelve days, and he says it makes him look bad. I tell him it makes me look bad. If you work for a good *goy*, they respect your religion. If you work for a bad *goy*, well that's a whole other story.'

I know this script by heart, but he lost one extra point by using the derogatory, yet commonly used word, for non-Jew.

'So, do you like New York?' he asked in return. (When does your visa run out and how desperate are you to marry for a green card?)

'I'm enjoying it a lot – it's very different from Melbourne.' (I don't need your crummy green card, you twit.)

'I've never been.' (What's Melbourne got that's not in New York?)

He was already looking at his watch. The conversation continued with the usual banter – he barely asked me about myself, yet I endured his tales of legal lechery and boardroom conquests. Why do I do this, I thought to myself? Why don't I just stop the conversation and say, 'Listen, you know you're not interested in me. I'm certainly not interested in you. Why don't we forget the humus: you go back to your fancy office, and I will go home where my computer respects me more than you do.' But no, we give them a chance because you just never know. But I know, I said to myself.

At 2.45 p.m., the waiter presented us with the bill for $25.75.

I motioned to get my purse.

'Oh no, its fine – I'll get it,' he said gallantly. 'The next one's on you.' (If you believe that, you're a real greenhorn!)

'Sure. Thanks.' (The next one – are you out of your mind?)

'No problem. Come on (Up, dog!) – I'll walk you to the subway.' Thankfully, it was only a couple of blocks. 'I'll give you a call later in the week,' he said, as he turned his head to look at some gorgeous thing who had just walked by.

'Sure, fine.'

Reader, I did not marry him.

Who are these Orthodox men? Many are intelligent, attractive, financially secure, sociable, caring and endearingly neurotic men. Why can't so many of them make a serious commitment? Like many of the women, they have tried to fuse a commitment to religion with an interest in all things secular, only to find themselves stranded in a community that does not value their intellectual interests or imagine the secret depths of their spiritual malaise. The growing shift towards the right by the Orthodox community, and the accompanying fear and closing down of intellectual curiosity leaves many modern Orthodox men somewhat alienated by the Orthodox world. (That is a whole other book that a man with nothing to fear will have to write.) However, while these single men pound the streets of Manhattan, London and Jerusalem, suffering from an overdose of cynicism, disillusionment and the loss of hope, they fail to understand that although they want a home infused with traditional family values, it is very difficult for independent women (the type of women they proclaim to desire) to adapt to Neanderorthodox Man.

I soon realised that I would have to play up my nurturing and enabling qualities to find a husband. I would have to be a mother. Few men appreciated my intellectual or acerbic wit. Even those who prided themselves on being politically correct would rather a woman fulfilled the traditional maternal and subsidiary roles. Sometimes, it seemed to me that the more a Jewish male espoused the feminist cause, the greater the likelihood that he would expect his wife to take on the feminised domestic roles. Naturally, he would be concerned about this, sharing his pain at the frustrating typical gender roles that he and his wife had fallen victim to.

The Orthodox establishment has failed to realise that a drive to encourage Orthodox women to have professional qualifications, without a concomitant reappraisal of their on-going ritual exclusion and the traditional childbearing role of Jewish women, was destined for trouble. At work, their non-Jewish colleagues value their sensuality, their assertiveness and independence. At home, Jewish men are often threatened by these same qualities. I'm already worried about what you girls will do if you can't find a Jewish partner.

I often fantasised about converting one of the lovely non-Jewish men I knew at work. (My psychoanalytical biographers will claim that I created these fantasies because I knew it was safe to do so. It's not as if I ever proposed to one of these men, or actually did anything about a particular fantasy – it was just a way of avoiding Jewish men and keeping them at a distance. Who do these psychoanalytical biographers think they are?)

Theoretically, there is a wonderful pool of potential Jewish men waiting to be created. These men are open to other religions, and would welcome the opportunity to join the Jewish community and embrace its cultural and spiritual dimensions. So, when you are older, you could seek out a nice non-Jewish man and convert him. With courage and foresight, the *Beth Din*, the court of law that oversees the conversions, could have such a positive, dynamic role in shaping and participating in the realities of contemporary Jewish living. For most couples, the conversion process is regarded as an obstacle course to be conquered, but the authorities could make it an opportunity to welcome new Jews into a civilisation that has so much to offer. The conversion process will bring Jewish women closer to their own religion. They will be in close contact with observant Jews, and have the chance to learn about their own heritage as adults, rather than as children forced to go to Sunday School or as teenagers compelled to study for an GCSE level Bible exam.

Non-Jewish men would alter the gene pool, possibly decreasing the incidence of Tay-Sachs (partly due to inbreeding amongst Jews of Eastern European Ashkenazi descent) and other inherited diseases. No matter which *Beth Din* oversees the man's conversion, the children will always be *halachically* Jewish, and for a community obsessed with its decreasing birthrate, this should be incentive enough to sanction and support these marriages.

Then, of course, there is the option Orthodox Jews don't like to talk about – marrying out, intermarriage, out-marriage, interfaith marriage, marriage-with-no-name. It doesn't matter what the sociologists and academics want to call it: a rose is a rose is a rose.

Admittedly, the ultra-Orthodox community has been a little sheltered from the issue because statistically it does happen less within their tight confines. Anyone who does marry out is more likely to have family ties severed and lose all contact with the community,[3] and we all know of rabbinical dynasties shamed by

3 A recent example is described in McBride, J., *The Color of Water*, Riverhead Books, New York, 1996. This recent poignant memoir by a man whose mother was from an Orthodox family and 'ran off' with a black man relates how the family sat *shivah* for his mother as if she was dead.

the stigma of an errant child marrying a non-Jew.

Yet amongst the modern Orthodox who have been exposed to the secular world and mix freely with non-Jewish people in their work environment, the issue of intermarriage cannot be ignored. As the intermarriage rate hovers around the fifty per cent mark in America and England, most of us have someone in our immediate and/or extended family who has married 'out'. In a family of four sons, it only takes two sons to marry out and fifty-per-cent of the grandchildren will not be Jewish according to Orthodox law.

I didn't appreciate this ten years ago when I refused to attend a close friend's wedding because she was 'marrying out'. At the time, I felt that I could not condone what I thought was a terrible thing. When my rabbi agreed with me, I felt vindicated. (It proved to be the last time I listened to a rabbi.)

Let's call her Jane. During our adolescence, Jane and I spent Saturday afternoons at youth group, Saturday nights hanging out together and planning how to get sick so that we wouldn't have to go to Sunday School the next morning. We both thought Jewish 'stuff' was pretty stupid and largely irrelevant.

During our twenties we were at different universities pursuing different careers and we mixed in different social groups. Nevertheless we managed to keep in fairly regular contact and always enjoyed long chats into the night. Then Jane told me about a man, let's call him Peter, and I knew it was going to be serious. She had made a concerted effort to meet Jewish men, and had had some lovely Jewish boyfriends, but none of the relationships lasted. She met Peter through her work, and suddenly she felt hope and happiness. After we all went out one evening, I knew this was it. Soon after, they were engaged. Although I was genuinely happy for her, I also felt this deep sadness that she was going to marry a non-Jewish person. For me, these conflicting emotions were about what I regarded as the choice between one's individual pursuit of happiness and one's responsibility to the community to maintain boundaries and cohesion. What right does a person have to put individual desires before communal needs? After all, I would never think of putting myself before three thousand years of Jewish civilisation. How can anyone be so audacious? OK, so I was fairly arrogant and naïve. (Now I find I am often putting myself before three thousand years of Jewish civilisation.)

I was disgusted with myself as I have many non-Jewish friends and work colleagues whom I enjoy and value immensely. But I was still overcome with a sense of inexplicable doom and despair that I could not share with her. I censored my own meek efforts to raise the issue with her, and avoided sending back the RSVP to the wedding. I was hoping she had forgotten about me when she rang about ten days before the wedding.

'Hi, how is it all going?' I asked nonchalantly.

'Fine – but, Sal, we haven't got your reply yet . . . you know, we will arrange *kosher* food.'

'Umm, well actually, I don't think I should be coming. I mean, I don't know, umm, it's just that well I don't really think I should, umm, come. It's sort of difficult to explain.'

I can still hear the silence at the other end of the phone, and it was two years before we spoke again. Although I did not attend the reception, ironically, I did attend the ceremony. On the day, I just felt that I could not stay away and I watched from the back of the room as a celebrant blessed their union. Several mutual acquaintances greeted me with contempt. All had heard I was not coming to the reception, and wondered what I was doing at the ceremony. Their disgust at my attitude chilled my spine. I am spineless, I thought to myself. Her mother cast me a piercing glance I will never forget.

Eventually, before I left Australia in 1990, I made a conciliatory gesture which fortunately she accepted. The history of our friendship was too important to me to forsake it entirely. Polite conversation masked any reference to the 'wedding incident' but our relationship was, in effect, ruined and ended. Since then my views have fundamentally changed, and every time I think about my friend's wedding, I am ashamed and deeply regret the way I behaved. I tried to make her realise that it was 'nothing personal' and that I had nothing against Peter, it was just that I thought intermarriage was a bad thing. Of course now I realise that it is *the most* personal thing. When I rejected her choice of partner, I was rejecting her most important decision and denying that part of her

life which was going to make her happy. I had to grow up and see a
bit more of life before I understood that.

Basically, I grew up in New York. Before I went there, I did not
know any Jewish families who had Christmas trees. I didn't even
know anyone who knew any Jewish families with Christmas trees.
But in New York, the 'December Dilemma' is a fact of life for
interfaith couples and the *menorah* competes with the Christmas
tree for equal space in the lounge. In the local newsagent's, season's
greetings cards cater to the interfaith market: Santa lights a
menorah, Jewish children wearing a Magen David sing 'Jingle
Bells', and a *dreidel* can be found in many a Christmas stocking.

When I interviewed families for a newspaper article on
interfaith marriages, people said things like: 'We put blue and
white decorations on the Christmas tree and I tell my children that
Christmas is Daddy's special day;' and, 'We light *Chanukah* candles
and we set out Christmas stockings for the children, so that they
can experience both. We make sure that *Chanukah* and Christmas
receive equal time and financial commitment.'

This was just so foreign to me. I kept meeting people who had
brothers and sisters in interfaith marriages. I met people who had
non-Jewish half-siblings because when their Jewish parents got
divorced, their father remarried a non-Jewish woman and had
more children, who according to Orthodox law, are not Jewish
because the mother is not Jewish. Some had non-Jewish step-
grandparents who liked to take them to church to hear Christmas
carols.

Life was clearly not as predictable and safe as that I had left
behind in Melbourne. Somehow, for all my maturity, I was fairly
naïve about the complexity of family life. My experiences initially in
New York, and further in England, have seen my views shift
dramatically. Now I have several good friends in 'mixed marriages',
and I know of many acquaintances who have non-Jewish partners.
In half the couples I know, the Jewish woman is married to a non-
Jewish man. Here is a growing market for the flexible
entrepreneurial rabbi willing to perform interfaith marriages in
churches, synagogues, mosques or temples. In the other half, the
Jewish man is married to a non-Jewish woman who has converted

to Judaism. It is interesting to me that the women are more likely to convert than the men. Perhaps this is because men require a circumcision, but it is more likely because a child's Jewish status is dependent on the mother. When 'push comes to shove' these Jewish men want their wives to convert so that their children will be Jewish.

Clearly, the Jewish community has a vested interest in encouraging Jewish people to marry each other. It's not a bad idea: it strengthens the community and helps to support communal institutions such as schools and religious bodies. Additionally, when two Jewish people marry it is also simpler for the children as there are less cultural gaps to close and the social cohesion of the community is maintained. Obviously, much as some communal leaders would like to be social engineers, ultimately we must respect the freedom of people to make their own choices. I am interested in how individuals and communal bodies respond to those undesirable choices.

For example, I have a friend in London with a very strong sense of Jewish identity from a traditional Jewish family. Her boyfriends throughout her teens and twenties were all Jewish. But she met a non-Jewish man at work, and although tormented by the implications of marrying a non-Jew, realised that this was the person she loved. He is an incredibly generous and thoughtful man, raised in a humanistic tradition, who wants his wife and daughter to enjoy their Judaism. He happily supported her request to have the baby named in a synagogue, and went along to the Reform synagogue where the rabbi welcomed them. They would not have had the same warm reception in an Orthodox synagogue, even though there is no question that their daughter is Jewish. Likewise, her family will not invite her husband to come to anything 'Jewish' like Friday night dinner or the Passover *seder*. The grandparents want their granddaughter exposed to Jewish rituals, and say that my friend and her daughter are welcome, but not the husband. She obviously will not go without her husband and it means everyone loses out. Her husband's tolerance is wearing thin, and my friend's willingness even to consider taking her daughter to the synagogue on the High Holydays is receding. Her parents have got to learn the same lessons as I did, otherwise they will be very unhappy people in their old age, and their granddaughter will resent the friction they caused within the family.

We do not live in an ideal world, and if a non-Jew and a Jew love each other and want to marry, it is not up to me to judge. If the woman is Jewish, it is less problematic as the children are Jewish, but we will lose the whole family if we act as arrogantly as I did with Jane. The community should welcome the family and encourage the parents to bring the children along to educational and social activities. I can only hope that Jane does not deny her children the opportunity to learn about their Jewish heritage. If she does, I will always feel that my intransigence was partly to blame.

Admittedly, where the marriage is between a Jewish man and a non-Jewish woman, the issues relating to children are more complex because Orthodoxy only recognises matrilineal descent. Once the marriage is a *fait accompli*, there is still no point in excluding these families and it may be worth gently encouraging conversion. If not now, the children may choose to convert as young adults. There are many Jews with a Jewish father who, as teenagers, felt that they wanted to convert to Judaism. This won't happen if their families are rejected by the community. I am not trying to make this sound like a numbers game where I want to increase the number of available Jews in the world, but it seems to me that people brought up in a world of two cultures often want some security and clarity. At least if you keep people near Judaism, they are in a better position to choose to reject it or embrace it.

I am sure I am on the right track, because I recently came across an important rabbinical response which came to the same conclusion. Rabbi Benzion Uziel (1880–1954), the Sephardic Chief Rabbi of Palestine (before Israel was established in 1948), dealt similarly with the issue of intermarriage. He recognised that rabbinical intransigence would most likely lead to a civil marriage, resulting in the loss of both the Jewish partner in such a marriage and the children born from it. Even though the desire to marry a Jew is not considered a valid reason for conversion, he supports a lenient approach to the conversion of the non-Jewish partner 'because this Jew or Jewess does not want to transgress, but rather wants to save herself or himself from this transgression'. It is, as Novak says:

> an extraordinary sociological insight in the very heart of a *halachic* judgement. What Uziel recognised is that the sociology of intermarriage has changed in modern times. Whereas in earlier times intermarriage was most often an expression of apostasy, in modern times it has become a consequence of greater social interaction between Jews and non-Jews. Thus the modern Jew who is drawn into a love relationship with a non-Jew, and who urges a non-Jew to seek conversion to Judaism, is attempting to reconcile his or her personal involvement with his or her own authentic commitment to Judaism. The motivation, then, is the exact opposite of that which seeks apostasy.[4]

We need more of this sort of compassionate reasoning and considered application of *halachah* which convinces me that Orthodoxy can recognise the changing realities of modern lives if its rabbinical leaders want it to.

However, the Orthodox community does not rationally discuss any of the alternatives to the image of the 'perfect Jewish family'. I mean who would get rabbinical approval? A Jewish mother married to a non-Jewish man, a single Jewish mother who has not married 'out', or a single childless Jewish woman? None gets communal sanction, and we have created an atmosphere that generally excludes women who choose alternative lifestyles. Yet, any children born of these diverse arrangements will still be Jewish and it seems short-sighted, arrogant and dishonest to dismiss their mothers. The boundaries and the imagination of the Orthodox community have got to change if we want young intelligent and articulate women to feel valued as individuals in their own right, not just as someone's wife or mother.

Not only does the Orthodox community largely ignore social trends, it often refuses to acknowledge the extent of damage to the

---

4 Novak, D., 'Modern *Responsa*: 1800 to the Present', in Hecht, N. S., Jackson, B. S., Passamaneck, S. M., Piattelli, D. and Rabello, A. M. (eds), *An Introduction to the History and Sources of Jewish Law*, Oxford University Press, 1996, p. 389

image of the perfect family. When we first got married, we lived in a large apartment block with very thin walls. Next door was an Orthodox family with a couple of boisterous young children. We only ever exchanged cursory greetings waiting for the elevator, and often I even used the stairs to avoid eye contact. We were regularly woken up in the middle of the night by screaming arguments between the husband and wife, the sound of sharp slapping and heavy objects being thrown around the house, or possibly at each other. It seemed that they never slept. I regularly heard the children being chastised and at times it almost sounded as if they were being hurled across the room.

I just didn't want to get involved. How could I intervene? What would have been my opening line? What practical advice could I have offered? I had one baby, and was expecting another; we were looking for a new place to live and the last thing I needed was to get involved in something that was beyond me (I conveniently forgot that I had almost ten years' social work experience) with people who were essentially irrelevant to me. (I conveniently forgot the maxim that 'all Jews are responsible for one another'.)[5]

As the family were known within the Orthodox community, I just assumed someone was dealing with the 'problem'. One day, some removal men arrived to pack up all their belongings. I saw the family on the steps.

'Goodbye,' I said. 'Good luck.'

'You too,' one of them said, pointing to my expanding tummy. 'You have been very quiet neighbours.'

And at that moment, I realised they knew we had colluded with their secret. Not only were we quiet neighbours because we tend to talk quietly and read books, but we were also 'quiet' about them to the outside world. Then, suddenly, they left the apartment, divorced and moved countries before we managed to find a new home. We did nothing to ruin the image and myth of that perfect Jewish family.

The *Talmud* is replete with epithets about the nature of marital relations. A husband shall 'love her as himself and honour her

5 Babylonian Talmud, Shevuot 39a

more than himself'.[6] 'He shall not afflict her, for God counts her tears. One who honours his wife will be rewarded with wealth,'[7] after all she is 'far above rubies'.[8] However, the rabbis of the *Talmud* were well aware that there were problems in marriages, and men who abused their wives were regarded harshly.[9] Nowadays, despite a culture of collective denial about many social problems, domestic violence – physical, emotional and psychological abuse – is gaining the recognition it deserves.

In the 1970s, Mimi Scarf pioneered some ground-breaking research with Jewish families in Los Angeles which indicated that a Jewish woman who is a victim of domestic violence usually comes from a home where there was a loving relationship with clearly defined gender roles (in stark contrast to the theory that women who get into abusive relationships were abused as children, thus perpetuating a 'cycle of abuse'). She probably had a close relationship with her father, expected to marry a 'nice Jewish boy' and spends her life raising children. She will keep quiet about the violence for a long time, if not her whole married life, because the reputation of her family, and the damage to the children would be too stigmatising. To the outside world, they are the perfect couple: courteous, charming and pillars of the local community. However, slowly she isolates herself from her friends and community because her self-esteem has been eroded, and her husband disapproves of her friends. She will be financially dependant on him, having been encouraged to stop studying or working so that she can be 'looked after' by her husband and have the time to devote to the family. She cannot tell her family, or, if she does, she minimises the extent of the abuse so much that her parents tell her she is exaggerating. If she goes to a Jewish social service or her rabbi, they will be incredulous, suggesting they have never heard of 'wife-beating' in the Jewish community. No one wants to believe her, and at some level 'she cannot believe it is happening to

6 Babylonian Talmud, Sanhedrin 76b
7 Babylonian Talmud, Bava Metzia 59a
8 Proverbs 31:10
9 Elon, M., op. cit., p. 482

her because Jewish men do not do this sort of thing. This does not happen to Jewish women.' [10]

Since Scarf's research was carried out, there has been widespread recognition of the problem, and Jewish activists around the globe have been following the lead of local government social services and voluntary sector organisations who have put all categories of abuse on to the political and social agenda during the last twenty years. Shelters for women, therapy and counselling services, helplines for children, community education and publicity campaigns about violence, men's groups to help men deal with their anger, official investigations and reports of abuse in residential homes, and support groups are all part of a system designed to help women and children at risk of abuse.

In 1980, the first refuge with a *kosher* kitchen was established in Far Rockaway, New York. Refuges have since opened in several major American cities, including Chicago and Los Angeles, catering to Jewish women, and in communities unable to fund a refuge, telephone support services and community education programmes have been established.[11]

Many of these services have eventually been copied in a number of other communities with large Jewish populations. For example, although a confidential helpline to help victims of domestic violence was established on a part-time basis in Leeds in 1986, Anglo-Jewry did not put domestic violence on its national communal agenda until 1992. When Judith Usiskin, a social worker with over twenty years' experience in the Jewish community, brought together a group of social workers, they realised for the first time that they shared a knowledge of many

[10] Scarf, M., 'Marriages Made in Heaven', in Heschel, S., op. cit., pp. 51–64
[11] See *Lilith*,Winter 1995–6, p. 43, which lists a range of resources, including Spiegel, M., *A Bibliography of Sources on Sexual and Domestic Violence in the Jewish Community*; Bnai Brit education kit to educate rabbis about family violence; and Jewish Social Services – Shalom Bayit: A Jewish Response to Child Abuse and Domestic Violence Kit. The American Jewish Congress has produced stickers, advertising the phone numbers for helplines, which are available to put up in places such as women's bathrooms in synagogues and community centres.

women who had experienced violence. As a result, they conducted an informal research project and found that twenty women in the past year had admitted to their social worker that they had been abused, and if a Jewish refuge had existed, they would have gone there. Judith felt this was clearly the tip of the iceberg, and a steering group was formed by sympathetic women. In an open meeting in the West London Synagogue in November 1992, she and her colleagues were given overwhelming support to establish an organisation to support women in situations of domestic violence. Subsequently, Jewish Women's Aid (JWA) was officially launched in June 1993 and £17,000 was raised at its first public meeting. Since then the organisation has increased public awareness about the problem, set up a telephone support service, established a series of educational seminars for rabbis and, in May 1997, the first British Jewish women's refuge was opened.

Jewish Women's Aid achieved one thing that most other organisations never manage: it attracted the attention of women who have been marginalised by the community establishment. Social workers and psychologists working in non-Jewish social services, architects, lawyers and businesswomen who have virtually no contact with the organised Jewish community were attracted to JWA and continue to give hundreds of hours of free professional time to the organisation. This bears out Schneider's research which also shows that in comparison to men, women are more likely to fund the development of services and grass-roots organisations concerned with social services and educational initiatives for women. Schneider also suggests that philanthropy in Jewish causes is a useful and important measure of how much religious identity still means to women who participate only minimally in other Jewish activities. She cites the example of the Jewish Theological Society which, in 1992, made its advertisement for the Jewish New Year about domestic violence and received lots of donations from women who had not previously donated.[12]

Unlike the synagogue which rejected an offer by one of its female members, a successful financial adviser, to help sort out its

[12] Schneider, S. Weidman, op. cit., 1993, p. 9

financial affairs, JWA welcomes and thrives on the camaraderie of women bringing their professional skills to the organisation. When marginalised Jewish women are attracted to Jewish women's causes that deal with social dysfunction, can we infer that when Judaism is not working, it becomes appealing to get involved? Do they want to save Jewish family life, or does it merely reinforce for them the prejudices and disillusionment with Judaism that contributed to their marginalisation in the first place? If the religious establishment continues to deny the potential of women and exclude their participation on spurious grounds, it will only have itself to blame if the daughters of these disenfranchised women move completely away from the community.

The stresses of unemployment, the isolation of marginalised poor families, social pressures, addictive behaviour such as gambling, mental illness and a general lack of communication between couples impact on the likelihood of domestic violence. However, stresses Judith Usiskin, while the factors affecting Jewish families are the same as those affecting other families, the different Jewish response to domestic violence (e.g. protracted denial, greater reluctance to report, family pressure to stay together, rabbis unwilling to believe a woman and fear of disgrace in front of non-Jews) makes domestic violence more difficult to deal with in the Jewish community.

Members of JWA worried that there might be hostility to their campaign, but Judith is quick to point out that the vast majority of the community has shown overwhelming support. When I took some information to the *mikveh*, I hesitated and spent time thinking of the best strategy. I was a bit concerned that the *mikveh* lady, who sometimes looks a little dour, might think it a bit too 'radical' and something she, too, did not want to get involved with. I feared that she would tell me that she would first need to check it with the men who take care of the administrative details of the *mikveh*. I decided on the gentle, but direct approach.

'Have you heard about Jewish Women's Aid – I have a few cards. I was wondering, would you mind, perhaps, handing them out?'

'Show me – what is this about?'

As soon as I mentioned domestic violence, her whole

demeanour changed. Her face shone, and suddenly she was my comrade-in-arms, my colleague in the struggle.

'Yes, yes, I have heard of this – a shocking business. I even know that sometimes the rabbis will not believe the women when they say that their husbands do terrible things. A woman does not make up such stories! Why would a woman lie about such a thing? Of course, leave me your information, and I will make sure the women see it.'

'Thank you very much,' I said, and I meant it.

'God bless you, and all the good work your group does,' she said as I left, and she really meant it.

The refuge in London received wide media attention and was publicly lauded by the community. It will be an interesting social 'experiment', and a model of religious tolerance to be emulated by the rest of the community. Although religious observance can't be imposed on the non-religious women, they will have to agree to certain standards because Orthodox women will only feel comfortable coming to the refuge if they know it will be *kosher* and that the rules of *Shabbat* can be adhered to. 'It will have to be tolerant of people's needs in a way that other organisations have not found so imperative,' suggests Judith; 'there is a strength in knowing that there is a woman's group that will take them in – a woman-led organisation.'

But there are hiccups. One Orthodox man in authority tried to derail a plan to appoint a Jewish liaison officer to work specifically with Jewish victims of domestic violence in Stamford Hill, a suburb of London with a very high proportion of Orthodox families. He felt that the problem was negligible and that rabbis were the best source of help. He tried to minimise the claims made by JWA, but fortunately he was unsuccessful in blocking the appointment of the worker. [13]

Judith acknowledges that some women have repeatedly complained about the attitudes of rabbis – particularly those who encourage the woman to go home and 'make peace'[14] – however,

[13] 'Row over plan to appoint adviser for battered Orthodox women', *Jewish Chronicle*, London, 8 April 1994, p. 11
[14] Goodkin, J. and Citron, J., op. cit., p. 57

she also is pleased that many rabbis have phoned her for professional advice.[15] One year, the Sabbath during *Succot* (Tabernacles),
the autumn holiday in which Jews erect a temporary dwelling for
eight days, was designated as a *Shabbat* in aid of JWA. Then, and at
other times during the year, many rabbis were requested, and
agreed, to speak from the pulpit about the issue. However, it
doesn't always have the desired effect. When I was in the
synagogue, the rabbi made mention of JWA, and one of the more
prominent men laughingly interrupted with: 'Does that mean I am
allowed to beat my wife today, or is she allowed to beat me?'

There was a sort of sneering laughter that makes my blood boil,
but I just put it down to sheer stupidity. However, in doing some
research for this chapter, I came across the following experience of a
member of the Israeli parliament, MK Marcia Freedman, who tried
to place the issue of 'wife-beating' on the national agenda in 1976.

No sooner had she begun to address the house, than she was
interrupted by laughter and heckling from the floor. One MK,
Mordechai Ben-Porat, interjected, 'And what about the second
motion, husband-battering by wives?' While Freedman asked
those present not to joke about the matter, another MK, Pesach
Groper (in Hebrew, the word does not mean 'groper'!), repeated the same question. And then, the Minister of Health,
Victor ShemTov, commented, 'MK Groper, you don't look like
your wife beats you.' The Minister of Police joined the fray.
'How do you know, you haven't seen his wife!'[16]

Since then, intense media campaigns and high-profile incidents
have alerted the public to the problems, resulting in a tremendous
shift in community attitudes and a willingness to listen to women.

15 Cwik, M., 'Peace in the Home? The Response of Rabbis to Wife Abuse
within American Jewish Congregations', *Journal of Psychology and Judaism*,
Vol. 21, no. 1, Spring 1997, pp. 5–67. This is a study of a hundred and twenty-
seven rabbis, representing different denominations, evaluated their handling
of wife abuse and their use of referral services.
16 cited in Swirski, B., 'Jews Don't Batter Their Wives: Another Myth Bites
the Dust', pp. 319–27, in Swirski, B. and Safir, M., *Calling the Equality Bluff:
Women in Israel*, Pergamon Press, New York, 1991, p. 321

The first Israeli shelter opened in Haifa in 1977 and now there are
several others in major cities across Israel: 'It is no longer ignored
or joked about.'[17] Women-to-Women, an American based organisation, has also been publicising the extent of domestic violence in
Israel and raising funds for the shelters.[18]

But why had some male attitudes barely changed in twenty years?
I had a chance to challenge that middle-aged 'respected' member of
our synagogue and I blew it. Did I doubt the cause? Did I fear being
regarded as a bit too militant, a 'bit of a feminist'? I tell myself that
I didn't want to embarrass him and cause a public débâcle. In that
case, I should have spoken to him alone, quietly in a corner, and
explained the seriousness of the issue. But I didn't because I knew he
would not really listen to me. I knew that he has to believe that it is
not really a problem, that women are making a fuss about nothing
and, besides, no one was going to tell him that he doesn't treat his
wife like a queen. I couldn't be bothered talking to a wall of denial
and incomprehension. It is going to have to start with our daughters
and our sons. Parents of sons are going to have to tell them that it is
not acceptable to be violent, and sisters of brothers are going to have
to be firm. I'm not saying people don't get angry (just ask your father
what I can be like!) but until the fundamental nature of power within
Orthodox relationships (and all other relationships) is addressed, we
are not going to get to the root causes of domestic violence.

---

[17] ibid., p. 326
[18] Kriegel, P., 'NY Group Helps Israeli Feminists', *New Directions for Women*,
January/February 1991; Snitow, V., 'Women-to-Women works for equality
between the sexes in Israeli society', *Jewish Exponent*, 26 July 1991; Rapoport,
G., 'Israeli battered women's havens funded', *Jewish Week*, 2 November 1990

Chapter 7

What usually happens, of course, is the establishment blame it on 'education'. The theory is that if Jewish kids receive a good Jewish education, they will never be violent, and of course they will understand why it is important to marry someone Jewish. In practice, until they start paying educators the sort of salaries that reflect a real appreciation of their worth and their skills, I can't take the claim that our Jewish schools are our most important resource too seriously. Hence, I wouldn't rely too much on Jewish schools to produce model citizens.

My first brush with a formal Jewish education was on the first Wednesday morning of my primary-school life.

'Will all the JEWISH children, please go to Room Three. That is all the JEWISH children, Room Three. Your teacher is waiting for you.'

Four or five of us would sheepishly leave our classrooms and head for Room Three. The other children stared at us as we walked down the corridor, heads hung low. It was punishment for not going to a Jewish school – not only did we have to suffer the indignity of being pulled out for Religious Instruction, we also had to get up early on Sunday mornings.

At Kew Hebrew School, *circa* 1967–73, from 9.30 a.m.–12.30 p.m. every Sunday, I was fed a steady diet of Jewish festivals, laws, Hebrew, prayer, Jewish history and Zionism. My resistance to Hebrew school usually started on Tuesday evening when I made excuses about not feeling well, in the vague hope of looking heroic and with a plan to spin it out till Sunday, when I would collapse and argue that I couldn't possibly go to Sunday School. Somehow my parents realised what I was up to.

'I hate Sunday School,' I screamed out behind the bedroom door I had locked.

'We don't care, you have to go,' they screamed back, as they tried to jiggle the key and pry open the door.

We went to Sunday school with another couple of kids living around the corner. Their father was a large ebullient man with a passion for big dogs. He tooted outside our door, and my brother and I joined them, all squashed up in a Mini-Minor, for the ten-minute car ride. Three hours later, my father returned the favour and brought us all home. Most of the time Sunday School seemed largely irrelevant, and on the whole the teachers are a blur. I do remember Miss Fonda, who taught me when I was six or seven years old. She is now married with children and when I am in Melbourne I occasionally bump into her.

'Hello, Miss Fonda,' I say.

'Judy, please,' she replies kindly, adult-to-adult, but I can't bring myself to be so familiar. I left part of my childhood at Kew Hebrew School.

Despite Wednesday morning Religious Instruction class, I was an extremely happy graduate of the distinctly non-Jewish North Balwyn Primary School and Balwyn High School. Although I managed to get into Melbourne University and marry a Jew, I am in conflict about the idea of sending you to a Jewish day school. While I think that I benefited tremendously from attending a non-Jewish school, obviously I want you to be Judah the Macabbee in a *Chanukah* play rather than the Virgin Mary in a nativity performance. I want you to be exposed to Jewish traditions, customs and literature and have playmates that you can visit on *Shabbat* afternoon. But I also want you to understand that non-observant Jews and non-Jews are just people who make different and equally valid choices, and are not demons to fear. I want you to love Israel unconditionally, fall in love with a *kibbutznik* and pick avocados while reciting Leah Goldberg's poetry. Yet, I want you to go to a school that will instil a sense of justice for the poor, challenge racial stereotypes and encourage you all to raise money for starving children. At the same time, I want you to worry about Jews in trouble spots around the world, and I'd like you to visit lonely old Jewish ladies in the local nursing home.

I have already started to garner application forms. Each one comes with threats and promises, coded in its own subtext. 'Applications for admission to the school will be considered only for children who are recognised as being Jewish by the Office of the Chief Rabbi of the United Hebrew Congregation of the Commonwealth.' (Don't think you can intermarry and come crawling back, and don't bother with a Reform conversion.) 'Children from a variety of backgrounds are encouraged to develop an enthusiasm for an Orthodox way of life.' (However, wealthy kids from irreligious backgrounds will be especially welcome.) 'There is a strong Jewish ethos in the school, which gives the children a pride and pleasure in their own religious and cultural heritage.' (You'll never be really British, so why fight it?) 'Wherever possible, teachers integrate aspects of the children's secular studies with Jewish learning.'(Who wins? God or Darwin?)[1]

One of my important selection criteria for a Jewish school is that it must teach the boys and the girls *Talmud* and all other Jewish studies in the same classroom. While the evidence points to girls learning better in single-sex schools when it comes to English and maths, it is not the same for Jewish studies. Boys must be in the classroom, because most teachers do not rate a girl's Jewish education as being important. Neither of you may want to be *Talmudic* scholars or female rabbis, but I will certainly make sure you both have the opportunity to decide. Sometimes, I have this vision that you will come home and accuse us of being too liberal – a sort of Orthodox version of that sit-com *Family Ties*, with Michael J. Fox: liberal sixties' parents with left-over hippie values – father in public television making documentaries, mother some sort of environmentalist architect, with three children typical of the eighties – their teenage son (Fox) poring over the *Wall Street*

1 See Goodman, A., 'Variant Text', excerpted from *Total Immersion*, Harper Collins, 1990, in Solotaroff, T. and Rapoport, N. (eds), *The Schocken Book of Contemporary Jewish Fiction*, Schocken Books, New York, 1992, pp. 86–109, for an hilarious exposé of the contradictions of providing a modern Orthodox education.

Journal, accusing the parents of permissive liberal values, and their daughter, a vacuous fashion fanatic.

I picture one of you coming home and telling me to put on black stockings. You'll beg us to transfer you to a more religious school, like the one where single female teachers do not get one of the limited parking spaces because priority is given to the married women. At eighteen, you will elope with a black-hatted Chassid in the black of the night, blaming us for not being rigid enough and accusing us of compromising with the secular world.

I'll understand. When I was eighteen I also thought I might like to elope with a black-hatted Chassid. I was at a women's seminary in Jerusalem, let's call it Gates of Hope. Ostensibly, we were there to study Judaism – its rituals, history, literature and culture. However, what I remember most were the little pep talks given by Mrs G, the 'house mother'. She gathered us together in the lounge and we would wait with shy longing for her words of instruction.

First were the deportment lessons.

'It upsets me,' I can recall her saying, 'that some of you are going on the streets with ladders in your tights. This is not the way of Jewish women. And girls, walk straight, walk proud, and take the chewing gum out of your mouths.'

Then, there was the cleaning routine.

'You have to think of cleaning the floor as a *mitzvah* – as you get ready for *Shabbat* on a Friday afternoon – don't think if it as a chore – think about what a holy task you are doing to welcome the Sabbath Queen.'

But my all-time favourite, directed to each girl, every one 'placid and housewifely, of no intellectual pretensions, but with a practised mothering ability which made her the ideal organiser of genius',[2] was the one about the rubbish bins.

Girls, when you marry, do not distract your husband from the

2 Goldstein, R., *The Mind-Body Problem*, Random House, 1983, Penguin, 1993, New York, p. 181. The protagonist, Renee Feuer has left the Orthodoxy of her youth, although she remains ambivalent about its worth. She is a philosophy graduate married to a brilliant mathematician and this novel is nuanced with sharp insights into the Orthodox world. This is a quote which Renee cites about Elsa, Albert Einstein's wife.

saintly task of learning – take out the rubbish bins yourself – for him, it is *bittel zman.*'[3]

I never forgot those little pep talks: partly because I felt so belittled and patronised by them, and partly because they carried such strong messages, constantly reinforced, about a woman's obligation to create a traditional, religously inspired Jewish home. To think that I thought I wanted to create this home! Twenty years later, my girlfriends and I still laugh at each other when we say, 'Ah, that makes me feel really fulfilled as a Jewish woman,' after we have washed the kitchen floor on a Friday afternoon.

In the coded language of the religious world, my community is divided into those who are '*frum* [religious] from birth' (FFB) and those who are *ba'alei teshuvah* (BT), a master of repentance: a Jew who was not born into the Orthodox world, yet makes a choice to lead a religious lifestyle. The word *teshuvah* means 'return', and in the act of return, the BT returns to the traditions of our ancestors and becomes part of the Orthodox world.

FFBs grow up in the enveloping security of a religious community, which like any total institution, provides one's friends, schooling, recreational activities, reading material, music and preferred holiday spots (like the Catskills in New York, Bournemouth on the English coast and Grindelwald in Switzerland). The community is designed to maximise the FFB's complete and 'natural' socialisation into the cultural norms and minutiae of ritual behaviour. The FFB requires no proof of identification and his or her impeccable credentials leave little question of a sullied reputation. The FFB has very little problem finding a spouse.

For the BT, life is a lot harder. He or she must be completely resocialised into the cultural norms and ritual expectations of the religious community. Although there have always been people who returned to Orthodoxy, the data suggests that there has been a significant increase in this feature of Orthodox life in the last two

[3] Mintz, J., *Legends of the Hasidim*, University of Chicago Press, Chicago, 1986, p. 86. He cites a 1959 Chassidic magazine for women in which 'a rabbi cautioned women not to have their husbands help them with the dishes too often as this would result in neglect of the study of *Torah*'.

generations.[4] (There have also been religious people who defected from Orthodoxy and now lead completely secular lives, but that is something the community conveniently prefers to ignore.) [5]

Two competing bodies of Orthodox outreach professionals and organisations have emerged to interest and educate spiritually lost and homeless Jews. One is the Lubavitch movement of Chassidim, who are adept at enticing non-Orthodox Jews to embrace Orthodoxy. They will go to the remotest places on earth, find its Jews and patiently instruct these virtual strangers in the finer details of ritual and even pay for a *kosher* kitchen. They have made it 'cool to be *chassidishe*'. The non-Chassidic Jews, on the other hand, have developed *yeshivot* (institutions geared to Jewish studies from a religious perspective), such as Gates of Hope, and the network of educational programmes which describe themselves as 'outreach' programmes. Millions of dollars, slick advertising campaigns, and rabbinical egos have been at the centre of this battle for Jewish souls. Inspired by the confidence that they possess the truth, both groups consider themselves responsible for saving the Jewish people from the ravages of assimilation, intermarriage and the high defection rate of Jews to Eastern religions.

The term *ba'alei teshuvah* became part of the contemporary Orthodox lexicon in 1972 when five schools were founded specifically for *ba'alei teshuvah*.[6] (Although, in the late 1950s, Yeshiva University in New York did establish an intensive programme of Jewish studies for men with a limited Jewish education, it did not have the accoutrements of the BT phenomenon as it developed in the 1970s.)[7] In America and Israel, the BT movement

[4] Danziger, M. H., *Returning to Tradition: The Contemporary Revival of Orthodox Judaism*, Yale University Press, New Haven, 1989. This is a comprehensive overview of the history and philosophies of the different schools attracting *ba'alei teshuva*.
[5] There is an organisation called *Chozrim b'She'ala*, meaning 'returning in question', which is a Hebrew pun on the term *ba'al teshuvah*. It was set up as a support group for people leaving Orthodoxy.
[6] Danziger, M., op. cit., p. 71
[7] Klaperman, G., *The Story of Yeshiva University, the First Jewish University in America*, Collier-Macmillan, London, 1969, p. 182

was galvanised by the 1967 Six Day War that reshaped Jewish consciousness. Imbued with the idealism of the age and the flower-power of the 1970s, many young Jews came to reject the Judaism of their parents as materialistic, shallow and devoid of spirituality. Some young people found comfort with Lubavitcher Chassidim while others preferred one of the other BT organisations in America. Some set out on the hippie trail to India with a short detour to Israel. In Israel, a small group of rabbis realised that a golden opportunity was staring them in the face. Here was a group of intelligent young men, disillusioned with the assimilationist Jewry of their parents, ready for the picking. If they were going to an ashram, why not a *yeshivah*?

So a small team of highly charismatic rabbis positioned them-selves at the Western Wall, the central bus station, and other popular tourist spots. They approached young men with backpacks who looked aimless and in need of a good meal. They challenged them: 'You haven't seen the real Israel until you have had a Friday-night dinner or gone to a *Torah* class.' Innocent recruits were offered a place to sleep for the night and a chance to attend some thought-provoking lectures about the wisdom of the *Torah*. Many young men found a spiritual home and cashed in their tickets to India.

The rabbis quickly realised that these wandering Jews craved the structure and discipline that religion could provide. It seemed that many of their emotional and psychological needs were chronically unmet by their families, and the hand-picked models of Orthodox homes allowed the young men to acknowledge these emotional gaps in their lives. An unspoken contractual obligation developed: we, members of the Orthodox community, will look after you, teach you, nurture your soul and provide the mystical dimension to life that you are looking for. In return, you will agree to live by the Orthodox laws of Judaism. You will study the ancient texts regularly, only eat *kosher* food, and observe the Sabbath by refraining from all work.

The young men were sent to various families to experience an 'authentic' *Shabbat*, and slowly encouraged to adopt the clothing of the Orthodox. Sombre suits started to replace their jeans, and as

Bobby became Benzion, Paul became Pinchas and Michael became Moshe, their external features began to make them indistinguishable from the next Orthodox Jew. The rabbis considered these new recruits as a great success. Choice, which until this point had been the hallmark of the *ba'al teshuvah*'s life, was regarded as the cause of his unhappiness and inability to mature. Now, with a set of legalistic structures and moral judgements imposed on his life, the only new choices were how many hours to study, when to start wearing the conformist garb, and the rate of ritual take-up.

The families of many of these young men were devastated. A few months ago they had an all-American son, taking a break before settling down to law school or medical school. Now, they had a son intent on spending countless hours in front of ancient tomes, and uninterested in pursuing any type of secular education. It seemed that to be successful, the *ba'alei teshuvah* had to cut their ties with their families and eschew modern culture much more decisively than those brought up in modern Orthodox homes. And when bouts of religious low self-esteem hit the stigmatised BT, he was repeatedly encouraged to remember that *'in the place where a ba'al teshuvah stands, a wholly righteous person cannot stand'*,[8] for the sacrifices of a BT made his commitment to Judaism more loved in the eyes of God.

But there was a missing ingredient to this new Jewish world order: the women. Only marriage would finally secure these newly-Orthodox men in the community. Tremendous social status is attached to being married, so this would help boost their egos and self-esteem. But where would these men find suitable partners? Very quickly the men discovered the painful reality that few of the ultra-Orthodox families would sacrifice their daughters to these men. Their daughters would have to marry people of their own kind. A BT did not have the years of intensive studying and learning to make him eligible for the daughter of a religious family. It would take years for the BT to catch up. And what of his family's credentials – did his mother use the *mikveh*? Was he conceived at

---

[8] Babylonian Talmud, Brachot 34b

an unholy time of the month? The BT is held accountable for the sins of his parents. A divorce in the family or a conversion without the proper authority was enough to sully him – not to speak of past affairs with non-Jewish women. Ultimately, a religious family wants its daughters to marry virgins, and there was no guarantee that these young men, no matter how much they repented the past, had not tasted the pleasures of the flesh.

When Noah built the ark, he realised that each animal desired a mate that understood its specific needs. Rabbis leading the *ba'al teshuvah* movement realised it was best to match kind with kind. As difficult as it would be to marry off male BTs to female FFBs, how much more difficult would it be for the women BTs to find partners in the Orthodox world.

Women from a non-Orthodox background would rarely be deemed innocent and deferential enough to marry young boys from Orthodox families. There would always be a lingering suspicion: could they educate their children properly, would they be familiar with the finer points of *kashrut* and, of course, the ultimate yet unspoken fear – had they also succumbed to the desires of the flesh?

In 1972, the first *yeshivah* (or seminary as they are usually referred to when discussing women) to cater for women from a secular background, or women willing to renew and dedicate their lives to a rediscovered Orthodoxy, was founded. In the women's seminaries the study of Jewish texts and Jewish law is not as rigorous as in the men's *yeshivot*.[9] Rather there is a distinct emphasis on personal development. *Mussar shmoozes*, a meandering list of character traits to aspire to, and the means to acquire good character traits are popular subjects. While being a good person is an important ethical imperative inherent in the Jewish religion, for the BT women, this translates into expecting women to adopt a demure and deferential role. There were never as many women's schools as men's *yeshivot*, but over the years they managed

9 This is particularly so in the *yeshivot* geared to the *ba'al teshuva*. In other places, the 'gender gap' still exists, but it is closing in some selected schools (see Danziger, M., op. cit., chapter 8)

to prepare a steady stream of women with the values necessary to forge generations of submissive Jewish women, ready to take out the rubbish bins and whistle while they worked.

Gates of Hope was established in 1978, and here I discovered Mrs G when I was there for six months in the latter half of the same year. I was the youngest by far, eighteen years old. Most of the women were in their mid-twenties and several in their thirties (ancient in my book!) Gates of Hope only existed for a few years, and eventually merged with another BT seminary.

During that time, and a subsequent three months I spent at a similar place in the mid 1980s, I remember feeling that I could not believe all the niceness was sincere, all the spirituality genuine. I now realise that a lot of subtle, conscious and unconscious, things were going on that I didn't really understand. At the time I just knew I didn't quite fit in, but I didn't have the words or the concepts to explain why.

Now, almost twenty years later, I have the words and the concepts. For example, despite our age, professional qualifications and life experience, the first act of infantilising the women was referring to us as 'girls'. In the eyes of the community, we were children in the knowledge of the *Torah*, and as single, childless women, we were a long way from adulthood.

I watched with a combination of intense curiosity and admiration as those I knew slowly began to take on the rituals and mind-set of an Orthodox Jewish woman. I learnt how to gauge how long a student had been there by her external appearance. Some arriving in jeans and a clingy short-sleeved top were transformed within a few weeks. Soon they were wearing the trademark long denim skirt and trainers with short socks. A loose-fitting pale blue cotton shirt hung neatly, conveniently avoiding her breasts. Sometimes it appeared that these women were suddenly scared of their own bodies.[10]

I was once chatting to a friend who is a psychotherapist and

[10] Roiphe, A., *Lovingkindness*, Summitt Books, New York, 1987. This novel fictionalises a mother-daughter relationship in which the daughter becomes religious and virtually rejects the mother and her lifestyle.

works with AIDS patients. He made an off-the-cuff comment about the similarities between a BT and a gay man coming 'out' to his family and friends, and more importantly, accepting himself for who he really is. Something clicked – it sounded wicked, but it rang true. Slowly, the gay person takes on certain clothing of the homosexual subculture. He has to perform several confessionals, admitting to friends that his life has changed, including his attitude to sexuality. All the assumptions his friends made about him were misplaced. He might lose friends and ruin certain familial relationships, but it is almost certain to launch him into a new self-consciousness from which he can never return to the previous, repressed self. The gay men and women who come 'out' and the Jews who take upon themselves the Orthodox lifestyle both challenge the public perception of how they function in the world.

A BT has to start wearing clothes that identify him or her as part of the group. It can be as obvious as the head covering, or as subtle as the muted tones of modest dress. Taking on new rituals can lead to an estrangement from one's friends, and visiting family becomes more complicated if they do not have a *kosher* kitchen. With allegiances to new friendships, there are shared new rules about sexuality. External appearance starts to make an even more important difference, and just as gay activists extol their new freedom of expression so, too, do newly Orthodox Jews often feel compelled to preach their newly discovered faith. They want to convince other Jews of the sincerity of their 'conversion' to the cause. They are filled with a desire to make other Jews more observant and filled with the fear of God. Their newly found personal status becomes a political statement in a way that gains social rewards.

In a reverse of this process, someone who is religious and actually wants to become non-observant has to go through some of the same processes. I knew one person who was too enmeshed in the Orthodox world to make a quick clean break. He had also inherited the mannerisms and demeanour of a *yeshivah bocher* (student): the spotless white hands, gaunt body, social awkwardness, downcast eyes, general ill-defined twitching, *yeshivish* speech – an English sprinkled with Yiddish words and rabbinic aphorisms which sounded like a coded language. I felt that his social inadequacies were never dealt with in a system that valued endless hours of study, poring over books. It is legitimate to stay up late at night in the library. One is protected from the usual adolescent insecurities of the opposite sex by complete sexual segregation. Shyness and unease are hidden behind a veneer of modesty and selflessness. Obsessive-compulsive behaviour finds its resting home in the demands of rigorous attention to detail and the repetitive minutiae of ritual practices. The social pressures of the *yeshivah* world are not always about virtuous religious piety, but sometimes a deep psychological need to be accepted and rewarded in the system. Letting go of these rewards and the accompanying religious esteem comes with a price: a pain of recognition and increasing alienation from the people who were once the most important and stable characters in one's life.

I recently read Karen Armstrong's autobiography[11] about her decision to be a nun in the 1960s, and her subsequent decision to leave the convent. While I was moved by her story, I was also struck by the similarity between convent life and that of the *yeshivah* which both seek to break the will of the individual in order to reconstruct a personality that is able to do the work of God. Armstrong writes that

> kneeling in the little convent chapel, I found myself plagued with doubts and fears. Had my desire to become a nun been a form of adolescent sexual escape? Or had the knowledge of the ugliness of my unformed body made me believe I was unfit for love, so that I had removed myself from the sexual arena simply to forestall a lifetime of rejection? It doesn't matter, I told myself. Even if it were true, a religious vocation can begin with all sorts of unworthy motives.[12]

I am not suggesting that Orthodox women are like nuns, but I think that the interplay between spiritual yearnings and psychological forces are not adequately acknowledged by those responsible for influencing people towards Orthodoxy. It would be

[11] Armstrong, K., *Through the Narrow Gate: A Nun's Story*, Macmillan, London, 1981   [12] ibid., p. 236

blasphemy to suggest that not everyone is cut out to be *frum*, but some of the people who came to Gates of Hope 'got' Judaism like they 'got' crystals a year ago and Transcendental Meditation the year before that. Suddenly they found out about being *frum*, and pow! they were into it. The rabbi's trick was to make them stick with it this time and not discover something else.

All the institutions attracted a range of students. The brighter ones worked out the underlying, and unstated, psychological dynamics at play. The same rules applied that every primary school kid recognises at a very young age: you can get attention by being extremely naughty or by being extremely intelligent. The average kid just gets shunted through the system and few people bother to notice that she's there. The 'naughty' kids, those that refuse to become *frum* and refuse to take on the religious expectations, receive lots of strategic attention from rabbis who begin to take a personal interest in them, making them feel extremely wanted and reassured. Subtle pressures to conform are increasingly applied and the girls come to feel that they are betraying a personal relationship with a particular rabbi if they do not become more observant. On the other hand, those who become very *frum* and models of pious return to their Jewish heritage, are rewarded with adulation from the staff and reverence from the other girls for their commitment. They might even get offered a husband which is the supreme accolade. These social rewards are very enticing and the school's insular and self-perpetuating system reinforced favourable behaviour. When major benefactors arrived at the school, the 'right' girls were paraded out to talk to donors. When you know that a million dollars is resting on the impression you make, you are grateful to the people who showed so much faith in your faith. How can you let them down?

The schools are not intrinsically bad, nor the rabbis intentionally manipulative. I think a lot of it is unconscious and derived from the fact that the rabbis really believe that they have the truth. For many people these schools enabled them to create a new, productive life, free from destructive influences that were literally killing them. However, what disturbs me, and has taken me twenty years of reflection to realise, is the lack of honesty and the lack of critical reasoning. There are different motivations for becoming religious, and they are not always 'for the sake of Heaven'.

The cloistered world of the *yeshivah* and the powerful embrace of traditional Judaism can offer protection from the real demands of the outside world. People who could not 'make it' out there are attracted to a system which rewards piety and a lack of material success. It's ideal if you have a weight problem and think you are a little ugly. Lynn Davidman, an American sociologist, has written the most illuminating book on the process of becoming an Orthodox woman. She noted, amongst many other things, that many women put on large amounts of weight as they become religious.[13] In their new, fairly guarded community, some women will fill themselves with food precisely because they cannot get physical comfort. And then they will have to purge themselves, because they are repulsed by the act of over-eating, as if this act of ersatz sex is itself a sin.

That happened to me. I was always a plump kid, and then went through a seriously thinned-out teenage phase, only to be unable to control my weight when I became more religious. Now, I just blame it on my pregnancies, and my clothes, in several different sizes, compete with each other to be taken out of the cupboard. But I know deep-down that there was an appeal about being in a system that professed to value my mind more than my body. I was led to believe that the system was not shallow, nor filled with 'Western values', that it cared more about my soul and intellect than my figure. Ultimately, it's not true of course, particularly for women, who are valued for their father's wealth and/or their own beauty.

For some newly observant people, the switch to religion is no more than a sophisticated form of rebellious virtue. I remember Beth, a model student. In her own family, no matter how hard she tried, she could not satisfy her parents. She was never considered as attractive as her older sister, nor as academic or as sociable. But at Gates of Hope, she was valued for herself. Typically, Beth's family felt extremely rejected. They were convinced she had joined some weird cult. As very assimilated Jews, they had no real concept

---

[13] Davidman, L., *Tradition in a Rootless World:Women Turn to Orthodox Judaism*, University of California Press, California, 1991, p. 170

of Orthodox Judaism, and could not identify with the extreme zealots they would sometimes see on the news, throwing stones at skimpily-clad women passing through the religious neighbourhoods of Jerusalem. Beth tried to explain that the seminary was not like this, but the more she tried to make them understand, the less they believed her. They wanted their little girl back, but Gates of Hope made her realise she did not have to be that little girl any longer. It gave her an opportunity to construct a new personality and rewarded her for precisely those things her family did not value. Her rebellion was to become Orthodox. This rebellion undermined the materialism of her parents, and she blatantly told them she did not value the life goals they had struggled to achieve. There is a certain asceticism that only the rich can afford; paradoxically they often expect their parents to bankroll their Nazarene aspirations.

In 1978, I became very friendly with an American woman named Caroline. At first I thought she was a bit odd. She had a perpetual smile, sat in the back of the class and never took notes, just scribbled these amazing drawings of strangely contorted figures. She rarely spoke in class, but when she did, wow! it was incredible. She just hit the nail on the head. Eventually, we started to talk, and I watched her transformation. Within a year she went from someone who knew virtually nothing about Judaism to a married lady wearing a wig, on the cusp of pregnancy (the first of six) and living on the West Bank. I found out that her academic record was brilliant and she had been planning to attend medical school. Her family always assumed that she would just follow her father's illustrious medical career. However, unbeknown to her family, she had no real career ambitions and felt imprisoned by her family's expectations to pursue a profession. She was proof of Cantor's thoughts about the differential impact of becoming Orthodox on men and women:

> many women as well as men could find relief in Orthodoxy's rigid division of labour and in the validation it provided for role fulfilment.[14]

14 Cantor, A., op. cit., p. 362

All Caroline really wanted was to be a full-time mother and a homemaker, but she knew that this choice would not be acceptable in her milieu. It would be seen merely as a failure to succeed in what her parents defined as the 'real world'. In a 'chance' encounter (religious people consider that nothing is by chance), a religious woman invited her home for her first real *Shabbat* experience. She was hooked on Judaism in a big way. She started to attend some classes, and found that the teachers, the lessons, the values and the lifestyle spoke to her in a language that she understood and did not feel alienated from. For the first time, she felt she belonged, receiving great accolades and valuable recognition when she chose the traditional path of the Jewish woman. I was pleased for her because she found a genuine place to belong.

When I went back to Australia we continued to keep in touch, and she sent me beautifully illustrated cards with words of inspiration. I admired the way that she revelled in the miracle of the everyday and somehow I never doubted her sincerity. She left Israel to return to America and lives in an Orthodox community on the East Coast. While I was in the States I visited her and we spoke on the phone, but I found it harder to communicate with her. Although I will always have a soft spot for her, I can't be myself with her. I can't be cynical, I can't voice scepticism, I can't be honest. It's the same way I feel about most of the women and the teachers I met twenty years ago, but in Caroline's case it bothers me. She was just too smart to become so religious.

I always worried when I saw some of the women lapping up the clichés without any sort of critical eye. My favourite obscenity was the religious rationalisation for the destruction of a third of world Jewry:

Of course the Holocaust was a terrible thing, but we only see one part of history out of its context. If you only see part of a movie, you are unable to see the whole plot, you are unable to understand the purpose and context of the few scenes that you saw. Jewish history is like a movie.

Do they think we are complete morons? Or the other stuff like:

You know I don't like the words religious or Orthodox or observant. I call myself a growing Jew, I want to continue to grow.

It is meant to make all the students feel comfortable, and while there is nothing objectionable about wanting to 'grow', the language is a deliberate attempt to make Judaism sound a bit like a contemplative Eastern religion. Of course, this is designed to make Judaism even more palatable (don't they think it is palatable as it is?) The most insidious teachers are the pretty ones, tilting their heads seductively with their gorgeous wigs firmly in place, their lilting voices bringing in lots of references to the Christian church to demonstrate their worldliness. The teachers with a university degree were at pains to make sure we knew they had a degree, and a couple of professors from Ivy League universities were regularly trotted out to show how you can be Orthodox, intellectual and really part of the modern world.

I am particularly annoyed when these same people profess that they don't value the secular world, but it is the secular world which gave them the titles which they use to gain credibility. I recently heard one Orthodox woman psychologist with a PhD give a lecture, and, in response to a question about women rabbis, she said that women who want the title of 'rabbi' are being petty and seeking status. Let's have a bit of honesty here: she was introduced as Dr X. It's clear how she likes to be known.

With hindsight, it feels like the rabbis thought most of the women who came to study at Gates of Hope were very ordinary women who just needed to get married. The rabbis, of course, tell these average women that they are 'special', 'unique', 'made in God's image', and that the greatest contribution they can make to the Jewish people is to get married and raise children. (That's true, as the demographics suggest the number of Jewish children is decreasing, and I don't want you to think that I believe there is something instrinsically evil about getting married and having children.) Religious families are more fecund than the average, and therefore it is essential to 'catch' these young women in the earliest stages of their exploration and return to Judaism. If enough pressure is applied, they feel compelled and obligated to stay, and fast footwork proceeds to ensure that a suitable husband is found fairly quickly.

The Sabbath is the focus of a BT's rehabilitation. On this special day of the week, when normal activities are suspended, we were sent to a range of families to participate in an 'authentic, straight out of the *shtetl*' experience. Unlike many of the other women who had never seen candles lit of a Friday night, I came from a family which was traditional and I was familiar with the rituals, so things were not so 'beautiful' or 'special' for me. (I have come to hate the word 'special'. I visited several types of families, some so 'special' they should be locked away.) In one type of family, the husband studied full-time in a *kollel*, a *yeshivah* for married men where they receive a small stipend for studying full time, and the wife worked, usually as a teacher or secretary, while their young children were left in childcare. The virtuousness of these families can't be matched in other families. They lived simply but neatly, and seemed to desire no material possessions. The women revelled in the esteemed role of *akeret habayit* – the cornerstone of the home, and took pride in their ability to support a husband studying *Torah*, arrange care of the children, have guests on *Shabbat* and be involved in charitable activities in the community. The women with large families (eight to ten is not uncommon) were socially rewarded by being carefully selected to be role models. Now I can't believe that, at the time, I had pretensions to be just like one of these self-sacrificing women.

In another type of family, the couple with professional degrees and interesting jobs are paraded around for the benefit of the career women in the student population. These students often fear that becoming religious will force them out of their careers, so the schools find dual-professional families that prove the religious lifestyle does not impinge upon the woman's self-fulfilment. These families are harder to find, but once ensnared, are highly valued recruitment tools. Often the men are lawyers, accountants, bankers and the women are psychologists, social workers and teachers (when they find a female chemical engineer, they are tempted to pay her to take in *Shabbat* guests). Other valuable finds are the female doctors and male psychologists. They are good examples of how people can combine professions and *Torah* observance in the modern world.

We were sent to families on a Friday night when the tablecloth was clean and the candles sparkled. It was also intended as a not-so-subtle instruction for the students as to how to make *Shabbat* and create that certain atmosphere that we would be expected to replicate and have wafting through our own homes in a couple of years. And we were instructed on how to dress: at the height of one Jerusalem summer, I was at a Friday-night dinner in a below-the-knees dress with a closed collar, pantyhose and sleeves that just reached the top of my elbow. They should have covered my elbow, and my hostess (not so discreetly) gave me a winter cardigan so that my elbows would be hidden. It didn't seem to bother her that I blushed bright red out of embarrassment.

Men in *yeshivot* for *ba'alei teshuvah* are receiving the same instruction, so that when couples marry, all of us will know the right way to hold the *Kiddush* cup to sanctify the wine, the minutiae concerning the ritual washing of the hands before eating bread, and the traditional *Shabbat* melodies which unite the guests in song.

We saw the perfect example of a husband-wife relationship and what was expected of each partner. Maybe they were in love, but it seemed to me that many families acted purposefully in a concilia-tory mode, giving young impressionable women the idea that Jewish husbands are attentive, caring and altogether a better catch – particularly religious husbands. It was also a model of a relationship with a caring, yet dominant man. For students without adequate male figures in their lives, this reconstructed 'new religious man' who will protect them is one of the most powerful and effective incentives to join the Orthodox world. On Friday nights, the world seems ripe for personal salvation, with the imminent arrival of a knight in a black coat.

The grand plan seemed to work. Over the last twenty years, many of the BT women have married the BT men from the parallel schools, and in many instances moved into ultra-Orthodox neighbourhoods. Their idyllic union found fertile breeding ground. In Israel, many of these newly married couples moved to areas with large communities of BT families and in the 1980s a few new developments on the West Bank were established specifically for them. The BT movement has influenced the structure and character of traditional Orthodoxy. Their insecurity and tenuous position in the community often compelled the BTs to behave more zealously, piously and meticulously. This ghetto-isation has created a BT subculture with negative connotations which could hinder their children's integration into the wider Orthodox community.

I found the gender politics between the teachers and the students disturbing. In an environment that was meant to place no emphasis on sexuality and almost deny its existence, the place teemed with a sexual tension very different from that found in discos or sex bars where the sex is for sale. For the rabbis involved, it is a legitimate and praised opportunity to have contact with a wide array of women, in stark contrast to their own FFB community where they barely speak to women. Unlike the FFB women, who have virtually no experience with men outside their immediate family, the BT women have unlimited access to rabbis and extensive male contact within the religious community when they visit families for *Shabbat*.

Of course, I didn't realise this at the time, but now I see that the rabbi/student relationships were based essentially on the power and charisma of the rabbis, and the students' needs to gain their favours and emulate their manner. The subconscious was working overtime, and I know some of the women married certain men because the men were highly recommended by the rabbi whom the woman wanted to please. I observed a manipulative streak in the forging of relationships between the students and the large families. If you are 'special' enough to be selected to visit one of the rabbis' families, there is an extra price to pay. Rabbis who work at a school for young women recognise the potential to recruit able helpers for their wives. The rabbis seduce the students, not with kisses or God forbid, any hint of sex, but rather with words of gratitude, and offers of becoming a valued member of their extended family.

Once I received the honour of an invitation for a *Shabbat* meal and it was suggested that I go and help the *rebbetzen* to prepare for *Shabbat*. It was suggested in the guise that I would see, first-hand, how a traditional Jewish home is made ready for *Shabbat* and the wonderful excitement of the children as they join in the preparations. I ended up vacuuming the floor, peeling and chopping vegetables, and, most insulting of all, I was asked to change the baby's nappy. When the meal was finally underway, and only a plate of gefilte fish separated me from the rabbi I idealised, I was too tired to observe that I had barely been noticed the whole evening. Eventually, though, it dawned upon me what was expected. There is no such thing as a free lunch. It was a subtle, more refined form of repayment that was expected and extracted. I was obliged to help with the kitchen duties and serving the meal. It was suggested that in the name of *chessed* – unyielding kindness – I might enjoy washing the dishes, but only in cold water because turning on the hot water means turning on the electricity which is forbidden on the Sabbath. I have heard of other instances where girls were sent to the rabbis' homes to help their wives clean the house for Passover. This basically involves purging the home of any crumb of bread, and any other trace of leavened goods. It is dressed up as 'good works', or 'learning first-hand what a Jewish home is all about', but essentially it is cheap domestic labour. However, to win approval one must be obliging in these tasks. Although the rhetoric is that the rabbis and teachers are there to challenge your mind and help you find your place in the world of the Orthodox community, much of the agenda is a systematic programme to transform a student into a particular mould. All of this was only further affirmation of my increasing sense that the students were not rewarded for their intellectual prowess, but rather for what they were able to contribute to the household. That, I imagined the rabbis joked amongst themselves, was the main advantage of teaching in a girls' school: it was a pool of cheap household help for their wives and large families. It never seemed to occur to the rabbis that the whole process devalued their own daughters, and that one day their students might have daughters too and have nothing to teach them but how to make a good chicken soup.

After I left Israel and went back to Melbourne in 1979 to pursue my university studies, I stayed in contact with several people I knew who had been through the BT 'system'. While many do have happy family lives, I know that during the last fifteen years, several couples have divorced and the women are now struggling as single parents. Most of these women are not religious any more. For several years, I maintained contact with one or two of the rabbis from my time in the *yeshivot*, and when I mentioned to them the high rate of divorce, they just shrugged their shoulders, as if to say, 'It's got nothing to do with us.' At one point, one of the rabbis admitted that they should have been more careful before encouraging the BTs to marry each other so quickly.

Back in Melbourne, I was also attending classes at Ohel Chana, the Lubavitch women's seminary in Melbourne. There were classes on the *Torah* portion of the week, Jewish law and the *Chabad* philosophy which underpins the Lubavitch movement. The contrast between university and Ohel Chana could have been the basis of a farcical comedy skit. I also went to occasional lectures for women on matters of Jewish law, and I found that sometimes, the image of women's learning is damaged by the women themselves.

I recently read Betty Freidan's *The Feminine Mystique* which was first published in 1963 and was struck by how much of it applies to Orthodox women's lives in the 1990s. She recounted a story that when she went back to her own college (Smith) in 1959:

> I picked up a copy of the college paper I had once edited. The current student editor described a government class in which fifteen of the twenty girls were knitting 'with the stony-faced concentration of Madame Defarge. The instructor, more in challenge than in seriousness, announced that Western civilisation is coming to an end. The students turned to their notebooks and wrote, 'Western civ coming to an end' – all without dropping a stitch.'[15]

I laughed out loud when I read those lines, because it reminded me of the girls in class busy crocheting *kippot* with ludicrous patterns

[15] Freidan, B., *The Feminine Mystique*, Penguin, New York, 1963, p. 134

for their boyfriends. Intelligent girls can spend hours poring over and discussing the intricacies of the patterns the same way a man dissects a page of *Talmud*. Not only did I not have someone to crotchet a *kippah* for, I couldn't crotchet. I still see women in their early twenties crocheting away: it amounts almost to sexual foreplay as they think about the man they are crocheting a *kippah* for. I'd be quite happy for rabbis to issue an edict banning crocheting *kippot* in class as this would be a first positive step towards raising the status of women's education and improving women's self-esteem.

Later Friedan asks another student, 'What courses are people excited about now?' and received the reply, 'I guess everybody wants to graduate with a diamond ring on her finger. That's the important thing.' This reminded me of the jokes people make about women's seminaries: that the young women want to graduate with an MRS degree.

During the late 1970s and early 1980s, I made friends whose weddings I went to (I went to twelve weddings one year!), but our lives rapidly went in different directions – by the age of twenty-one, they had a baby and all I had was a new Nissan car. Part of me wanted to fit in, I wanted to be as devout as these women, but I couldn't bring myself to that point of uncritical and loving submission to a higher authority. I used to feel a little guilty that I had disappointed them by pursuing my secular studies. Even now that I have the external trappings of a husband and children, too much time and experience have passed for me ever to feel that I could re-enter that world. Only one significant, lasting friendship endures from those years and, while I am always happy to see women from that community and like to know what is happening in their lives, I feel that chapter of my life is closed.

I continued to attend various lectures geared to an audience of *ba'alei teshuvah*, but I stopped in the late 1980s when I found myself increasingly alienated and somewhat disturbed by the content and the tone of the lectures. However, I do continue to read various studies about *ba'alei teshuvah*,[16] and have realised that a major

16 Aviad, J., *Return to Judaism: Religious Renewal in Israel*, University of Chicago Press, Chicago, 1983; Davidman, L., op. cit.; Kaufman, D., *Rachel's Daughters:*

difference between myself and the others is that I never really defined myself as a BT in the American sense, i.e. totally secular Jew from assimilated family who becomes ultra-Orthodox in a matter of weeks, months, years.

I am from a very traditional family – we were *kosher* (with occasional minor lapses), we celebrated *Shabbat* (with occasional minor lapses) and I was very aware of my ethnic identity as a Jew. What I lacked was a serious Jewish education, and several of the other more advanced *yeshivot* for women assumed a minimum level of competency in Hebrew texts which I did not have because I did not attend a Jewish day school. When I decided to be more observant, it was more about having consistency in my practice of Jewish rituals, and consciously deciding to link myself with hundreds of years of tradition. I just needed an education to help me fill in the gaps: I did not need a whole lifestyle. I was not attempting to reject my parents' values, nor seek a more ethereal and spiritual frame of reference. Rather it was about continuing my parents' traditions which had been interrupted by the war.

However, for some BTs this sudden power to alienate their parents and multiply their inadequacies gave them great satisfaction. It was the only socially rewarding way of devaluing everything that they had struggled for.

So, by the time I went to America in 1991, I no longer identified myself with the BT movement, nor did I occasionally wonder if I could be an ultra-Orthodox Jew. Despite repeated attempts by well-meaning friends to introduce me to men in black hats, I knew that I couldn't marry one of them. However, amateur anthropologist that I am, I still found it fascinating to get a glimpse of the contemporary 'outreach'[17] movement in New York. It is much less focused on a central *yeshivah*, but rather on educational programmes that fit around the frenetic pace of professional life on the Upper West Side.

Newly Orthodox Jewish Women, Rutgers University Press, New Brunswick, 1991
[17] outreach work is referred to as *kiruv* from the verb 'to bring closer'

At first, I was taken by the advertising campaigns. 'Call 1 800 44 hebrew, and find out where you can take a Hebrew class in your neighbourhood.' I am serious. Toll-free Judaism. I found the tactics too corny (it was my Australian sensibilities) and the rabbis worryingly demagogic and unaccountable. I have heard a prominent rabbi in the outreach movement say enthusiastically, 'For the price of a chicken, you can make a BT.' I have seen it happen at the 'Turn Friday Night Into Shabbos' events which are geared to helping unsuspecting Jews take their first sip of chicken soup towards redemption. A small group of well-intentioned enthusiasts will plan a Friday-night event at their synagogue. The prayer services are led by unusually young, bearded and 'special' rabbis who approach the task with the requisite zealotry and clarity of purpose. Dinner (at carefully arranged tables, with specially recruited, unbetrothed men and women poised to 'get to know each other'), festive singing of traditional *Shabbat* songs and a lecture by the resident charismatic rabbi all follow. Outreach workers understand that the key to success is the power of myth-making and nostalgia, so the romantic images of the *shtetl* and the cohesion of family life are sharply juxtaposed with the anomie and rising divorce rate in conglomerate cities like New York. Discussion is encouraged so that the usual theological traumas are vented and the predictable questions of suffering rise to the fore – 'Why do bad things happen to good people?' repeats itself in various guises.

Those who attend a Friday-night event are monitored – their name is put on a list and soon after, they start to receive literature about classes in Basic Judaism, and phone calls inviting them to attend a 'Beginners' Service,' and other events geared toward the BT. Some in the BT business claim that 'there is a haemorrhaging taking place in American Jewry, and unless we do something about it now, we will bleed to death as a people within the next few decades'.[18]

---

[18] See the literature of the National Jewish Outreach Program, which describes its basic charter as 'saving American Jewry from extinction'. Its envelopes to solicit funds are emblazoned with the sentence, 'Concentration camps and gas chambers aren't the only ways to exterminate the Jewish people.'

These shock tactics are cheap and, once again, I found it disturbing that the BT movement relies on the infantilisation of the returnee. It creates a dependency on people in authority, who will always know more than the returnee and will use this knowledge to undermine any attempt at an individualistic expression of Jewish belief.

I suppose what especially disturbed me was that most of the organisers had an air of moral superiority. They almost felt sorry for people who were not religious. I remember the pain of one woman who told me that she finally observed her first Sabbath without 'cheating a bit when no one was looking', and then had to fly to Texas the next day to be bridesmaid at her brother's wedding to a non-Jewish woman. She felt she couldn't share her distress with the people who had influenced her to become religious for fear of ruining her reputation as someone who had 'made it'. She didn't want to disappoint them.

The world was divided into 'us' – safe, reliable, trustworthy, and 'them' – uneducated, vulnerable and ripe for the picking. People were either religious, or 'not yet' religious. Relationships were not genuine or equal, rather they were fostered with this ulterior motive.

Judaism is a history, a literature, a culture and a religion with lots to offer, and it is disappointing that millions of Jews worldwide know very little but fairy tales and myths about Judaism. Therefore, I think that the hundreds of caring and idealistic families and teachers who have taken the *ba'alei teshuvah* into their fold and taught them about a three-thousand-year-old religion are doing a great communal service. However, to reduce the immense richness of the Jewish cultural heritage to cheap marketing slogans and quick-fix spiritual savvy merely makes Judaism a disposable fashion accessory destined to be replaced when something more sexy comes along. Those of us who struggle with it every day deserve to be taken more seriously.

Chapter 8

If New York has some of the worst of things, it also has some of the best of things. In New York I discovered real and serious study. I was living on the Upper West Side of Manhattan and attended classes at Drisha Institute. Drisha was founded in 1979 by Rabbi David Silber, and offers women classes in a range of topics, including *Talmud*, Bible, philosophy and Jewish law. The first thing you notice when you walk in is that there are books everywhere – as it should be – but the same books that you will find in a men's *yeshivah* – volumes of the *Talmud* stand next to a range of biblical commentaries, they are no books of apologetics written in substandard English which are found overflowing in the *yeshivot* for *ba'alei teshuvah*.

It is different from all the other places because it does not assume a lesser intellectual standard from women, and it does not censor the texts which women have access to. It also has a 'scholars' circle' which is a small group of women who study full time and receive a stipend – just like the élite of the men's *yeshivah* (although they cannot go on to be rabbis as their male counterparts can – but that is a whole other chapter!).

Monday nights at Drisha became sacrosanct, and nothing got in the way. My teacher had rabbinical ordination from the Conservative JTS, the Orthodox Yeshiva University, and a master's degree in English Literature from Brown University. His vocabulary was majestic and he was so smart that I took two classes with him – because I couldn't get enough. The first class was *Mishnah*, the code of laws which is the basis of the *Talmud*, the Jewish legal cannon, and the second class was *Midrash*, a body of varied literary works which expand and interpret the meaning and intent of the Bible.

The classes I attended were small – it may have been the subject material, but I think it was more because my guy had yet to be discovered. He was not a flashy type, nor a trendy populist, rather a quiet, thoughtful, reflective individual who was just frighteningly clever. We did not cover a lot of ground each week, but that didn't really matter – each verse was treasured, and resonated with meaning. His literary and psychological approach to the text brought the characters and issues alive. The text was regarded as a challenge to work with rather than to be in awe of. This twist in the dynamic and the change in the relationship which I, as the reader, had with the text, was deeply exciting for me, and changed my whole view of learning. I have never been so challenged before.

I suppose that is why the classes attracted such an interesting mix of students. There was an intriguing (was she a spy, I kept wondering?) Polish academic, with heavy kohl around her eyes, who made disconcertingly original comments; there was a completely eccentric Princeton academic with a PhD in something incredibly ancient who was so totally unaware of her socially inappropriate behaviour that she became endearing; and there was my good friend Julie, a rabbinical student at the Jewish Theological Seminary, who, in September 1996, became the first woman rabbi on the Upper West Side (at the Society for the Advancement of Judaism – a Reconstructionist synagogue). I suppose that is what I really enjoyed about the place: it was rare to meet such a broad cross-section of women equally committed to Jewish knowledge, yet secure enough to respect each other's individual lifestyles.

The opportunities I have had obviously make me think about the sort of education I want you two girls to have. I wonder what will become of your curiosity. How will I be able to nurture your natural intelligence and foster that additional 'spark' called imagination? How can I ensure that you have all the opportunities you deserve to fulfil your potential? Based on the evidence to hand – the answer is simple – keep you away from most forms of formal Orthodox education. It's a sorry state of affairs, but the handful of high schools which give girls equal opportunities for study are exceptions to the rule.

I am not sure who said, 'educate a Jewish boy and you will have a Jewish man, educate a Jewish girl and you will have a Jewish family', but the dictum seems to work in subtle ways that undermine young girls and socialise them into very traditional roles. It starts at playgroup where the 'mummies on the bus go chatter, chatter, chatter, and the daddies on the bus read, read, read'. It gets worse at kindergarten with the *Shabbat* party on Friday afternoons. The 'mummy' lights the candles, and the 'daddy' has the honour at the head of the table to say the blessings. Is there an Orthodox day school that lets the 'daddy' light the candles once in a while, and lets the 'mummy' say the blessing over the wine and the bread?[1] It seems to me that it is precisely because if you 'educate a Jewish girl and you will have a Jewish family' that a girl's education needs to be taken more seriously. Isn't it time we were encouraging and creating the sorts of Jewish families in which daughters are given many of the same options as their brothers?

I once interviewed Rabbanit Chana Henkin, another pioneer of women's education. She wanted to provide women with a programme of intensive intellectual rigour, and in Jerusalem, where the gender divide is even more pronounced, her institution, Nishmat, was amongst the first places to teach women *Talmud*, with the discussion in English. It attracted a lot of American and European women with advanced secular degrees, but limited Jewish education. As she said:

> In *yeshivot* for men, there are no notebooks, but in the women's *yeshivot*, they are all busy taking notes. While the men get smart, among the women, only the notebooks get smart . . . It is important not to confuse a lack of textual skills with a lack of analytical skills . . . Women's learning has largely been presentational – women are presented information as a *fait accompli*. Yet a law student learns to go to the source, and Jewish women need to have the same familiarity with the sources. If we speak down to them, we will lose them.[2]

Bravo, I say.

---

1 This is permissible according to Jewish law, but custom has dictated a social norm that has defined the roles very clearly; see footnote 22 on p. 71.
2 *Forward*, 10 January 1992

If we accept that knowledge is power, then women must acquire the same tools that men take for granted and use against women to keep them in a dependent position. Women will not be able to challenge the decision-making process until they have the skills to understand the development of the law and the ability to interpret the law. One can only choose to reject 'male' knowledge claiming it as the source of women's oppression, if one knows about it. We risk putting ourselves beyond the debate by marginalising our concerns as 'only' women's concerns.

On the other hand, it is easy to fall into the trap that Jewish education is only about sitting in a *yeshivah* poring over *Talmudic* tomes one can barely lift. There is an argument that women want to learn different things. They want a woman's perspective – they don't want to learn what a lot of dead white males had to say about the religion. If women want to learn women's history – great, women's literature – great, laws applicable to women – great, but I think there is a danger that some women have been exposed to Judaism only through the prism of women's experiences and that is only half the picture. In the long term, I think that this approach is naïve and superficial, especially when the community doesn't expect women to take their intellectual interests seriously – a workshop here, a lecture there, a monthly seminar perhaps – it all seems to be considered enough.

Until recently, the majority of books written for Orthodox women were still written by male authors with a specific agenda to socialise women into the traditional domestic roles expected of Jewish (nay, all) women.[3] In design, these books written by men remind me of the comment Betty Freidan made about male editors: 'the deciding voice on these magazines [women's magazines] was male, the formula of the housewife was man's,'[4] and she remarked that, 'the very size of their print is raised until it looks

3 Miller, Y., *In Search of the Jewish Woman*, Feldheim, New York, 1984, and Feldman, A., *The River, The Kettle, The Bird: The Torah Guide to Successful Marriage*, CSB Publications, Jerusalem, 1987, are two of many examples of the genre written by men.
4 Freidan, B., op. cit., p. 48

like a first-grade primer'.[5] Yet, as women begin to take control of
what they learn, they will gain the confidence to define the debate
with the rabbis and to participate as partners in a dialogue. As
women learn *Torah*, they will begin to transform the meaning of
Torah. As women learn, they can begin to write the books that
other women will turn to for advice and information.

Women love books. We love to dust them. We love to arrange
them alphabetically. And now that we can read, we love to create
book clubs so that we can talk about them, preferably while
cracking pistachios and nibbling dried papaya in Hampstead
Garden Suburb. I am known as the 'mother of all book clubs' –
wherever I am found, there is a book club following soon after.
The first one I co-founded was the most fertile in Melbourne – a
bunch of primigravadas, trying to get pregnant, pregnant or just
delivered (with the obvious exception of me who didn't even have
a date on a Saturday night). We met monthly all having read the
same book, discussed it for an hour and a half, drank coffee and
gossiped for about an hour.

One woman confessed that her husband was not so keen on her
coming, 'You are always so aggressive in bed when you come home
from that book club. Anyway, why can't men join?'

Clearly he was jealous, and why not? Eight vibrant, attractive
intelligent women discussing literary trends, narrative form,
character development, metaphor and the existential dilemmas of
the author. Which man wouldn't want to be in the club?

In the Melbourne book club (which still meets and apparently
does not miss me) we read a range of books – South American,
Russian, Czech, English, American and occasionally Australian.
Although the books were not always of Jewish content, I read them
with a Jewish woman's eyes, with a Jewish woman's sensibilities. I
tried to empathise with the characters, their conflicts and
contradictions. I suppose Freud would call it projection. That is
probably why I was very uncooperative when it came to Australian
literature – it felt so empty, so devoid of suffering and angst, the
cultural references were very alienating and foreign. (Funny thing

5 ibid., p. 58

that – born in Australia, educated there and always happy to tell people I am Australian when I travel, yet I find that when it comes to its literature, most of it fails to move me.)

At first glance, my London book club looks homogenous: despite the age-range of mid-twenties to mid-sixties, we are all educated middle-class white Jewish women, including a couple of lawyers, a doctor and a businesswoman. However, religiously, politically and socially, the group is so varied that it is unlikely we would ever meet each other in 'normal' life. That's why I enjoy it so much because through our own perspectives we ask different questions and seek our different answers from the women we read about.

Yet, every meeting ends with the same question, 'What next?' and we answer with the same questions. 'Do we want to do a Jewish book?' 'A woman's book?' 'A Jewish woman's book?' 'What is a Jewish woman's book – does it have to be written by a Jewish woman, or can it be about a Jewish woman?'

We have found that even books manage to bring out the guilt in women. Details are scant but we know about Miriam, the daughter of Benayahu, in Yemen, who was a scribe and copied the Five Books of *Torah*. Typically, she felt guilty, and wrote a note in her own hand which said, 'Do not condemn me for any errors that you may find for I am a nursing woman, Miriam, the daughter of Benayahu, the scribe.'[6]

Another apologised for combining motherhood with her career. (It could have been the 1990s!) In an anonymous footnote by a woman, cited by Solomon Schecter in one of his scholarly research works, a woman writes, 'I beseech the reader not to judge me harshly when he finds that mistakes have crept into this work; for when I was engaged in copying it, God blessed me with a son, and thus I could not attend to my business properly.'[7]

Women have been involved in literature for far longer than most of us realise. Recent scholarship has unearthed the literary

6 cited in Henry, S. and Taitz, E., op. cit., p. 115
7 cited in Amram, D., *The Makers of Hebrew Books in Italy*, The Holland Press, London, 1963, 1988, p. 32

endeavour of women which testifies to a vibrant and creative life that we have marginalised and forgotten about as we teach our children the highlights of Jewish history: Expulsion, Inquisition, Pogroms, Holocaust and Generic Persecution.[8]

Diaries and letters have been an important focus for scholars and one of the most famous diaries is that of Glückel of Hameln, written 'to drive away the melancholy that comes with the long nights' after the death of her husband. She was born in Germany in 1646, married at the age of fourteen, widowed at the age of forty-four, and in between, had twelve children.[9] Her strength and determination to provide for her family, in the face of the hardships endured by the Jewish community, has made her popularly revered as a role model and inspiration.

However, often when men write about the lives of Orthodox Jewish women, they choose to reconstruct the events in a way that suits a broader religious and political agenda. In a fascinating and extensively documented study, Don Seeman, who describes himself as an 'ethnographer of suppressed memory', recounts the life of Rayna Batya. She was a granddaughter of Rabbi Chaim of Volozhin, and the wife of Rabbi Naphtali Zevi Yehudah Berlin, known by his acronym, the Netziv.[10] Exact dates of her birth and death are unavailable, but her first child was born in 1832, when her husband was fifteen years old (yes, fifteen) and we guess she was about the same age.

Her nephew, Baruch Epstein, the author of the *Torah Temimah*,

---

[8] Umansky, E. and Ashton, D., *Four Centuries of Jewish Women's Spirituality*, Beacon Press, Boston, 1991, is an excellent anthology of primary documents written by women from 1560–1990. See also the references mentioned in footnote 3 on p. 23.

[9] *The Memoirs of Glückel of Hameln*, Schocken, New York, 1977. There are several editions of this memoir. This edition is translated by Marvin Lowenthal. See also Zemon Davis, N., *Women on the Margins: Three Seventeenth-Century Lives*, Harvard University Press, Cambridge, 1996 (one of the women she analyses is Glückel).

[10] Seeman, D., 'The Silence of Rayna Batya Torah, Suffering, and Rabbi Barukh Epstein's "Wisdom of Women" ', in *Torah U-Madda Journal*, Volume 6, 1995–6, pp. 91–128

a commentary on the *Torah*, had long conversations with his aunt who expressed her frustration at her exclusion from religious life. In Epstein's 1928 Hebrew memoir, *Mekor Barukh*, he devotes a chapter, 'Wisdom of Women', to Rayna Batya and repeats some of their conversations:

> More than once I heard her complain and bemoan in sorrow and pain, with unpleasant countenance and a bitter soul, the pain of the bitter fate and narrow portion of women in this life . . . men have received 248 positive commandments, while oppressed and disgraced women were only given three! . . . Even more than this was she disturbed and pained by the desecration of women's honour, and by their lowly position, inasmuch as it was forbidden to teach them *Torah* (referring specifically to *Talmud* study). Once she said to me that if Eve (i.e. all women) had been cursed with ten curses, then this curse, the prohibition of learning *Torah*, was equivalent to them all . . . [11]

In essence, Epstein portrays a brilliant woman, noted for her lack of housewifely skills, ensconced in the milieu of some of the greatest *Talmudic* scholars of her day, who is deeply aggrieved at her exclusion from study and ritual.

In 1988, an edited English version of *Mekor Barukh* was published, entitled *My Uncle the Netziv*. Written from an Orthodox perspective, this abridged memoir systematically omits or tampers with Rayna Batya's expressions of frustration, outrage and despair. Further, it deletes references to her study of Jewish legal texts and homiletics. Rayna Batya was 'too hot to handle' and an alternative paradigm of a saintly woman, relatively happy with her lot and married to one of Orthodox Jewry's leading lights was created.

Here is Orthodox history being rewritten to suit a broader religious and political agenda, particularly one that seeks to obliterate a woman's pain. Rabbinical leaders tell us that women's twentieth-century disquiet is a product of modernity and the

[11] ibid., pp. 93–4. He translates and cites from *Mekor Barukh*, Vilna, 1928, p. 1950

adoption of values antithetical to a '*Torah*-true' way of life, because after all 'our grandmothers were satisfied. They never complained.' But clearly they did complain, and I would suggest that Rayna Batya is also an archetypal representation of many intelligent women who wanted more than what was offered to them. However, Rayna Batya was different, because unlike all the other women who left Orthodoxy and chose the Enlightenment, she did not reject the Orthodoxy that rejected her.

What are Orthodox 'historians' afraid of? They understand that when they tamper with history, it affects our understanding of women's participation in the past, and informs our own involvement in the future. Thus, they consider it their ethical duty to suppress and censor knowledge so that the lives of *Torah* scholars and their families are pasteurised to create role models and imagined realities to which we should be aspiring. But if we have been fed lies, how can we claim integrity?

As Seeman points out

> . . . the pain associated for some people with a life of *Torah* (where it is other than the voluntary self-sacrifice valorised by tradition) can hardly be acknowledged. In practical terms, this attitude is associated with a narrowing of legitimate *halakhic* and theological debate within Orthodoxy, often justified by fallacious references to an idealised past in which cultural conflict (such as that with respect to women's *Torah* learning) simply did not exist. [12]

Nevertheless, this sort of research and exposé consoles me and gives me hope. Personally I find compelling accounts of women like Rayna Batya more appealing than revisionist attempts to convince me that my foremothers were all happy with their lot. There is nothing interesting in happy women. Conflict produces the sort of anguish which forces Orthodox women to question and evaluate their relationship to Judaism in ways that men do not have to, because they are not excluded.

[12] ibid., p. 118

There are too few Rayna Batyas left willing to stay the distance, but if Orthodoxy is strong and vibrant enough, it can respond and adapt to women's spiritual needs. However, if Orthodoxy is scared of itself, its women, my daughters, will leave. How will historians of the future explain that one?

Sometimes, women in conflict create alternative opportunities to channel their search, and in recent years, women have been commanding control of *Rosh Hodesh*, the first day of the lunar month, to create a sacred space in which to explore their identity. The New Moon is mentioned in the Bible as a day to 'blow with the trumpets over your burnt offerings' (Numbers (10:10). In the *Talmudic* passage discussing the laws of work on *Rosh Hodesh*, the commentators agree that while men are expected to work on the New Moon, women are not. This is because while Moses was on Mount Sinai receiving the Ten Commandments, the women did not participate in building the Golden Calf and refused to hand over their gold jewellery. God rewarded them with the observance of the New Moon, which is symbolically linked to the menstrual cycle after which women renew themselves like the moon. Interestingly, some have made the point that *Rosh Hodesh* was not the appropriate reward for refusal to worship the Golden Calf:

> Justice would suggest that women's loyalty be rewarded with priestly power and leadership. Aaron [Moses' brother] should have been deposed and the righteous women ordained in his place.[13]

Nevertheless, women were instructed not to work, although the nature of this 'work' is debated (e.g. spinning, no, sewing, yes, laundry, no, giving charity, yes). Most amusingly, a ban on gambling was declared in the Middle Ages partly because

13 Litman, J., Glass, J. and Wallace, S., '*Rosh Chodesh*: A Feminist Critique and Reconstruction', in Berrin S. (ed.), *Celebrating the New Moon: A* Rosh Chodesh *Sourcebook*, Jason Aronson, Northvale, NJ, 1995, pp. 23–32, p. 24. More than forty essays divided into sections, 'Teachings of *Rosh Chodesh*', 'Approaches to *Rosh Chodesh*', 'The Cycle of the Month' and 'Poetry, Prayers, Songs and Meditations', form the basis of this very useful and eclectic collection.

'mischievous Jewish women' were squandering family money to gamble during their free time on *Rosh Hodesh*. [14]

During the last twenty years, there has been such a proliferation of *Rosh Hodesh* groups that it can be likened to a social movement and part of the second wave of feminism. It seems to me that the consciousness-raising groups of the seventies and the idea of creating a 'safe space' for women to raise issues which will get a sympathetic hearing impacted on the nature and structure of the 'sacred space' which *Rosh Hodesh* groups provide. Just as *Rosh Hodesh* groups are as varied as the women who join them, each group is free to develop its own ceremonies and set of rituals as there are no prescribed formulas. I have attended groups which start with prayer, groups which start with passing a burning candle to each person, who speaks about something important that has happened in the previous month, and groups that start with coffee and cake. Some groups form as a branch of the local synagogue, some have no affiliation, some are geared to a particular age-group, some purposely try to be cross-generational. Activities can focus on a Jewish holiday happening that month, a guest speaker, someone's experience or some creative activity. [15]

One group of women in Montreal has been using its local synagogue every *Rosh Hodesh* for nearly fifteen years. The women meet for the morning prayers and read from the *Sefer Torah*, this being one of the special activities marking *Rosh Hodesh*. They also consider it a suitable space for young girls to celebrate their *bat mitzvah*. [16] This use of sacred time to blend feminine spirituality, women's concerns and Orthodox practice has made *Rosh Hodesh* groups very popular amongst Orthodox women exploring the connections between Orthodoxy and feminism.

14 Agus, A., 'The Month is for You: Observing *Rosh Hodesh* as a Woman's Holiday', in Koltun, E., op. cit., pp. 84–93; Kaufman, M., *The Woman in Jewish Law and Tradition*, Jason Aronson, Northvale, NJ, 1993; '*Rosh Hodesh*, the Women's Festival', pp. 228–31
15 Adelman, P., *Miriam's Well: Rituals for Jewish Women Around the Year*, Biblio Press, New York, 1990
16 Joseph, N., 'Reflections on Observing *Rosh Chodesh* with My Women's Tefillah Group', in Berrin S., op. cit., pp. 111–16

Chapter 9

But perhaps the ultimate bonding place is the *mikveh*, the ritual bath. Apparently it has become 'hip to dip'.[1] On my own first visit to the *mikveh*, I knew that I was about to be initiated into a secret society. The *mikveh* is to women what the morning *minyan* is to men. The rules of membership are similar: attendance is regular, it has to be on time and you should be clean before you go in. Bonding is strong and quick. In the late afternoon of the twelfth day, before I go to the *mikveh* after nightfall, I take a long luxurious bath, clouded with fragrant bubbles. I pack my special bag of essential items – a towel, a comb, and my favourite lace slip. (At least that was BC (before children); AD (after delivery) it is more like a rushed shower, stuff a towel into a Sainsbury's plastic bag and leave home without a change of undies.)

When I am there, I sometimes feel like I am in a parallel universe.

'Lice.'

'Lice? What do you mean, lice? Didn't she check her hair before she came to the *mikveh*?'

As the senior *mikveh* attendant, supervising each woman who ritually immerses herself in the *mikveh*'s pure rainwater seven days after her period on the night she will resume sexual relations with her husband, Mrs D was used to such tricky questions.

---

[1] Mann, S., 'Lucky Dip: Ancient Ritual and Modern Romance', *New Moon*, June 1992, pp. 20–3. Research into women's ritual observances in England found that nineteen per cent of women who attend the *mikveh* do not observe *kashrut* or some of the other key practices. 'This suggests unusual and unexpected patterns of personal religious choice emerging in the UK, as has been found in the USA. One interpretation is that ritual practice is coming to be seen as a means of achieving personal satisfaction or psychological growth rather than as a response to divine authority;' see Goodkin, J. and Citron, J., op. cit., p. xiii.

'Apparently, she just got home and found the lice in her hair,' the junior *mikveh* attendant replied meekly. 'She's left her telephone number, and asked that you call her back with the answer.'

Mrs D sighed and started to ring around the rabbis who specialise in the intricate rules of *taharat mishpachah*, badly translated as 'family purity.'

'It's always impossible on a Sunday night. Weddings, *bar mitzvahs*, fund-raising dinners: no one's at home,' she said as she put the phone down.

I had the distinct feeling that she resented having to call these men for the official answer and defer to their authority. After all, she had been a *mikveh* lady for over twenty years and knew the intimate secrets of women's bodies better than any male rabbi.

'So can she go to her husband tonight?' asked the junior.

'Go where?' I thought to myself. What a great euphemism for sex. That's what the lice was really about: sex. I overheard this conversation one evening at the *mikveh*, but when I was spotted, the voices of the attendants went all *sotto voce*. I would hear no more of the lice, and decided it was time to go home. That is the difference between me and the more pious woman: I'd go to your father with lice and pass them on.

Here's the birds and bees lesson, kids. I'll give it to you once, and don't ask me again. I am considered off-limits during my period and the following seven days.[2] When these days are finished, I go to the *mikveh*, a ritual bath, immerse myself in the warm rainwater, put on some sexy underwear and rush home for a night of unbridled passion. (Don't tell anyone I mentioned the sexy underwear.)

Ante-marriage *kallah* classes for blushing brides are usually given by the wife of the rabbi who is going to perform the

---

2 The laws are based on the biblical verse: 'Thou shalt not approach to a woman in the impurity of her menstrual flow, to uncover her nakedness' (Leviticus 18:19). Historically, the law evolved to extend this separation to twelve days – this combined the five days designated for the period (even if it was less), followed by seven 'white' days, in which the woman has to check there are no traces of uterine blood. During this time, physical intimacy of any sort, including kissing, and holding hands is restricted.

marriage, or any other woman deemed suitably pious and knowl-
edgeable in the specific laws of sexual relations. They are often on
a one-to-one basis and consist of about eight to ten hours of
instruction. Sometimes, these ante-marriage *kallah* classes are
anti-marriage classes. I mean, finally you have found someone
half-decent to marry, someone you are about to share your cheque
book with, and all of a sudden you are having lessons about when
you can have sex, when you can't have sex, how often you should
have it, where to have it, how to have it and why bother?

As if the promise of a honeymoon every month was not enough
incentive to use the *mikveh*,[3] some teachers appeal to the more
literary minded with tales of pious women being rewarded for using
the *mikveh*. Like the one about the man who left his wife to go on a
long journey, and told her that he would be back on a particular
evening. As that day approached his wife prepared for his return by
going to the *mikveh*. When her husband returned, he was delighted

'Since you have bathed in anticipation of my return, I shall
present you with a gold piece with which to buy the garment of
your choice.'

'Allow me,' she replied, 'with that gold piece to purchase a book
or to hire a scribe to copy a book for lending to students, enabling
them to pursue their studies.'

Subsequently, the woman became pregnant, and gave birth to a
boy. While all the brothers of that boy were devoid of learning, this
boy was the exception. [4]

Another woman refused to have sexual relations with her
miserly husband until he agreed to purchase books and devote
them to charitable purposes. Her husband complained to a wise
man, who told him, 'Blessed is she for having brought upon thee
pressure to perform a worthy deed.'[5]

Most of my friends got married at least ten years before I did,
so for at least ten years I was excluded from all their giggly

---

[3] Babylonian Talmud, Niddah 31b
[4] Sefer Hasidim, Margulies edition, 1973 Mossad Harav Kook, paragraph
874, p. 490
[5] ibid., paragraph 873, p. 490

conversations about their *kallah* classes. Coded messages between blushing brides escaped me and I relied on stolen glances at their reference books for clues about the sexual habits of the Orthodox woman. It felt a bit like that moment when you have ripped open the sealed section of Cosmopolitan magazine and realise that there is no going back, no way you can actually hide the fact you peeked. Then when I got married, I was privileged to have *kallah* classes with a very learned woman in New York, from whom I learnt the sources of the law and their historical development. Unlike most of my friends who were told 'what' to do, I was told 'what' *and* 'why'.

Finally, I became part of the gang, and girlfriends felt a moral obligation to instruct me in the ways of the world. It struck me how much of their personalities had been hidden and their sexuality suppressed in the guise of modesty. Given half the chance, they were desperate to talk about 'going to' their husbands.

Those in the know, know where to find the *mikveh*. There is no neon sign announcing a *mikveh* – they are discreet buildings, usually in a Jewish neighbourhood, near a synagogue, or in a quiet street. Although the external façade of each *mikveh* varies, depending on its architect, the internal construction of the *mikveh* is standardised, dictated by specific guidelines regarding the height, breadth, depth and water temperature of a *mikveh*.[6] The *mikveh* is open every night and on any given night there could be up to sixty women coming to the *mikveh*. I have been to the *mikveh* on the first night of Passover, when everyone gathers for the *seder*, and on the first night of *Rosh Hashanah*, the New Year – both highly inconvenient times for the women who supervise the *mikveh*, but on both occasions, they made no fuss and were genuinely happy that I had come to use the bath.

When I arrive, I exchange pleasantries with the receptionist, hand over my £5 and enter one of the individual bathrooms. After a quick shower and hair wash, I wrap myself in a towel, press the buzzer indicating that I am ready, and wait patiently for the

6 Babylonian Talmud – see tractate Mikva'ot for specific details about the construction of a *mikveh*. Kardish, S., *A History of Mikvaot in Britain*, Vallentine Mitchell, London, 1996

'*mikveh* lady'. Oops, wedding ring! I take it off – for the next few minutes, I belong to no one. It's just me in my birthday suit and some holy water. This kindly, post-menopausal woman oversees the immersion of each woman with Solomon's wisdom. She can discern between the new bride who needs gentle reassurance during her first year of marriage, and the seasoned mother of several children nearing the end of her childbearing years.

She looks me in the eye and says, 'Eyes, teeth, ears?'

I nod, 'All clean.'

Coyly, she points in the direction of my belly button.

'Yes, clean,' I smile.

'Make-up, nail polish?'

'No, nothing.' I am so proud of myself.

'Wait a minute,' she says.

I love this bit – she takes out the nail brush from her pocket and gently swipes away a few loose strands of hair from my shoulder.

'OK, you're ready. Go down carefully.'

I move towards the actual *mikveh*, best described as a three-foot-square sunken bath where a pool of stored rainwater gurgles happily, and drop my towel gently into the *mikveh* lady's hands. Guided by the handrail taking me down several steps into the water, I reach the bottom of the pool, my head slightly above the warm water. I glance at the *mikveh* lady who nods. Pausing for a moment, I take a deep breath, and immerse myself completely underwater.

My head now above water, the *mikveh* lady pronounces the word *kosher* (which literally means fit or proper), indicating that I was in fact completely immersed, without any hair left out of the water. As I recite a special blessing for this occasion, she does the hippest thing – she takes my towel and drapes it over my head, so that my hair will be covered when I say the blessing. It's the wildest thing – I am stark naked and she puts a towel on my head. What a religion!

Then I immerse myself again.

'*Kosher*,' she exclaims.

And again.

'And . . . *kosher*.'

What am I? A piece of meat? I wonder what she thinks about our bodies. She has seen it all: ante-natal lean, post-natal flab, big bums, floppy boobs. The women who work out, the women who are stretched out.

As I emerge, she hands me my towel and quietly disappears – sometimes muttering a wish for a healthy life and good tidings. It all takes less than a minute, but in a corny way, it is the most precious minute of each month – completely unadorned, I feel refreshed and renewed for sensual pleasures. I have been transformed from a piece of bloody flesh into a Jewish woman.

As I get dressed quickly, roughly dry my hair, and fumble with my stockings, I fantasise about being a *mikveh* lady. Part social activist, I plan a Lysistratian[7] revolt – no sex until there are equal rights for women, a support group for women experiencing domestic violence, and a counselling service – after all, the *mikveh* is the only place that women can come to knowing their husbands have no idea what they are really doing, and the '*mikveh* lady' is a crucial part of a system to protect women.[8] Women who want to celebrate their menopause could come for one last congratulatory dip, and I would offer women who have been sexually abused or raped the option to come to the *mikveh* as part of their recovery process. The *mikveh* would be a place of renewal and healing, encouraging women to seek solace in a warm dip.[9] I'd blow the whistle on single Orthodox women who are enjoying premarital sex and encourage them to use the *mikveh*, even though theoretically premarital sex is a definite no-no. After all, it's the

7 In Aristophanes' play *Lysistrata*, the women threaten to withdraw all sexual favours until the men stop fighting. See Cantor, A., op. cit., p. 432, which mentions that this strategy was used successfully in one Canadian community. Women refused to go to the *mikveh* until the community compelled a recalcitrant husband to give his wife a religious divorce.

8 Blustain, R., 'Orthodox at Turning Point on Domestic Violence' and '*Mikveh* Ladies Looking for Signs of Trouble', *Forward*, 29 December 1995, p. 1

9 see Goodman, J., 'Masectomy: Twelve Months after Surgery. A Bathing Ritual for the End of Mourning', *Lilith*, Fall 1995, pp. 25–6. The author recounts her personal experience of using the *mikveh* and includes the traditional prayers and verses which she recited.

1990s and you can't expect the unprecedented number of single thirty-five-year-old Orthodox women to remain celibate.[10]

I'd let other women know that some women don't actually wait the full twelve days because their husbands are getting impatient, and some women with a short menstrual cycle who are having trouble conceiving a child are also not waiting the full twelve days before resuming marital relations. A banner, 'You're not the only one', would be hung outside the *mikveh*'s front door. I would alternate the activities each month to maximise the number of women who would attend, and my publicity information could be picked up on any evening; women could also make a confidential call to my office. Forget the stockings – I am wasting valuable time.

As I leave the *mikveh*, I often recognise a familiar face, and we nod knowingly – this is not the time to stop and make small talk. My car is parked around the corner, and I make a quick dash. Your father, waiting for the familiar noise of the car, turns on the front porch light when he hears the engine stop. Before I have a chance to put the key in the lock, he opens the door, beaming contentedly. I place a kiss on his cheek, as if we are newly reunited lovers. It has been a long time.

Inevitably, one of you starts crying just at the crucial moment. I go nuts. We burst out laughing.

'I bet that little brat knows exactly what is going on,' I say.

'Don't be ridiculous, they're only babies.' He always sticks up for both of you.

'Two is old nowadays. Soon Avigayil will be asking questions.'

'So, you'll tell her.'

---

10 I once saw an advertisement, 'Wanted: *kosher* cutie for *tefillin* dates.' This requires substantial deconstruction: '*tefillin* dates' suggests a man who has phylacteries ready for morning prayers, should he end up staying the night at the home of his female date; the request for a *kosher* cutie suggests that the male wants someone Orthodox willing to play outside the rules. It is impossible to quantify how often this happens, but the point is that Orthodox circles are not immune from sexual pressures, particularly in the modern Orthodox community where marriage is delayed and women are in highly visible, professional jobs. See also Goldman, A., *The Search for God at Harvard*, Random House, New York, 1991, for an exposé of this issue.

'Tell her what?'

'Everything. Better you than me. You're her mother.'

'Stop kissing me. GET OFF ME! I can't do this now. I've got more important things to think about.'

'Oh, jeez, are you crazy!' (I think he meant to say Jesus Christ, but stopped himself in the nick of blasphemous time.)

'Listen, how does this sound? Avigayil, Elisheva, it's time we had a little chat. First, put down your play-dough. Now, I worry about your sex life, well not exactly your sex life, but rather how you will understand your sexuality and the sort of relationship you will have with your body.'

'Mum! You are so embarrassing!'

'Look, I'm sorry. Really sorry, but I'm setting you up for an obsessive personality and an eating disorder. With all those rules of keeping *kosher* and the list of forbidden foods to preserve your spiritual purity, it is only another short step to controlling your own diet and ending up an anorexic.'

'What has that got to do with sex?'

'Good question, Avigayili – conceptual leaps have always been your forte. Thing is that there seems to be a higher incidence of anorexia and bulimia, eating disorders that partially reflect a fear of a woman's sexuality, amongst Jewish women.[11] I think that in the religious community an eating disorder often reflects the tension between the expectations of the community and the needs of the individual woman. Although I did not grow up in a tightly controlled community that forbade television and magazines, I was always interested and confused by the young women I knew in such communities who still absorbed the contemporary messages about waif-like beauty and had an obsession about their weight. Perhaps because a woman's control of her body in such a sexually segregated, highly organised, male-dominated and male-driven society is the only thing she can cling to, the problems of eating disorders are accentuated. It seems to me that the young neo-anorexic women on the streets of Stamford Hill and Borough Park

11 Fishman, op. cit., p. 97; *Israel Women's Network Newsletter*, Vol. 10, no.1, January 1997, p. 4

are displaying their fears of autonomy and individuation.'

'How do you spell that Mummy?'

'I–n–d–i–v–i–d–u–a–t–i–o–n. Do you know what that means?'

'Only Daddy knows the meaning of words he can't spell.'

'Well, it means that because Orthodox families are generally more intact and enmeshed, you know, very nosy and in each other's pockets, it might be more difficult for young women to separate from their families. One reaction is to develop abnormal eating patterns. This usually gives the young woman the attention she desires and may prolong her separation from the rest of the family. These young women know that there is only one route out: marriage and children. However lacking knowledge of men and their own bodies, the thought of marriage and sexual intimacy is too frightening. As for the hallowed precept of pregnancy and the blessed virtues of having their own children, this represents the last semblance of any control. As their slim, taut figures are transformed into huge, shapeless blobs, pregnancy is a very real reminder that there is no escape. But a young woman cannot admit this to anyone because being pregnant is the most self-satisfied statement a woman can make to her community. It says, in one glance that, 'I am married, fertile and destined to domesticity.' Anyway, they don't even realise that being pregnant is a lot less complicated than coming to the *mikveh* and standing around in your birthday suit!'

'Mum, are you sure that's the way all those happy brides in taffeta really think? Are you sure there's not a bit of projection going on over here?'

'This is how you thank me? I am telling you all this because no one else is going to. But I have digressed a bit. This whole *niddah* thing is difficult, but I have to tell you that I value the time I have to myself each month, and that although not giving Daddy a big cuddle is a real pain, it is actually very meaningful when we are together. In fact, I think that one of the reasons that I was attracted to Orthodoxy is the value it places on women's sexuality. I know full well that historically menstrual blood was regarded as a sign of impurity by many cultures and tribes who used it to justify the separation of the sexes, the subjugation of women and repressed sexuality.[12] It wasn't just the Jews, although being obsessed with detail, the rabbis managed to organise all this blood into a complex system of rules and regulations. But I quite like the system. I like the idea of being 'off-limits', and I like the idea of being appreciated anew each month. I like the romance involved, and I like the fact that sex is not taken for granted. (In fact, men are considered impure when they, as we so quaintly say, 'spill seed', and there are some men, particularly amongst the *Chassidim*, who dip themselves in a *mikveh* every Friday before *Shabbat* – or in some cases every day – in order to cleanse themselves.)[13]

'Mum, you are so embarrassing. Tali's mummy doesn't talk like this.'

'I know it sounds very un-nineties, very un-cool, but hey, I never said I was the most hip mother around, just the most enlightened Orthodox one. Look, there are women who decry the use of menstruation to enshrine the power base of men. Their arguments are usually that any notion of menstruation as a form of divine punishment or defilement is offensive (I would agree with that one), and that modern sanitation negates the need for a 'purifying' bath. Basically, they regard the whole set of *niddah* laws as 'senseless and irrelevant to modern society'.[14] Other women have embraced *taharat hamishpachah* as part of a spiritual quest[15] or as part of a feminist view on the patterns of birth, death and rebirth.[16] There are some Reform rabbis who think the *mikveh* is pretty funky – recasting it as a place to 'take back the water', offering it as

---

12 See Young, S., *An Anthology of Sacred Texts by and about Women*, Pandora HarperCollins, London, 1993, for a selection of writings from religions including Judaism, Christianity, Islam, Hinduism, Buddhism, Shamanism, Confucianism, Taoism, many of which deal with the rituals associated with menstruation, and the separation of menstruating women from their community.

13 Mintz, J., op. cit., p. 50-1

14 Priesand, S., *Judaism and the Modern Woman*, Behrman House, New York, 1975, p. 25

15 Frankiel, T., *The Voice of Sarah: Feminine Spirituality and Traditional Judaism*, HarperCollins, New York, 1990, p. 82

16 see Adler, R., 'On Tumah and Tehara', in Koltun, E., op. cit., pp. 63–71

a place to dip on *Rosh Hodesh* and a woman's resource open during the day hosting an array of classes,[17] while other Reform rabbis have abandoned the practice together. And Moroccan women talk about observing these laws as 'our way,' asserting that keeping the laws is their way of culturally defining themselves as women and Jews. *Niddah* has been observed as an important context 'in which women can finesse their husbands in the game of authority. Therein may perhaps lie one of the causes for the profound attachment to *niddah* by these women who viewed it as one of the main symbols of womanhood.'[18]

'But, mum, why do you do it?'

I feel a bit like those Moroccan women. It defines me as a Jewish woman. It is that simple, and that complex. What right have I got to stop going to the *mikveh* when I know that some women travel hundreds of miles to visit a *mikveh*, and that communities under oppressive regimes have built hidden *mikvehs* in private homes for women's secret use.

'But, mum, you can't do things for other people. It has to be for you.'

'That's what your father says. My obligation drives me: but I can rationalise my actions in ways that suit my feelings about my Jewish identity. Look, you will have to work out your own answers, but I've got a punchline I have been storing up for years.'

'Is it going to be embarrassing?'

'Virginia Woolf says a woman needs a room of her own, but I say, "Every Jewish woman needs a womb of her own." '

'Mum, you are really strange. No wonder dad prefers you to stay at home rather than leave the house.'

'Enough already!' Suddenly he speaks. 'Just kiss me, you idiot.'

[17] Goldstein, Rabbi E., 'Take Back the Waters: A Feminist Re-Appropriation of *Mikveh*', *Lilith*, no.15, Summer 1986, pp. 15–16
[18] Wasserfall, R., 'Menstruation and Identity: The Meaning of *Niddah* for Moroccan Women Immigrants to Israel', in Eilberg-Schwartz, H. (ed.), *People of the Body:Jews and Judaism from an Embodied Perspective*, State University of New York Press, Albany, 1992, p. 323

Chapter 10

Your father has a way with words, but he makes up for it when he takes you to the synagogue on *Shabbat* mornings.

I like it when you go to the synagogue with your father on Saturday mornings. You like it too.

'Do you want to go to *shul* with Daddy this morning?'

'Cake! Crisps!'

You've got it all sussed. After the services, light refreshments, starring crisps and chocolate cake, are served by the honourable women of the Ladies' Guild. If you behave yourself, you can have as much cake and as many crisps as you want. It's a win-win situation.

We belong to a small community just beyond the intense Jewish hubbub of north-west London. There is only one Orthodox synagogue and, as in other Orthodox synagogues, men and women are separated by a *mechitzah*, a partition. However, in our *shul*, the separation between men and women is not unreasonably oppressive for women. (What exactly is reasonably oppressive?) Men and women are on the same floor and the partition is a few brass poles, rather than a thick net curtain, wooden slats or an upstairs balcony.

I have mixed feelings about the separation. While I know some people regard it as an affront to equal rights for women, I quite like the idea that my family status is anonymous. When we are not seated together, I am not automatically regarded as someone's wife and mother, rather I can have some time to myself. Although sitting separately usually means that I can still see the action, and I can even make eye contact with the rabbi, I can never be part of the action. That all happens on the men's side.

I watch you as you play with your father. I watch as the other men smile sweetly at you and pat you on the head. I watch as they encourage you to touch the *Sefer Torah*, almost bringing the Holy Scroll to your very lips to kiss it. But it's wrong – they are all conspiring to raise your expectations. How could you possibly know that you are being set up to fail? In a few years' time, those same men will be telling you that your days in the men's section are numbered. Some older men will take you on to their laps and whisper sweet nothings – 'You will be a big girl soon. You will have to sit with the ladies,' or, 'You can help them cut up the cake.'

I think of a smart answer – 'I'm no lady, and you can cut up your own cake,' and make a mental note to teach you to say this.

Then magically, you will be banished from the men's section.

'Go Shoo,' 'Get Out,' 'Tsk tsk, didn't your mother teach you better?'

All of a sudden it will be my fault that you don't know your place.

So, there are days when I don't want you to go to *shul*: I know there will be disappointment ahead. Life will be less disappointing if you stay home and help me make lunch, especially after your *bat mitzvah* at the age of twelve. In a strange twist, Orthodox Judaism will transform a young girl of twelve into a woman whose emerging sexuality and sensuousness is too threatening to handle. Funny thing – I thought it was the women's magazines which made innocent girls into seductive women, but no, it's the synagogue.

And it's not just the girls we have to think about; as the mother of two young sons, my friend Esther makes me aware of what it feels like to have boys. 'In *shul* we enjoy having our little boys on our laps, exploring through the small bag of toys and *nosh* we have learnt to bring for them. But as they grow older, the gender lines are drawn, and they sit on the other side of the *mechitzah* with their fathers. Does Orthodox Judaism remove our sons from us?'[1]

So what do I do? Keep you away? That can't be the right answer if I want you to know the liturgy and the traditional service. If I want you to develop a relationship with a formal God, I have to encourage you to go to the synagogue. Although I am still fond of

[1] Takac, E., 'Frogs and Snails and Puppy Dogs' Tails', *Generation: A Journal of Australian Jewish Life, Thought and Community*, Volume 6, nos 1 and 2, October 1996, p. 41

the *shul* I attended as a child, I did find it the most incomprehensible and boring experience. My memories of it are as quite an austere building. Visitors often admired its architecture and commented on the stained-glass windows designed by a famous artist, but the windows reminded me of the image through a kid's kaleidoscope.

The people were kind and harmless. I went because it was an outing with my father, and I wanted to spend time with him. As a young child, I sat with him in the men's section and was doted on. My grandfather had a seat in front of my father, and my brother, uncle and cousins surrounded us. I dubbed it the Berkovic bloc. Since those halcyon days, my grandfather and father have died, my brother and older cousin have moved to other communities in Melbourne and another cousin lives in Israel. My uncle remains faithful to the synagogue, and on the few occasions I have visited and seen him sitting alone in the Berkovic bloc, it was as if the whole family had disappeared before my eyes. He is a survivor again, bereft of family.

When I became *bat mitzvah*, and was shooed away from the men's section, just as I know you will be, I compensated by making a grand entrance to the women's gallery upstairs. I would methodically count the steps each time I went up and went down – there were about thirty. I would climb to the top of the stairs, listen for the squeak as I opened the door and separate the deep red heavy velvet curtains at the entrance. There I waited for the men to notice me. They never did.

I always giggled when other women got lost in the folds of the curtains, not knowing how to pull them apart deftly as they opened the door. Unlike them, I always made a Scarlett O'Hara-like entrance. I would walk down a few stairs towards my aunt and sit next to her (I've already told you my mother was never there), but within a few minutes I was complaining that I was bored in *shul*, and started to play with her gloves or her hat.

The one day of the year that was different was *Rosh Hashanah*, the New Year. On *Rosh Hashanah*, Mrs K and her fur coat came to *shul*. She sat next to my aunt and always made some attempt to chat to me. Although I don't remember what we talked about, I remember that I spent hours stroking that fur coat. I was very aware that the real action was happening downstairs and we, the women, were the audience staring down at a theatrical perform-ance. I always felt irrelevant.

Spiritual moments were as rare as hen's teeth. The only one which stays with me came during the recital of one sentence during the High Holyday services on *Rosh Hashanah*, the New Year, and *Yom Kippur*, the Day of Atonement. Like most syna-gogues, we employed a rabbi's assistant for the High Holydays to add extra formality, conduct some of the singing and lead some of the prayers. Our *shul* hired Mr S, a kindly, gentle man from the ultra-Orthodox community. He came with his wife and young son, and they all came to be loved by our congregation. Somehow you felt you were getting the genuine article: a sincere man of faith and devotion. It seemed right that he should be negotiating with God on our behalf. Everyone was also very fond of his wife, a modest and perceptive woman who radiated an optimism that hid the pain of illness.

Mr S did not have a particularly beautiful or melodious voice, but it carried authority. There is a certain prayer – *Avinu Malkeinu* – which includes the usual litany of requests from God such as happiness, health and prosperity. He led the congregation in this prayer, and I still have a very clear image of his knobbly fingers and raspy voice. As he got to the verse *shelach refuah shlemah*,[2] he was crying and screaming desperately, with no self-censorship, as if the synagogue was empty. Yet the thousand people who packed the synagogue knew he was crying for his wife, who suffered with cancer for many years and eventually predeceased him. It was a pure voice that went up to the heavens, an unadulterated voice beseeching and bargaining with an invisible God. I was embarrassed for him, but I was deeply moved by his plea as he stood there, crumpled underneath his huge prayer shawl.

I would glance at his wife. What was she thinking? Was she blushing like a schoolgirl? Was she embarrassed? Did she realise

2 In English, 'send complete healing to all sick people'

what he was doing? Mr S was saying that prayer with all the devotion he could muster. It was an act of love more erotic and more romantic than the kiss or embrace of an attractive young couple.

'Hey God, are you listening up there? My wife is really sick! Help, please help her.'

This public declaration of his love with the congregation as his witness, was the most moving moment of my entire *shul*-going life. I think about the S family occasionally and wonder how he felt when she died. Did he think his prayers were in vain, or did he think that his prayers prolonged her life beyond her allocated years?

Until I left Australia, my experience of prayer was limited mainly to visiting three or four synagogues which were not radically different from each other – men with longer beards at one, women with shorter skirts at another.

When I went to Israel, my horizons started to expand. I sat in some small Chassidic *shtiebls* of Jerusalem where I could not see anything, but closed my eyes and enjoyed the melodies. I attended services in large formal synagogues with a distinctly tourist feel to them. I prayed at *kibbutz* synagogues where the informality of the *kibbutz* pervaded the services. I went to a Moroccan *shul* where the customs were foreign to me, but I sat fascinated by the scrambled and unfamiliar Hebrew pronounciation of the words and the women's ululations outside the synagogue doors. I expected some sort of mystical, out-of-body experience at the Western Wall, the holiest site we have access to, but I got hassled by beggars for money instead. All the time I was looking for a place to pray with a community of faithful people whose values I shared. I was looking for the Holy Grail.

Yet wherever I went, I always remembered the synagogue of my childhood, for it also hosted our family's significant religious events.

'Ah, your big day will come,' said my father.

No prizes for guessing what I was complaining about: the fuss about my brother's *bar mitzvah*. Of course, my father was referring to my wedding – when I would be at the epicentre, and my brother relegated to ushering the photographers around the appropriate relatives. Naturally, my brother got married before me and I ushered the photographers around. So much for that theory.

When my brother stood up to recite his *Torah* portion, I remember the deliberate hush that descended upon the synagogue It was the day of his formal initiation into The Club. The day linking him to the mantle of tradition of his father and grandfather. The day linking him to Adam's *bar mitzvah* in the Garden of Eden. Who, I have been trying to find out, did the catering?

A boy's *bar mitzvah*, literally 'son of the commandment', at the age of thirteen, is the day he must assume responsibilities for the Jewish laws: he is considered a *man*. He counts, and his studies are enthusiastically encouraged. The idea of a *bar mitzvah* has biblical roots – Levi, the son of Jacob, is called Ish, man, at the age of thirteen,[3] and according to the commentaries, Jacob and Esau 'grew up' at the age of thirteen.[4] The name *bar mitzvah* occurs in the *Talmud* where it is applied to every grown Israelite.[5] Nowadays a young boy prepares for his *bar mitzvah* by learning to read from the *Torah*, and is instructed in certain rituals of prayer, most specifically the wearing of *tefillin*, the phylacteries. Depending on his family, and his own level of interest, the young boy's preparations will vary from intensive and serious study of the text and preparation for singing the tunes, to learning to recite the minimally required blessings and a few passages by rote. There is usually a luncheon or party for friends and family to celebrate the event – I have been to some lavish *bar mitzvahs* where I felt it was like a wedding without a bride, and others where an elegant and simple afternoon tea did the trick.

An Orthodox girl becomes *bat mitzvah*, literally, 'a daughter of the commandment', at the age of twelve. She is considered a *woman*. But she does not count. It is the day when she must leave the men's section of the synagogue. Susan Alter poignantly reflects –

3 Genesis 34:25
4 Genesis 25:27
5 Babylonian Talmud, Bava Metzia 96a

the ultimate achievement of my womanhood would carry with it
my total exclusion from any further opportunity to be close to
the *Sefer Torah* . . . What so confused me was that for my
brother exactly the opposite was true. Being a mature adult,
'becoming a man' as it were, and assuming responsibilities for
doing the *mitzvot*, brought with it an even closer identification
with the *Torah*, not only in the spiritual sense, but also in a very
real and physical way.[6]

The idea of an equivalent for girls first appeared, not surprisingly,
in Reform circles as part of a general ethos towards religious
equality. The idea of a *bar* and *bat mitzvah* was reconceptualised into
the practice of confirmation for all youth at the age of sixteen. The
rite was first officially mentioned in 1810,[7] and in Berlin girls were
confirmed for the first time in 1817 and in Hamburg in 1818.

In 1922, Judith Kaplan, daughter of Mordechai Kaplan, celebrated the first recorded *bat mitzvah*. Kaplan, the founder of the
Reconstructionist movement of Judaism, used to say that he had
four good reasons for instituting the *bat mitzvah* – his four
daughters.[8] Judith recalls –

Everything was in readiness except the procedure itself. On
Friday night, after *Shabbat* dinner, Father took me into his study
and had me read aloud the blessings which precede and succeed
the *Torah* readings. How severely he corrected my diction . . . He
then selected a passage from the weekly portion . . . which I
practised reading in both Hebrew and English.[9]

It started a trend so that nowadays, in most Conservative and
Reconstructionist congregations, young girls can be called to the

6 Alter, S., 'The *Sefer Torah* Comes Home', in Grossman, S. and Haut, R.
(eds), op. cit., p. 280
7 see entry for *bar mitzvah* in the *Jewish Encyclopaedia*, Funk and Wagnalls,
London, 1916, for detailed historical information about the development of
the *bar mitzvah* in different communities around the world.
8 quoted in Scult, M., *A Biography of Mordechai M. Kaplan*, Wayne State
University Press, Detroit, 1994, p. 301
9 ibid., pp. 301–2

Torah and perform the same rites as thirteen-year-old boys.[10] Nowadays, Reform synagogues vary in their practices, and while some have maintained the practice of confirmation at sixteen, others have returned to the traditional practice of a *bar/bat mitzvah* at the age of thirteen in which the girls and the boys have the same ceremony.[11]

The Orthodox community, despite protestations to the contrary, does not remain immune to evolving rituals in other branches of Judaism. An account of a *bat mitzvah* in an Orthodox synagogue in 1944, in Brooklyn, New York, highlights the rabbi's enthusiasm and support for the idea which was initiated by the girl's mother.

A *bat mitzvah* was necessary on two accounts: it enabled the Jewish girl to realise her 'responsibilities in a Jewish sense', and it eliminated the feeling that 'in Orthodox synagogues the girls do not count'. The service was held on a Friday night and she chanted the *Kiddush* blessing over the wine, and gave a speech.[12]

Although celebration of the *bat mitzvah* is virtually ignored in a few small Orthodox groups, the majority of the Orthodox community has been working on ways to create some sort of parallel ritual to the *bar mitzvah* which 'has a meaningful function in the context of *Torah* observance'.[13] The real debate is about content and form of the *bat mitzvah*.

I remember my own *bat mitzvah* in the early 1970s. My

10 Hyman, P., 'The Introduction of *Bat Mitzvah* in Conservative Judaism in Postwar America', in Moore, D., *Yivo Annual*, Vol. 19, 1990, Northwestern University Press, Illinois, pp. 133–46
11 Schneider, S. Weidman, *Jewish and Female*, Simon and Schuster, New York, 1984, Chapter 3 explains how each denomination of Judaism celebrates a *bat mitzvah*.
12 Joselit, J., *The Wonders of America: Reinventing Jewish Culture 1880–1950*, Hill and Wang, New York, 1994, p. 129. Chapter 3, 'Red Letter Days', discusses *bar* and *bat mitzvah* in more detail. The book also contains many wonderful photographs of Jewish memorabilia.
13 Berkovits, E., *Jewish Women in Time and Torah*, KTAV, Hoboken, NJ, 1990, p. 81

synagogue organised a class for the *bat mitzvah* girls on a Sunday morning, and we planned to have a ceremony for about six of us on an arbitrary Sunday afternoon somewhere in the middle of all our twelfth birthdays. We had weekly lessons much like young girls around the world were having on topics such as how to observe the Sabbath and Jewish festivals, read from a prayer book, and run a *kosher* home. Some girls also research some aspect of Jewish tradition or do a project considered relevant. This was all preparation for some sort of group presentation of songs and prayers in the synagogue on a Sunday afternoon which was to be followed by a party for friends and family. In addition to the boring classes, we had some extra classes on Sunday mornings with the human dynamo, Zippy (a diminutive of *zipporah*, meaning bird, but the idea of her zipping around was most apt). Somewhere I still have the notes she painstakingly prepared for us, and I will always credit her with having a significant impact on my religious development. We used to sit around a table and think we were so grown up discussing the meaning of life. She explained to us the laws of the *mikveh*, and even arranged for us to visit one. What was she thinking?

However, like others who have noted that 'the practice of processing girls in batches on an arbitrary Sunday afternoon was widely perceived as degrading, contrived and lacking status both by the girls themselves and by women in general',[14] I felt the idea of a *bat mitzvah* ceremony was a waste of time and decided against being part it. (Besides, the thought of being flounced up in some white wannabe wedding dress was too revolting!) My parents, whom I would classify as the-people-least-susceptible-to-social-pressure-that-I-have-ever-met, did not mind. However, around the time of my twelfth birthday, my grandparents moved out of our home and into their own flat across the road from the *shul*. This was very exciting for my grandfather as he was to become one of a group of elderly men who attended the synagogue every day come rain or shine. My parents decided to make a small *Kiddush* (food and drink offered after the services) in their honour and for my *bat mitzvah* as well. Unbeknown to them, I was desperately in love

14 Goodkin, J. and Citron, J., op. cit., p. 15

with some pimply fourteen-year-old who attended the synagogue. I feared being the centre of attention because I did not think I was pretty enough, and I did not want to be embarrassed in front of this now nameless young boy. Cowardly, I ran out of the hall and hid in a park not far from the *shul*. It was several hours before I was found. My parents were worried till they found me, and then they were furious. It was a *bat mitzvah* that was talked about for a long time in my family!

In the twenty-five years since I sabotaged my *bat mitzvah* (what will my psychoanalytical biographers make of that?) there has been an increased interest in finding a way to make the *bat mitzvah* ceremony meaningful and more relevant to young women. This has coincided with the increased opportunities for girls' education in the secular world. Their secular education is often far superior than their level of Jewish education. Eventually, an imbalance is created whereby women can view the general world as well-informed adults, but once their Jewish education ends at twelve, they are equipped intellectually to understand the Jewish world only as children. As long as Judaism is based on relative ignorance, myth and nostalgia, there is little hope that young women are going to feel any sense of pride or commitment in upholding the tradition.[15]

Nicky Goldman demonstrated how the time of a young girl's *bat mitzvah* can have a lasting impact on her relationship to Judaism. She interviewed six girls and their mothers from two different Orthodox communities. In one community, the girl's only option is to give a speech: either in the synagogue or at a celebration in the synagogue hall or girl's home. In the other Orthodox community, girls have the option to read from the *Sefer Torah* in a women's service, and then give a speech later on. (Male relatives listen from behind a *mechitzah*.)

The obvious was inevitable: the girls who learnt to read from the *Torah* expressed a much stronger degree of involvement in the whole process, and a sense of the *bat mitzvah* having a lasting

15 Fishman, S., op. cit. Chapter 8, 'Educating the New Jewish Woman', gives a succinct overview of the traditional approach to women's education and some of the contemporary challenges.

impact on their Jewish practices. One of the members of the community where women's services are permissible explains why:

> Because the congregation is so well educated Jewishly, they are not afraid to search for new ways. This, almost from the start, they started to do, expanding women's roles within a traditional Jewish framework. It is not an option to join a Conservative synagogue where women could do their egalitarian thing. They are very committed to Orthodox tradition.[16]

We need to know more about what women are thinking and feeling as they pioneer these tremendous changes. It was refreshing to read a mother's account of her daughter's *bat mitzvah*, and especially to hear about the daughter's experience:

> My classmates' reaction when I told them I was preparing to *layn*[17] went from shock to amazement. The girls did not believe that I would actually go through with it. Many of their mothers would not allow them to attend, saying, 'It is not right.' I had already been told by my mother to expect such a reaction . . . I guess in my heart I really did not want to do anything that would make me stand out. [18]

These young women are brave, but, as Goldman points out, there is a risk of frustration for the *bat mitzvah* girl afterwards. She has invested all this energy into learning how to read the *Sefer Torah* but, unlike a boy, she will have rare opportunities to utilise those skills again.[19]

Avigayil, Elisheva – will you want to read from the *Sefer Torah*? And will my friends forbid their daughters to attend? Would they rather we imitate the trends of the time? If I had to arrange a *bat mitzvah* tomorrow, would they rather I set up a disco and have you

16 Goldman, N., 'The Celebration of *Bat Mitzvah* within the Orthodox Community in the United States Today', Spring 1991, paper submitted as part of Jewish Life-Cycle Course at Brandeis University
17 to read from the *Sefer Torah* using the traditional cantillation
18 Penkower, Y., '*Bat Mitzvah*: Coming of Age in Brooklyn', in Grossman, S. and Haut, R., op. cit., pp. 265–70
19 Goldman, N., op. cit., p. 18

dancing to the Spice Girls to honour your arrival at Jewish womanhood? When the time comes, will our relationship be honest enough for both of you to tell me what would be meaningful for you? Goldman draws on the work of Caplan, who suggests five criteria for creating a *bat mitzvah* ceremony: it must have a religious element, be a public performance, provide a challenge to the girl's intellectual capacities, be a unique event for her and include something of personal significance to her.[20] Whatever we decide to do, I will have to be a role model for each of you at your *bat mitzvah*, and this is the most daunting aspect. Your *bat mitzvah* will be my coming of age as a mother.

The increased consciousness and popularity of the *bat mitzvah* ceremony in the 1990s has led some women to have a restrospective *bat mitzvah* ceremony in their fifties or sixties [21] – or even in their eighties. When Judith Kaplan celebrated her eighty-second birthday, she decided to hold another *bat mitzvah* ceremony (the biblical life span is seventy, so when a person reaches eighty-two, another coming-of-age ceremony is appropriate). Second time round she observed that in some communities, 'all the bad aspects of the *bar mitzvah* institution have been taken over by the *bat mitzvah*. A lot of us hoped it would be different.' [22]

Perhaps the problem lies with the nature of the modern day *bar mitzvah*, rather than the unfulfilled desires of women to have a comparable *bat mitzvah*. We have to separate the religious ritual from the lavish parties which often accompany a young boy's rite of passage. I don't want young women thinking that if they have a comparable black-tie dinner and receive expensive gifts that they will have achieved the same as their brothers. Rather, we need to look at ways of creating meaningful *bat mitzvah* services drawing on ritual and tradition. The essence is the access to the *Sefer Torah* and the lessons that can be drawn from it. I would like your *bat mitzvah* to reflect a sense of partnership between you and your community.

[20] cited in Goldman, N., op. cit., pp. 4–5
[21] Fishman, S., op. cit., pp. 130–1; Schneider, S. Weidman, op. cit., 1984, p. 142
[22] Goldman, A., 'Celebration of a Gift: First *Bat Mitzvah* Plans her Second', *New York Times*, 19 March 1992, B1–2

It is a creative opportunity to draw on our collective history in order to express your individuality, but it is also a time when the community has to acknowledge its responsibility to educate you and welcome your potential.

Many young boys celebrate their *bar mitzvah* with a service at the Western Wall in Jerusalem. Now we can offer our daughters the same option: Yael Schneider celebrated her *bat mitzvah* with the Women of the Wall, a group of women who regularly pray at the Wall and arrange for a *Sefer Torah* to be available.[23] Blu Greenberg has written about *bat mitzvah* celebrations on *TuB'shvat*, a lesser known holiday which is the New Year for Trees, as well as *Rosh Hodesh* and *Purim*, when the young girl was able to read from the *Torah* and the Scroll of Esther.[24] Others have suggested a *Yom Limmud*, day of learning, in the child's honour; spending some structured time with women in the community to learn about women's lives; an oral history project about the women in one's family; and preparing a speech on a topic of interest to the *bat mitzvah* girl.[25] Wouldn't mother-and-daughter workshops to explore issues around the *bat mitzvah* and Jewish women's identity be a great way to understand each other better? Maybe we could recreate traditional rituals that speak to girls of the 1990s.

When it comes to presents, you will probably get the usual stuff for twelve-year-old Jewish girls: cookery books, prayer books, aprons, perfumes and craft materials. But Wolowelsky suggests:

> the real preference should be a *Kiddush* cup; the *bat mitzvah* is now obligated to recite *Kiddush* just as is an adult man. In many homes, only the *ba'al habayit* says *Kiddush* on Friday night, yet the sons at the table often have their own *Kiddush* cups as symbols of their adulthood. The same should be true of the daughters in the family who have reached the age of *mitzvot*.[26]

23 Schneider, S. Weidman, *Lilith*, editorial, Fall 1995, p. 2. See pp.216–17 for more on the Women of the Wall.
24 Greenberg, B., 'Feminism Within Orthodoxy: A Revolution of Small Signs', *Lilith*, Summer 1992, p.14–15
25 for suggestions see Schneider, S. Weidman, *Jewish and Female*, pp. 133–42; Strassfield, S. and Strassfield, M. (eds), op. cit., pp. 60–81
26 Wolowelsky, J., op. cit., p. 54

Will anyone give you a *Kiddush* cup, or will I have to?

Will I also be the one to suggest that the *bat mitzvah* seems an appropriate time to celebrate the changes in a young woman's sexual development as her twelfth birthday often coincides with her menarche? While the *bar mitzvah* does acknowledge a boy's puberty and emerging sexuality, a girl's tremendous biological changes are not formally acknowledged in Judaism. By twelve, Orthodox communities expect girls to have been fully socialised into modest behaviour, including speech, public demeanour and dress, by following the example of her mother. Perhaps the communal fear of transgressing the boundaries of modesty has limited the public celebration of the *bat mitzvah*. This may also help to explain why the *bat mitzvah* ceremony has more recently become a metaphor for the power struggle between some sections of the Orthodox rabbinate and *bat mitzvah* girls.

Four days before Sharon Kalker's daughter was to celebrate her *bat mitzvah* in January 1997, the *Va'ad Ha'rabbonim* (organisation of rabbis) of Queens (a New York borough with a large modern Orthodox community) issued an edict that the women's prayer group in which she was about to celebrate her *bat mitzvah* by reading from the *Sefer Torah* was disallowed. Significantly, the *Va'ad* did not ban the prayer group on *halachic* grounds, but on a sociological premise that *poretz geder bemesorat Yisrael*, that it was 'breaking the fences of Jewish tradition'. In a sort of rabbinic betrayal, the *Va'ad* implicitly questioned the decision of the highly respected legal authority, Rabbi Simcha Krauss of Hillcrest, under whose auspices the *bat mitzvah* was to be held. In response, an extra one hundred women turned up to the *bat mitzvah* and the *New York Times* placed an article on women's prayer groups on the front page of its metropolitan section.[27]

Personally, I think the *Va'ad*'s decision was not really about that young girl's *bat mitzvah*, rather it was about the authority to transmit tradition. These rabbis were questioning the foundation of the Jewish home that has always entrusted women to pass on the

---

[27] Onishi, N., 'Reading the *Torah*, an Orthodox Women's Group Takes on Tradition', *New York Times*, 16 February 1997

tradition and educate their daughters 'properly'. The rabbis were really saying that the women who participate in prayer groups and give their daughters fanciful notions are not considered 'fit mothers'.

Yet even unfit mothers and their wayward daughters have an obligation to pray:[28] Hannah's model of prayer in which she 'spoke in her heart, only her lips moved, but her voice was not heard'[29] is lauded as the prototype of sincere devotion. When Miriam led the Jewish women in songs of praise (Exodus 15:20) it was probably the first women's prayer group. According to the biblical commentator Abraham Ibn Ezra, the women who 'assembled at the door of the Tent of Meeting' (Exodus 38:8) came there in order to 'pray and hear the commandments'. We have a record of the song of praise by Deborah (Judges 5) and of the women who came to hear the reading of the *Torah* (Nehemia 8: 2-3). Women were official mourners and sang at funerals (2 Chronicles 35:25). Women sang and danced as they welcomed heroes home (Samuel 1, 18:6-7). Later, throughout Eastern Europe, women composed the rich body of prayer and devotions discussed earlier. In Italy, Debora Ascarelli and Rachel Morpugo wrote poetry replete with biblical associations,[30] and in Kurdistan, women gathered together, and sang a traditional dirge on the 9th of Ab, the day of national mourning.[31] In the past, Orthodox women wrote *techinot*, prayers of supplication, and these could be invoked by a *bat*

28 Maimonides, Mishneh Torah, The Laws of Prayer, Chapter 1; see Weiss, A., *Women and Prayer: A Halachic Analysis of Women's Prayer Groups*, KTAV, Hoboken, NJ, 1991, for an English language, accessible overview of the *halachic* obligations for women.
29 1 Samuel 1:13
30 Adelman, H., 'Women's Voices in Italian Jewish Literature', in Baskin, J. (ed.), op. cit., 1994, pp. 50–69
31 Sered, S. Starr, *Women as Ritual Experts : The Religious Lives of Elderly Jewish Women in Jerusalem*, Oxford University Press, New York, 1992, pp. 128–9, describes the ritual. See Sabar, Y. (trans. and ed.), *The Folk Literature of the Kurdistani Jews: An Anthology*, Yale University Press, New Haven, 1982, Chapter 10, 'Lel Huza: Women's Lamentations for the Ninth of Ab', pp. 71–83, for an account of what the women chanted.

mitzvah girl. Why aren't we writing for our daughters? Are we so illiterate that we are unable to compose meaningful prayers?

So when we walk to *shul* together, you stopping to admire the leaves, me hurrying you along, I think about the wonderful tradition of women's liturgical lives, of women participating in synagogue life, of women belonging to the community of worshippers, of women leading other women in prayer, and I wonder what went wrong. How did this rich tapestry of women's devotional lives get transformed to the situation in the 1990s where a woman who wants to create a meaningful *bat mitzvah* for her daughter is condemned? When did the synagogue become irrelevant to the majority of Orthodox women, and Orthodox women irrelevant to the synagogue? Sometimes I think we allowed this situation to develop because those of us carving out a new way are always glancing over our shoulders, seeking approval from those we have given the mantle of religious authority. However, we must not capitulate to the 'right wing', allowing them to set the goal posts and proclaim themselves as the 'true' interpreters of the law. Yet, even though I am deeply concerned about the relevancy of Orthodox Judaism in the lives of young modern women, I still find it difficult not to defer to old men in long black coats and wisdom-white beards who bear the confidence of their convictions. Sometimes, I feel as if I am betraying 'the family' if I seek to challenge their authority, and I am not sure if that feeling will ever go away. Maybe this psychological control is a good thing, ultimately keeping me close to those who have preserved the tradition for hundreds of years. But I fear it may drive both of you away.

Chapter 11

I console myself with the knowledge that even a hundred years ago, Sarah Schenirer, a woman far more pious than myself, recognised that the limited role of women in formal prayer was negatively affecting the social fabric of her community:

And we pass through the Elul [month before the Jewish New Year]days.

The trains which run to the little *shtedlach* [towns] where the *Rebbes* live are crowded. Thousands of Hassidim are on their way to them to spend the *Yamim Noraim* [solemn Holydays] with the *Rebbe*. Every day sees new crowds of old men and young men in the Hassidic garb, eager to secure a place in the train, eager to spend the holiest days in the year in the atmosphere of their *Rebbe*, to be able to extract from it as much holiness as possible. Fathers and sons travel, and those who can afford it make this journey several times a year. Thus they are drawn to Ger, to Belz, to Alexander, to Bobo, to all those places that have been made citadels of concentrated religious life, dominated by the leading figure of a *Rebbe*'s personality.

And we stay at home, the wives, the daughters, with the little ones. We have an empty *Yomtov* [Holyday]. It is bare of Jewish intellectual concentration. The women have never learned anything about the spiritual content that is concentrated within a Jewish festival. The mother goes to *shul*. The service rings faintly into the fenced and boarded-off women's gallery. There is much crying by the elderly women. The young girls look on them as beings of a different century. Youth and desire to live a full life shoot up violently in the strong-willed young personalities. Outside the *shul*, the young girls stand chattering; they walk away from *shul* where their mothers pour out their vague and heavy feelings. They leave behind them the wailing of the older generation and follow the urge for freedom and self-expression. Further and further away from *shul* they go, further away to the dancing, tempting light of a fleeting joy.[1]

Since the 1970s, some synagogues have tried to grapple with women's spiritual needs in many practical ways. Some synagogue members have recognised, like Sarah Schenirer, 'how fathers and daughters are strangers, living in different worlds; how the happiness of family life is shattered by the breaking away of maturing girls'. [2]

In Manhattan, Lincoln Square Synagogue is built like a circular amphitheatre so that men and women sit facing each other on opposite sides of the rotund, separated by a piece of clear perspex. (Hence it's nickname, 'wink and stare'.) The place where the cantor stands to lead the service and the *Torah* scroll is read aloud, is at the centre of the synagogue so that everyone can see equally.

When I first walked into Lincoln Square Synagogue, the married women were obvious from their hats and they barely took any notice of me. However, the single women eyed me from head to thigh to toe. After all, 'a woman is jealous only of another woman's thighs'.[3] I felt the shivery anxiety of being watched and became increasingly self-conscious. I fumbled with my prayer book, and then lost the place. A well-dressed woman in her early fifties sitting next to me watched from the corner of her eye.

'Can I help you find the place?' she asked kindly.

'Oh, I think I've got it. Thanks anyway.' I regained my composure and found the right page. I could see the woman still looking at me to check that I had the right place.

I was in time for the central piece of the *Shabbat* morning service – the reading of the *Torah* portion of the week. Here, as in all Orthodox synagogues around the world, two men approach the Holy Ark, which is usually raised on a platform, and ascend several steps. As the congregation sing in anticipation of the Ark being

---

[1] cited in Grunfeld-Rosenbaum, J., 'Sara Schenirer', in Jung, L., op. cit., 1964, pp. 410–11. The spelling in this excerpt is reproduced as is.
[2] ibid., p. 411
[3] Babylonian Talmud, Megillah 13a

opened, one of the men moves aside the heavily decorated velvet curtain that is draped over the Ark, and the Ark door is opened. Most synagogues have several *Torahs*, and one is selected to be read from that week. The other man takes out a scroll and hands it to the rabbi or cantor. In a thunderous voice, it is proclaimed: 'Hear O Israel, The Lord is One.'

And the community affirm this belief as they repeat the verse.

The *Sefer Torah* is taken through the men's section, and it is kissed by touching it with the fringes of the ritual prayer shawl worn by all the men.

But that day, something which at the time seemed amazing to me, happened. The *Sefer Torah* was taken through the women's section and brought within kissing distance of the women. Some women kissed it, some simply bowed their heads as it passed them, others took a prayer book and touched the *Sefer Torah* with their prayer book and then kissed the book at same spot. It was as if the *Sefer Torah* had a life of its own and commanded a reverence rarely accorded mortal beings. As the *Sefer Torah* approached my seat, I did not know what to do. My heartbeat accelerated. I had never been confronted with the possibility of handling the *Sefer Torah* – if anything my schooling had reinforced the notion (albeit a false one) that a woman is too impure to touch certain sacramental objects. I hesitated, and envied the woman next to me who confidently placed the spine of her prayer book on the *Sefer Torah* and kissed that spot. Two more steps by the man holding the *Sefer Torah* and he would be staring in my face. I hesitated and then quickly bowed my head. I had never felt so inadequate as a woman – why couldn't I liberate myself from the irrational ancient taboo that clouded my judgement? I was sure everyone was bemused by my awkwardness. As the *Torah* was read, I kept thinking about the way I had mishandled the situation. I was too embarrassed to lift my head because I was sure the women were staring at me, wondering what planet I came from.

At Yedidyah, a Jerusalem congregation, founded in the 1970s and well known among Anglo-Americans in Jerusalem, members make a genuine attempt to involve women. 'From the very first,' says Dr Debbie Weissman, 'the women's issue was central to our ideology. But we recognised that we had to move gradually. We didn't want to offend anyone, and we have never tried to pressure people into changes.'

Women are able to see everything that happens; the *Sefer Torah* is taken through the women's section and they are allowed to touch it; a woman can give a sermon; women can say the *Kaddish*; there are a range of *bat mitzvah* ceremonies for girls, including the option of a women's prayer group so that she can read from the *Sefer Torah*. Weissman claims that they have authoritative sources to back up their practices.

> In many cases the rabbinic source – either a text or a living authority – will say that there is nothing against it. In rabbinic parlance, that is often the closest you will get to an affirmative response.[4]

Some rabbis use a different strategy to appeal to women by minimising the importance of the synagogue. They claim that women who place inordinate emphasis on synagogue attendance and public ritual are imitating the Christian Church. Rather, it is in the home, they argue, that real Jewish identity is forged, and women are entrusted with this formidable task. Cynthia Ozick, in her compelling seminal essay 'Notes Toward Finding the Right Question', rebuts this position when she suggests that:

> in all the history of the synagogue – one of the oldest institutions in the world – there never was a time when the synagogue was, if not slighted, then as aggressively diminished as it is now. And why is it only now that 'The synagogue is secondary!' becomes a battle cry of the traditional rabbinate? The emphasis on family and home has not been diminished; why, then, should the significance of synagogue worship quite suddenly be reduced? Answer: The synagogue becomes a focus of disparagement only at that moment when women begin to make equal claims on it.[5]

4 cited in Beck, M., 'Orthodox *shul* points the way for women', *Jewish Chronicle*, 31 March 1995
5 Ozick, C., 'Notes Toward Finding the Right Question', in Heschel, S., op. cit., pp. 127–8

Even more powerfully she reflects:

In the world at large I call myself, and am called, a Jew. But when, on the Sabbath, I sit among women in my traditional *shul* and the rabbi speaks the word 'Jew', I can be sure that he is not referring to me. For him, 'Jew' means 'male Jew'. When the rabbi speaks of women, he uses the expression (a translation from a tender Yiddish phrase) 'Jewish daughter'. He means it tenderly. 'Jew' speaks for itself. 'Jewish daughter' does not. A 'Jewish daughter' is someone whose identity is linked to, and defined by, another's role. 'Jew' defines a relationship that is above all, biological. 'Jew' signifies adult responsibility. 'Daughter' evokes immaturity and a dependent and subordinate connection. When my rabbi says, 'A Jew is called to the *Torah*', he never means me or any other living Jewish woman. My own synagogue is the only place in the world where I, a middle-aged adult, am defined exclusively by my being the female child of my parents. My own synagogue is the only place in the world where I am not named 'Jew'. [6]

I had a similar experience recently. Currently, our synagogue is without a rabbi, and different men come each week to lead the services. One young man studying for the rabbinate visited our community and gave a brief speech at one point in the service. He expounded on the idea of parents influencing their children. Fathers teach their sons . . . like father like son . . . fathers bless their sons . . . you get the drift. As I am now convinced that nothing is going to change unless women start to talk directly and honestly with men to try and make them understand our perspective, I decided this might be a good time to try out this theory. After the service, I went to have a chat with this rabbi-in-waiting.

'Hello, I enjoyed your sermon. Would you mind if I made a little suggestion?'

'Go ahead.' He was still smiling. (A *pisha*, the boy is a *pisha* and I have to grovel.)

'When you talk about fathers and sons, it is actually very

alienating. I feel completely excluded. I influence my daughters. Language is very important, it is very symbolic. If you are going to be a rabbi in a community, then it might be worth thinking about how to include women when you are addressing the congregation.'

'But, I don't like to change the meaning. It was just a saying that everyone knows. Like father, like son.'

He was really annoyed with me.

'Yes, I understand that. But there is also the saying 'like mother, like daughter'.[7] Anyway, the point is that when women come to *shul*, it might be worth thinking about how to include them when you are addressing the congregation.' (I was practising the broken-record technique I learnt in assertiveness training.)

He started to raise his voice, and his arms were flailing about.

'But, but . . .'

'Look, I'm not angry,' I said, appeasing him. (I hate it when I do that.) I could see the president of the *shul* out of the corner of my eye. 'Forget it. Have a nice *Shabbat*.'

Women concerned about these sorts of issues should be on the selection committee when a new rabbi is recruited. They have to ask tough, hard questions and they should expect satisfactory answers. The same women on the planning committees of new synagogues can put forward their feelings about the *mechitzah*. While I accept the separation in the synagogue, women don't have to be upstairs or behind an impenetrable wall. The modern world beckons young women, and as long as we insist that our daughters' destinies are relegated to invisibility behind the *mechitzah*, we will have only ourselves to blame if they choose visibility elsewhere.

Some women are choosing visibility outside the formal synagogue in a women's prayer group where they can have an active participatory role. The act of women praying together is not new. In fact, women praying together is often lauded. In 1896 it was reported that

women's services, which are held every Sabbath afternoon at the Manchester Jews' School, celebrated their third anniversary. As

7 Ezekiel 16:44

the interest in them is in no way abated, we may consider that they show signs of permanent existence. We have always approved the special services for women, whether they are held in London or Manchester, from the time they were first suggested by the Reverend Simeon Singer [compiler of the Singer's prayer book] . . . [8]

A few years later, Sarah Schenirer recognised that women's exclusion from prayer would lead to estrangement from the tradition, and in the Orthodox Beth Jacob schools that she established, the women prayed together. That continues today, and at many religious schools for girls, the girls are expected to attend prayers regularly. At the Orthodox Lubavitch summer camps I went to, there was a distinct emphasis on women's prayer and we were expected to be on time for morning and afternoon prayers.

However, the contemporary women's prayer group has become a form of spiritual resistance and political challenge to male authority as they differ in one central regard from the groups of young schoolgirls or happy campers praying together. In addition to the usual prayers, women at a women's prayer group read from a *Sefer Torah*.

Until recently, most Orthodox women had never come close to an opened *Torah*, nor had the opportunity ever to read directly from it or say a blessing on the *Torah*. Gael Hammer recounts an unusual incident which changed her relationship to the *Torah*:

The year was 1956 and the State of Israel was in crisis in Sinai. The late Rabbi Izak Rapaport, arguably the most conservative Av *Beth Din* [head of the rabbinical court] seen by Melbourne, made an announcement one *Shabbat* in Toorak *shul*. In emergencies, he said, it was permitted and even encouraged for women to be called to the Reading of the *Torah* to petition the Almighty for the success of His holy cause, and to donate funds to that cause . . . One quarter of the female congregation rose to sit in a pew at the side of the men's section. Nervously we gave our names to the *shammas*, who relayed them to the *yammod* caller. Being the youngest and probably the bravest of the group, I was elected to go up first. It may be difficult for men, accustomed to such activities to the point of disinterest, to understand my overwhelming feelings upon being called to stand before a congregation for the first time, in front of an open *Torah*, and to watch the *yad* move across the text in honour of my being there ... The experience was enough to colour my world view on Jewish practice and to fuel my spiritual journey for the next forty years.[9]

The first women's prayer group, also called a *tefillah* group, started in 1970 in Riverdale, New York. It was developed under the spiritual and *halachic* guidance of Rabbi Avi Weiss. A recent newsletter of the Women's *Tefillah* Network lists over thirty prayer groups worldwide, although the main concentration is in the New York State area. Women have been taught the *trop*, the special musical cantillation, and these prayer groups have become an important and poignant place for women to celebrate a *bat mitzvah*, name a baby, celebrate a wedding, share a bereavement and give sermons.

Even as I learnt and began to understand the historical precedents and the legal rulings which are the framework for the services, I was still reluctant to attend my first prayer group. It was what a dear friend calls the 'black hatter' in me – that little bit of me which clings to the world of men in severe garb and black hats where the different roles of men and women are distinct and valued. Sometimes I latch on to it, precisely because there is a certain security in something that remains impervious to the outside world, although rationally and intellectually I cannot really be a part of that world.

There's a classic Jewish joke about the man who finds himself stranded on a desert island. He promptly goes about building two synagogues. Years later when he is found, his rescuers ask him why he built two synagogues.

'Well this is the one I go to,' said the man, 'and this is the one I would never dream of going to.' I felt that way about women's prayer groups.

Yet, I finally decided to go because I was unhappy with my non-participatory role in the synagogue, and I felt so alienated from the experience, that I stopped going regularly. My flatmate was a long-time supporter of women's prayer groups and I never doubted the sincerity of her motivation or religious observance. I was searching for a place where prayer would have some genuine feeling. I was willing to try anything once, and after all, I wanted to convince myself that this was a bunch of man-hating, angry, naïve, heretical, single (if they were married, they would have lunch to make and children to care for) women who were trying to make a political point (after all, that is the way that their opponents had portrayed them, and until this point, how would I have known any better?). So I went.

The room was filled with melodious chanting. The singing was beautiful, the atmosphere serious yet joyous, and suddenly, when I realised that a woman was carrying the *Torah*, a woman was reading from the *Torah*, and a woman was receiving the honour of standing next to the *Torah* while it was being read, I felt that I could belong. These groups are usually held once a month, so it doesn't mean that I am no longer seen at a regular service. It does mean that I have options, and that I can take you to a place where you will have role models and where you can participate.

I also realised that the men who suspect women's prayer groups of being a cult or witches' meeting would be pleasantly surprised to know that the women's service virtually apes their own. Only the voices are more in tune, and there is no idle chatter about the stock market. The Orthodox women are not creating a new ritual, but are conducting a rather ordinary Orthodox service. In fact, the women continue to defer to male authority and 'where *halachic* decisions are concerned, however, they accept the normative hierarchies of Orthodox life'.[10] The men do not realise that the

10 Fishman, S., 'Negotiating both sides of the Hyphen: Coalescence, Compartmentalization and American-Jewish Values', 1996, *Judaic Studies Program*, University of Cincinnati, 1996, p. 24

women have had years of psychological and social conditioning to overcome in order to create and participate in such a service: as a result they approach every aspect with desperate reverence.

Unlike the *gabbai* (lay-person organiser of the men's service), who has to fend off competing men who all want the honours, the *gabba'it* (the organiser of the women's service) has to hustle for women who want to take part.

'Oh no,' one woman says, 'I don't want to lead the services, I have a terrible voice.'

'No, no,' says another, 'I don't deserve the honour. Give it to someone else.'

The *gabba'it* uses therapeutic words of encouragement with the women, giving them permission to participate and reassuring them if they have any *halachic* queries about the validity of their endeavour. Women's prayer groups reflect the maturation of women's spiritual desires and the raised consciousness amongst Orthodox women who are publicly challenging their exclusion from certain rituals, prayers and synagogue life.[11] I think that one of the spin-offs of egalitarian prayer in Reform, Reconstructionist and Conservative synagogues was that some Orthodox women began to question their own status and began to feel that they wanted more out of the ritual experience.

Herein lies part of the antagonism towards prayer groups. Rabbis regard women's prayer groups as a response to the impact of feminism on the Jewish world. Orthodox women who want to bring feminism into the synagogue will not be tolerated. Women seeking to accommodate the ideology of feminism within the parameters of *halachah* will be publicly vilified.

The best known negative response came from five *Talmudic* scholars at the Rabbi Isaac Elchanan Theological Seminary (RIETS). Founded in 1897, RIETS is the rabbincal school of Yeshiva University in New York, the showcase of modern Orthodoxy, where it is possible for students to acquire a secular degree in professions such as social work, psychology, law and business in an

---

[11] Berkovic, S., 'A Scroll of Their Own: Women Mount a Challenge to Orthodoxy – from Within', *Jerusalem Report*, 11 March 1993, p. 34

Orthodox setting.[12] The rabbis, in what it known as the 'RIETS Five response', condemned the groups for three reasons: the women appear as if they are imitating a male quorum (although the women never refer to themselves as a *minyan*, and carefully leave out the prayers that require a quorum of ten men), a women's prayer group represents a significant change in tradition that cannot be justified, and the women involved are imitating the ways of the non-Jews. In other words, the rabbis were questioning the women's motives. They claimed that the women are inspired by modern fads of feminism and that prayer groups do not reflect genuine spiritual desires but are politically motivated.[13] But why is a man's motivation for coming to the synagogue never questioned, his degree of observance never queried, his quest for honour never suspected and his pursuit of a free whiskey after the services never, ever held against him?

In Israel, the most prominent prayer group is held at the Western Wall and conducted by a group called Women of the Wall. Well, actually, it is not held at the Wall because that has been forbidden by the Israeli government. In April 1996 they were banished to the south-eastern corner of the Old City, a short distance from the Western Wall.[14] The history of the Women of the Wall dates back to its first service on 1 December 1988. It was during a time when the 'Who is a Jew' issue dominated Israeli politics, and threatened a split between different denominations of Jewry, as the validity of non-Orthodox conversions was under threat. In response, a group of women attending the First International Conference of Jewish Feminists in Israel decided to demonstrate their unity with a prayer service at the Western Wall.[15] They planned their operation with

12 Klaperman,G., op. cit.
13 For a fuller discussion of this, and extensive footnotes detailing responses for and against women's prayer groups, see Haut, R., 'Women's Prayer Groups and the Orthodox Synagogue', in Grossman, S. and Haut, R. (1992), op. cit., pp. 135–57.
14 The *International Committee for Women of the Wall, Inc., Newsletter*, Summer 1996, has details of the Israeli government's decision and its implications.
15 Haut, R., 'The Presence of Women', in Grossman, S. & Haut, R. (1992), op. cit., pp. 274–8, powerfully describes the rage against the women.

military precision because they would have to smuggle in a *Sefer Torah* to the women's section, and risk the ire of both men and women. They were verbally abused, and felt the threat of physical violence. Despite opposition, a small group of women continue to meet at the beginning of every month and hold a prayer service. The Women of the Wall is more than just a prayer group. It exists in a public space in a democratic country, held to ransom by theocratic authorities who do not recognise the democratic rights of women. The attempt to silence the Women of the Wall is a symbolic attempt to silence all women who challenge the ruling rabbinic hegemony.

In England, there are some parallels with the American experience, but also some obvious differences. Although the RIETS response was a damaging blow to women's prayer groups, the women involved were not bound to its rulings as there is no central locus of control which binds the community together. The rabbis who composed this response were giving their independent, albeit well-respected, opinion. However, in England, the centralised control of the Chief Rabbinate and 'the hard hand and outstretched arm' of Anglo-Orthodoxy mean that women cannot act independently. The majority of Anglo-Jewry is nominally affiliated with the United Synagogue. Therefore, when a group of women in the United Synagogue want to act, they must ask permission of their rabbi, who is ultimately under the control of the Chief Rabbi. There are only a handful of independent modern Orthodox communities which are not bound by the Chief Rabbi's rulings (although they will clearly take his opinion into consideration).

This was highlighted by England's first attempt to hold a women's prayer group in November 1992 at the Stanmore synagogue, one of the largest Orthodox synagogues in the country. It was led by Rabbi Dr Jeffrey Cohen who vocally and courageously supported the women. However, a few weeks before the prayer group was about to take place, the United Synagogue announced its refusal to loan the participants a *Sefer Torah*. The group was advised by Chief Rabbi Sacks not to use the *Sefer Torah*, but rather to read the words directly from a printed Bible. Rabbi Cohen was bound to respect the ruling of his 'superior' and retracted his permission to read directly from the *Torah* parchment scroll.

The group accepted the decision and issued a statement:

> The Stanmore *Tefillah* group is made up of women belonging to the United Synagogue who accept the authority of the Chief Rabbi and his *Beth Din*. As such it will not disregard that authority . . . and will not be using a *Sefer Torah* at it first service . . .

However the subtext was more poignant, and was articulated by Doreen Fine who reflected the anguish of the women:

> There is an enormous need to belong. What else have we got if we haven't got our community? There is a need to be accepted and a reluctance to put ourselves outside the pale . . . we sincerely believe that the use of a *Sefer Torah* would enhance and intensify our commitment to *Torah*, *tefillah* and *mitzvot*, as well as providing the spiritual uplift that is so lacking in the society in which we are living.[16]

The women do continue to meet, and read the relevant *Torah* portion from a printed book.

Only one synagogue could help the women further: Yakar, one of the handful of mainstream Orthodox synagogues not bound to the Chief Rabbi's rulings. It allowed a group of women to hold a prayer service with the use of a *Sefer Torah* from Yakar. When I went to the first service at Yakar, a reporter from the *Jewish Chronicle* wanted to interview someone sitting next to me. She refused, and then whispered to me that when she went to have an interview at one of the Jewish schools regarding admission for her children, she was asked what she thought about 'women's issues'. She said she agreed with the Chief Rabbi and felt women's prayer services were not appropriate. 'If they knew I was here,' she said to me, 'there's no way my kids would get into that school. It's not up to me to jeopardise my kids' opportunities.' Of course, I am thinking why would she want to send her kids to that particular school, but then it occurs to me that all the Orthodox schools are likely to have a similar position. Where am I going to send you?

Sharon Lee, who has been the prime mover in the establishment of women's prayer groups in England, says the prayer groups give women an opportunity for dignity, for the chance to give a speech, to be participants rather than spectators. It also allows mothers to be role models to their daughters, and gives the daughters an option to celebrate their *bat mitzvah*. It is where I named both of you and said prayers of thanksgiving.

Yakar has also been instrumental in supporting women's prayer groups on *Purim*. On this day, *Megillat Esther*, the Book of Esther is read, and 'women are obligated to read the *Megillah*, for they too were in that miracle'.[17] There are several sources which concur that women reading the *Megillah* for other women is perfectly permissible.[18] There is documentation about the reality, like Mrs Singer who arrived in Manchester in 1904 from Galicia. Her daughter related:

> My mother was a very proud woman, and she went to the *shul* every Saturday. On *Purim* . . . about ten women used to come in and they used to sit around my mother and she used to say the Book of Esther in Hebrew, and they all used to say it after her, because none of them had been taught anything . . . she was a very well-learned woman.[19]

Yakar had its first women's *Megillah* reading in 1994, and I was there. Avigayil was too, five months old, sleeping quietly in her buggy. About seventy women came, many with their children, and

---

17 Babylonian Talmud, Megillah 4a
18 Berkovits, E., *Jewish Women in Time and Torah*, KTAV, Hoboken, NJ, 1990, pp. 92–9, gives a detailed explanation; Berman, S., 'The Status of Women in *Halakhic* Judaism', in Koltun, E., op. cit., pp. 114–28, was one of the earliest contemporary articles to articulate the central issues facing Orthodox women who want more involvement in ritual life and the *halachic* process.
19 quoted in Burman, R., ' "She Looketh Well to the Ways of Her Household": The Changing Role of Jewish Women in Religious Life *c.*1880–1930', p. 242 in Malmgreen, G., *Religion in the Lives of English Women, 1760–1930*, Indiana University Press, 1986, pp. 234–59

we all sat quietly following the reading from our own copy of the *Megillah*. Now I'm telling you, so that you can tell your children.

Nevertheless, as far as the majority of English rabbis are concerned, a women's service is yet another affront to tradition imported from the source of radical Orthodox feminism, New York. The United Synagogue is filled with rabbis who harbour a romanticised, and often inaccurate, notion of a '*Torah*-true' community in which the more restrictive position is legitimated as the more authentic. This shift towards a narrow Orthodoxy, which is usually not shared by the communities they serve, impedes women who are seeking changes that would enhance their participation in religious life without compromising the law.

A good example of this happens on *Simchat Torah*, the celebration of the completion of the cycle of reading from the *Torah*. In many places women are given a *Sefer Torah* to hold and dance with. One rabbi of a young vibrant London community was asked if women could hold the *Sefer Torah* on *Simchat Torah*. Although he acknowledged that it was permissible, he gave a ruling influenced by 'wider communal issues'[20] (i.e., the antagonism towards women's prayer groups). He admitted that he put sociological concerns before *halachah*. Sometimes, a rabbi knows that according to the law, something is permissible, but to preserve male power, he argues that the 'the honour of the community' is being eroded if women have public positions of authority or are seen to participate in the male preserve of ritual life. On the other hand, sometimes rabbis are ahead of the women in their community. One rabbi in another London community with a high percentage of young professionals told me that when he offered the women in his community the *Sefer Torah* on *Simchat Torah*, they didn't want to take it. They almost reeled in horror at the thought, as if they believed they would defile it. Their ignorance of Jewish law masquerades as a maternal concern to preserve the authority of their husbands and the finely tuned status quo of their families. After years of conditioning into a submissive role, the majority of women are unprepared to risk the crown of a good name to join in

[20] see letters and reports in the *Jewish Chronicle*, 7 and 14 October 1994

any activity perceived to be divisive and calculated to destroy the very fabric of the community.

I think some rabbis fear prayer groups are part of a bigger strategic plan to increase the opportunities for Orthodox women to participate more fully in religious life. How strange that at a time when the synagogues are struggling for men to enter the doors and pray, the rabbis seem to fear their power being even further eroded by women clamouring to pray to God. Here is a group of women, prepared to sit behind a *mechitzah*, wear modest clothing, keep *kosher* homes, go to the *mikveh*, yet once a month they would like to pray together. If the rabbis were more in tune with the women's needs, they would realise that participation in a women's prayer group has great potential to enhance the level of observance in Jewish homes. I recognise the danger that women are potentially creating a separatist religion, revisiting upon men the exclusion that women experienced. But I think what is more important is that for some women who have stopped attending the regular services, women's prayer groups has been a powerful re-entry point into the community.

Goiten has pointed out that 'the exclusion of women from the Temple service led inevitably to their being more drawn than men to the popular faiths and cults which were widespread in the ancient Near East'.[21]

It was the women who opposed Jeremiah's fight against the influence of the cult of the Queen of Heaven (Jeremiah 44:16–18). Centuries later, about ninety years ago, the failure of the institutions of Orthodox Judaism to accommodate to the needs of women was an important contributory factor in the development of Liberal Judaism (*c*.1911).[22]

Liberal Judaism is not an ancient Near East cult, but don't the rabbis realise that women are now leaving Orthodoxy for variations on the same theme? It is not the educated and devoted Orthodox women who are destroying Orthodoxy: it is the rabbis

[21] Goiten, S. D., 'Women as Creators of Biblical Genres', in *Prooftexts: A Journal of Jewish Literary Theory*, January 1988, Volume 8, no. 1, p. 21
[22] Burman, R., op. cit., p. 240

who fail really to listen to these women and seek *halachic* support for their requests.

Clearly, beyond Orthodoxy, the idea of women's egalitarian inclusion in ritual and leadership is not a new idea. Lilian Helen Montagu (1873–1963) was born in England into a wealthy Orthodox family. In 1902 she formed the Jewish Religious Union with Claude Montefiore. This later became the Liberal Jewish movement in Britain, and in 1926 she formed the World Union for Progressive Judaism. She never sought ordination, but she assumed a religious leadership role, leading prayer services and preaching on spiritual matters.[23]

Montagu's contemporary Ray (Rachel) Frank (1864–1948) was also born into an Orthodox family (are you beginning to notice a trend?) in California. She was a teacher, preacher, writer and journalist. In 1890, she conducted the High Holyday services for Jews in Spokane and, in 1893, she attended classes at the Cincinnati Reform rabbinical school. Although she was never formally ordained, her reputation as an eloquent speaker and prayer leader spread nationwide. Many referred to her as a prophetess and one newspaper claimed she was a female messiah. In a letter written in 1890, she explains extensively what she would do (and not do) if she were a rabbi. Clearly aware of the tension between the different branches of Judaism, she wrote:

> If I were the rabbi of what is termed the reform type, I would not be funny or sarcastic at the expense of my orthodox brother. If I were orthodox in my ideas, I would not apply harsh names nor deny a state of future bliss to my brother of modern opinions.[24]

Perhaps I should post Ray Frank's letter to all the rabbis listed in the phone book.

The story of German-born Regina Jonas, who sought ordination, has been recently brought to public attention. She studied at

23 see Umansky, E. and Ashton, D., *Four Centuries of Jewish Women's Spirituality*, Beacon Press, Boston, 1991, pp. 115–16, pp. 156–60
24 Marcus, J., *The American Jewish Woman: A Documentary History*, KTAV/ American Jewish Archives, 1981, p. 383

the Berlin Academy for the Science of Judaism and her thesis was 'Can a Woman Become a Rabbi?'[25] (Guess the answer!) Although her thesis was accepted, the principal Rabbi Leo Baeck refused to sign her ordination papers for fear it would split the community. She was then privately ordained by Rabbi Max Dienemann in 1935, and six years later, Rabbi Leo Baeck did sign a certificate confirming Jonas' ordination. She died in Auschwitz in 1944.[26]

More recently, in the Reform movement, Rabbi Sally Preisand became the first woman rabbi in America in 1972, and, in 1975, Rabbi Jacqueline Tabick became the first woman rabbi to be ordained at the Leo Baeck College in England. In Israel, the Reform Hebrew Union College ordained the first woman rabbi, Na'ama Kelman, in 1992. Since then, almost twenty women have been ordained in England [27] and scores more in America. When the Reconstructionist Rabbinical College was opened in 1968 in Philadelphia, it started on the premise that women could be ordained, and in 1974 Sandy Eisenberg Sasso became the first Reconstructionist female rabbi.

In the Conservative movement, the vote to admit women students into the rabbinical programme for ordination by the Jewish Theological Seminary precipitated a split within the faculty and led to the resignation of some scholars. [28] Eventually, in 1985, Amy Eilberg became the first Conservative woman rabbi, and now

---

[25] ibid., p. 889

[26] Monchi, V., 'A Job for a Jewish Girl', *Jewish Chronicle*, 16 December 1994, p. 25

[27] see Sheridan, S. (ed.), *Hear Our Voice: Women Rabbis Tell Their Story*, SCM Press, London, 1994 – collection of essays and personal reflections primarily by English women rabbis

[28] see Greenberg, S. (ed.), *On the Ordination of Women as Rabbis: Studies and Responsa*, Jewish Theological Seminary of America, New York, 1988, for detailed (generally positive) responses by faculty members to the decision to ordain women rabbis, and Weiss Halivni, D., *The Sword and The Book*, Farrar Strauss & Giroux, New York, 1996. Weiss Halivni, a brilliant *Talmudist* and Professor of Religion at Columbia University, was at the time, on the faculty of JTS. He voted against ordination and his letter of disagreement to the faculty, which led to his resignation, is included in this fascinating memoir of his intellectual and religious development (pp. 110–14).

about half of its rabbinical students are women. The steady increase of women rabbis and cantors employed as pulpit rabbis, hospital chaplains, teachers and directors of communal projects have been instrumental in writing new gender-inclusive prayer books and specific prayers which reflect women's concerns, such as pregnancy and childbirth.

Yet, historically, there have also been learned Orthodox women whose opinions were sought after.[29] Many daughters of Chassidic dynasties were petitioned for blessings, gave learned discourses and wore the ritual four-cornered fringed undergarment worn by men.[30] Some were even regarded as rabbis. One of the best known was Hannah Rochel Verbermacher (1815–1892) from the Polish town of Ludomir. She was the loved and longed-for daughter of a couple who had been unable to conceive for ten years. When they visited the Seer of Lublin, a Chassidic master and miracle worker, he predicted they would have a child who would become a great holy rabbi. The learned men who vied for the honour of circumcising the unborn saint were most disappointed when Hannah Rochel was born. However, her father cherished the prophesy of the Seer, and taught her the *Talmud* and *Kabbalah*, mystical works. The latter was especially forbidden to women.

As a teenager she was betrothed to her childhood sweetheart, but when the engagement was announced, Hannah Rochel was forced to stop seeing her fiancé until the wedding day. Upset by this restriction, she withdrew from her friends and community. Her mother died soon after, and on one of her regular visits to her mother's grave, Hannah Rochel lost consciousness. When she woke up, she discovered that she was alone in the graveyard. It was midnight and it seemed as if the spirits were swarming everywhere. She was terrified, and started to run, but soon fell into an open grave. That is where she was found by her father. When Hannah

---

29 see Brayer, M., *The Jewish Woman in Rabbinic Literature, Volume 2: A Psychohistorical Perspective*, KTAV, Hoboken, NJ, 1986, pp. 15–17. He refers to the 'Lady Rabbinists' in South Germany during the late fifteenth century who excelled in learning.

30 see Kaufman, M., op. cit., pp. 81–5, for a brief biographical sketch of fifteen such women

Rochel opened her eyes, the first thing she said was, 'I have just returned from the Heavenly Court, and I have received a new soul.' She broke off her engagement and declared that she would not marry because she had transcended the world of the flesh. She donned the *tefillin* and *tallit* which forms the raiment of Orthodox Jewish male observance and absorbed herself in prayer. She was nineteen years old when her father died, and she insisted that she say the *Kaddish*, the mourner's prayer recited by male mourners. She converted her father's small house into a synagogue, and there she prayed three times a day like a man.

Over the years, her wisdom was recognised and she was regarded as a rabbi by many people. She exercised extreme modesty and when men came to her court, she gave all her teachings and blessings from behind closed doors. No one was allowed into her room. Her celibate life allowed her to transcend sexual differences, thereby permitting her to take on male characteristics. Indeed, as a 'false male', her popularity continued to grow, and certain men became more anxious about her increasing power.

Marriage was considered the solution to the problem of this spiritually ambitious woman and the communal leaders put her under great pressure to abandon her ways and fulfil the traditional role of a Jewish wife. Aged forty, Hannah Rochel was threatened with excommunication,[31] and soon after, she agreed to marry her elderly secretary. However, the marriage was never consummated and ended in divorce. Some say when she surrendered her *tallit* and *tefillin* to her husband, she compromised her authority. After a second unconsummated marriage and divorce, her spiritual powers left her and her following declined. It is said that she spent her last years in the Holy Land, quietly meditating at Jerusalem's Western Wall in her *tallit* and *tefillin*. Later, she became involved with an errant messianic group and eventually died in obscurity at an old age.[32]

[31] Babylonian Talmud, Sanhedrin 7b. The *shofar*, the ram's horn, blown on the Jewish New Year, was in the Middle Ages used to announce an excommunication.
[32] for more information about the Maid of Ludomir, see Rapoport-Albert, A., 'On Women in Hasidism: S. A. Horodezky and the Maid of Ludomir',

There was Rabbi Asenath who lived in Kurdistan in the seventeenth century. She was the daughter of Rabbi Samuel Barzani and famous for her knowledge of the *Torah*, *Talmud*, *Kabbalah* and law. She wrote:

> I was the daughter of a king. Who are the kings? The rabbis. I was raised on the knees of scholars, I was the joy of my father. And no work did he teach me except the work of Heaven, to fulfil what was said, 'And thou shall meditate upon it by day and by night.'

After the birth of one son and daughter, she prayed to God to terminate her menstrual cycle so that she could devote herself to *Torah* study.[33] God fulfilled her request. Here was another 'false male', neutered of her femininity to succeed in *Torah* study. After the early death of her husband, she became the head of a *yeshivah*, and eventually became recognised as the chief teacher of *Torah* in Kurdistan. She was given the title *tanna'it*, female *Talmudic* scholar, and was well known as a healer, especially sought after by women. As a mystic, it was reported that she knew the secret names of God and often pronounced the names of angels. [34]

I thought I might make a mystic, someone others would talk about in a reverential tone. When I was about fifteen, I wanted to see what it felt like to put on my father's prayer shawl and phylacteries. I planned the operation carefully because I did not want to be discovered. I was not worried about getting into trouble, but I was worried that my parents would laugh at me for looking a little silly. They would have thought it fanciful and added the incident to their repertoire of amusing stories about their children. (The others including the first time I plucked my eyebrows and the time my brother was knocked down by a tram.)

---

pp. 495–525 in Rapoport-Albert, A., and Zipperstein, S. (eds), *Jewish History: Essays in Honor of C. Abramsky*, Halban, London, 1988, and Winkler, G., *They Called Her Rebbe*, New York, Judaica Press, 1990
33 Sabar, Y., op. cit., p. 123
34 see Zolty, S., op. cit., pp. 141–4. Her book surveys other learned women who led their communities and were well respected.

I clearly remember bracing myself as I stood erect and carefully held the *tefillin*,[35] two small black leather boxes, crafted from the skin of *kosher* animals, in the palm of my hand. Each small box contains a small piece of parchment with passages from the *Torah*. I fingered the two black leather straps attached to each box. I positioned one of the boxes on my left bicep, practising to be a man. The box firmly in place, I took the longer strap and wound it seven times around my forearm below the elbow. With each circular motion a little more of my flesh bulged. It was just like the way my father's and my grandfather's forearms bulged slightly as they put on their *tefillin*.

I stared at myself in the mirror and the image scared me – a girl in man's clothing. In the Orthodox world, only Jewish men embrace a uniform replete with the *tefillin*, prayer shawl and skullcap, but my predilections for religious cross dressing were too strong to suppress. The strap remained wrapped around my palm. I was thrilled and ashamed at the same time. I could not bring myself to pray for fear of insulting God, and I knew I had done something which I could not tell my friends about, for we all knew that:

> The clothing of a man shall not be on a woman, neither shall a man put on a woman's garment: for all that do so are an abomination to God. [36]

I put the things away and gave up the idea of being holy. I was too cynical for the task and too conservative to rise to the challenge. I am not extraordinary: I could not be a Bertha Pappenheim, Henrietta Szold, Sarah Schenirer nor a Maid of Ludomir or Asenath. To be extraordinary, wrote Szold, is 'to rise above human feeling. It means to be intensely human, it means to raise ordinary feelings to an extraordinary plane.'[37] These women were intensely human, willing to go beyond the boundaries, breach acceptable

[35] The use of *tefillin* is based on the verse, 'And it shall be for a sign unto thee upon thy hand, and for a memorial between thine eyes, that the law of the Lord may be in thy mouth; for with a strong hand did the Lord bring thee out of Egypt.' Exodus 13:9
[36] Deuteronomy 22:5
[37] Fineman,I., op. cit., p. 117

limits and forgo the earthly delights of children. Most days I am still coming to terms with the disappointment of not being as radical as I would like to believe I am. That's when I think I would be better off trying to make the perfect Orthodox doughnut.

'You must try and come next week,' smiled the *rebbetzen* condescendingly, 'it will be a beautiful affair.'

'What are you planning?'

'Mrs T, a very special lady, will be teaching us about *Chanukah*.'

'That sounds very interesting. I will try and make it.'

I assumed it would be a lecture about the historical significance of the festival, some traditional customs associated with it, and perhaps a story culled from folklore. But perhaps not:

> If we succeed in instilling in our girl students that the purpose of their studies is to aspire to emulate our matriarchs, who did not study, then we have succeeded in educating our daughters.[38]

Then I remembered that our matriarch Sarah made little cakes by her tent to feed the passing angels.[39]

'Good, good,' the *rebbetzen* nodded her head. 'She will be making doughnuts – you know it is customary on *Chanukah* to eat oily, fried foods to remind us of the oil which burned in the Temple.'

'Yes, I know,' I shocked her.

'Oh. You do? I am sure a lot of the mothers will come.'

---

[38] cited in El-Or, T., *Educated and Ignorant: Ultra-Orthodox Jewish Women and Their World*, Lynne Rienner, Boulder and London, 1994, p. 65. On the other hand, Zolty, op. cit., p. 69, cites Rabbi Sorotzkin, a leading Lithuanian scholar, expounding the importance of women's education in the 1940s. He comments on the verse in Genesis (12:8) that Abraham 'pitched *his* tent (*oholoh*) west of Beth El'. The word, as it is written without the vowels, could be read as '*her*' tent [*oholah*]. This would indicate that he pitched his wife's tent first and then his own. We know that, according to tradition, these tents were not ordinary tents, rather they were tents for learning. We see that Abraham, the first patriarch, set up two types of tents for learning: the first for women and the second for men. Sarah, the first matriarch, was engaged in educating the women, specifically teaching monotheistic beliefs, while Abraham was teaching the same beliefs to the men.

[39] Genesis 18:6

At the time I was employed by a Jewish welfare organisation to liaise with a range of Jewish children's services. One was a mother-and-toddler playgroup, set up by the ultra-Orthodox community and funded by a Jewish charity. It was often hard to gauge the age of the young mothers as it was not unlikely that a mother of four children would only be twenty-five, yet look closer to thirty-five. Most of them had attended the local schools which were affiliated with their branch of Chassidism or the Beth Jacob movement. Each week a locally respected *rebbetzen*, Mrs N, presided over this group of young mothers who came for some emotional support, stimulation for the children and household tips. The *rebbetzen* had organised an activity for the week before *Chanukah* and encouraged me to come.

When the appointed Tuesday morning came, I could still find a spot in the car park. So, doughnuts was not to be a sell-out session. But then I remembered that most of the women do not drive, because in most Chassidic circles it is considered immodest. They *schlep* the kids, the buggies, the juices, the nappies on the bus, and occasionally, when exhaustion takes over, they take a mini-cab driven by an Orthodox Jew (but that's another story). I walked into the building, a dilapidated airless cold building, with paint flaking off, yet deemed suitable for young children (it's been a temporary arrangement for several years). I am shocked to find thirty women scurrying for a place in front of Mrs T's cooking utensils (Usually a maximum of ten women turn up to the playgroup.) It is standing room only and I nudge my way into a safe spot. I am transfixed – forget Mrs T, she hasn't started yet. I am transfixed by all the women who have come to get an education.

Then Mrs T arrives.

'*Shah, shah,*' says the *rebbetzen*. 'Mrs T is going to demonstrate how to make doughnuts. I want you all to be very quiet.'

And quiet they are. They take out their note pads and pens and sit poised for the holy words of Mrs T. A few more women turn up, but there is no room left, so they leave, disappointed. A friend shouts from the crowd. 'I'll take notes and, God willing, I'll go over them with you.' And for the next forty-five minutes, Mrs T proceeds to mix flour, beat eggs, boil water, fry oil, squirt jam, sprinkle sugar and anything else I may have forgotten that you need to do to make doughnuts. And the women are riveted. I mean, glued to their seats, immovable. They take copious notes and ask intricate questions.

'Is it better to use strawberry or apricot jam?'

'Caster sugar or icing sugar?'

'What temperature should the oil be?'

All questions are treated with the utmost respect and receive a thoughtful response. I am dying. The excitement on the women's faces was too depressing. Most of the women were in their late twenties to early thirties, with an average of five to six children each. Their yearning for knowledge, any knowledge, was over-whelming. The detail, the persistent questioning in pursuit of the perfect doughnut was incredible – clearly, these are intelligent women who are ready for so much more.

After the doughnuts were made, Mrs T posted the recipe and instructions on the wall. As I watched everyone clamour to read them, the thirst for knowledge was palpable and something that their foremother, Sarah Schenirer, would have been proud of. It was just depressing that all this energy was diverted from their intellect to their intestines.

Mrs T and the *rebbetzen* are important role models to these women, and the women, in turn, to their children. These women provide their sons with the prototype of a wife to look for. For the daughters who want to be like their mothers, the socialisation process is virtually painless and highly effective. They are socially rewarded by their community and they are comforted by the knowledge that their system seems almost impervious to change. Fine. But what about the daughter who wants to be a different sort of wife, a different sort of mother? What about the son who wants to be a different sort of husband, a different sort of father? Who can they look to? How do they begin to construct a different sort of religious identity and a different set of role expectations? At some level, men and women are equally trapped in the sharp gender divide of the ultra-Orthodox community because neither is allowed the freedom to explore alternative means of expression. Do they have to leave their community, and if so, where do they go?

Of course, there are many Orthodox women leaders already: revered women teachers, respected counsellors, admirable activists, highly regarded academic scholars and women who, in their daily life, create an environment in their homes and amongst their communities that encourages those around them, men and women, to uphold the tradition. This latter type is exemplified for me in a mother of ten children whom I knew in Melbourne, and who now lives in a Chassidic neighbourhood in New York. Over the years we have stayed in touch with occasional phone calls and news about each other via mutual friends. Recently when I was in New York for a brief visit, I had no time to see her, but I phoned her from the airport before coming home.

When I first rang, one of her children said, 'She's *davenning mincha.*'

'What?' The line was bad, and I couldn't understand

'She's *davenning mincha,*' he said again.

'She's *davenning mincha?*'

'That's right,' the little boy answered, obviously amused that it seemed I did not understand this hybrid of Yiddish and Hebrew.

'OK, I'll call back in ten minutes.' I understood exactly what he said, it was just that it took a moment to register because I couldn't imagine that my friend would find time to say the afternoon prayers. But she was *davenning mincha*, no doubt with at least five or six children watching her, guarding her and making sure that their mother had her own few moments of spiritual space. What a privilege for a child! What an amazing woman!

And what about you, Avigayil? Who will be your role models? And Elisheva, whom will you look up to? How will you decide who is important to you? What are the values that are going to inspire you? Who, will you seek to emulate? Will I be adequate enough? How do I encourage you both to think about women role models when the overwhelming majority of people in positions of leadership and authority within the Orthodox community are men? How will you come to respect your rabbi if he ignores your interests? How will you come to identify with your rabbi if he is unable to share your concerns?

Despite all I have said, you might find it strange that I still like

my rabbis old, bearded, hatted and severely dressed. It's familiar
and it is what I have learnt to expect. However, I can rarely talk
meaningfully to these rabbis, as they do not appear to understand
the nature of an Orthodox woman's disquiet in the maelstrom of
modernity. It's a sad indictment, but a male rabbi is largely
irrelevant in my day-to-day life. Often a woman's rabbi is her
husband's rabbi, and although he may play a major role in
ceremonial events, he is not someone women always feel meaningfully connected to. Some lucky women have a close relationship
with a rabbi-cum-mentor who regards their issues seriously and I
envy them, but most questions which a woman needs to be asked of
a rabbi are dealt with via her husband, man-to-man. For single
women, the issue of a rabbi is even more fraught, as it is improper
for a male rabbi to become too intimate with a single woman. As a
single woman, most relationships I had with rabbis were based on
the notion that they felt compelled to find me a husband.

When I think back to my teenage years, and those years that lie
ahead for both of you, I clearly remember a couple of male rabbis
that I respected, but there were none that I could identify with or
get close to. Now I am beginning to appreciate the impact of this –
poignantly described by Blu Greenberg who reflects on her
experience in *shul* on *Yom Kippur*, the holiest day of the year. She
noticed that:

> through a slight opening in the *mechitzah*, I see a young boy,
> fourteen or fifteen. His eyes fix on the rabbi. His lips are parted
> and every few seconds he faintly shapes them to complete a
> familiar Hebrew phrase the rabbi has begun. As I observe him, I
> realise that something more than listening is taking place: here
> the boy relates to the rabbi, not only as scholar and leader, but as
> role model and future mentor . . . Today there are no Orthodox
> women to serve as role models. No equivalent status of
> leadership is conferred upon Orthodox women.[40]

While some Orthodox rabbis agree that a woman can be as

---

[40] Greenberg, B., 'Is now the time for Orthodox women Rabbis?', *Moment*,
December 1993, p. 52

learned as a man, as competent an educator and pastoral worker as a man, they have suggested that the title of 'rabbi' is problematic and favour a gender-specific term. For example, Rabbi Avi Weiss suggests recasting the primary roles of rabbis to determine what women can do and selecting titles accordingly; for instance, an educator would be *moratenu*, our teacher. Rabbi David Silber stresses the need to give women the tools to participate in the interpretative process, educating women as *poskot*, legal arbiters, on issues affecting women, such as the laws of family purity. 'There is nothing magical about *halachah*. It is knowing the facts and having some sense. To give a woman a title is not the point.' [41]

However, for many women it is exactly the point. Technically, someone earns the title of 'rabbi' after studying certain sections of the *Talmud*. In traditional *yeshivot*, the study for *smichah* or ordination is not about preparing someone for the pulpit or pastoral duties associated with today's rabbinate: rather the acquisition of the title 'rabbi' is a formal indication of a certain amount of textual knowledge at a proficient level. (According to the Orthodox requirements of *smichah*, the male and female students of other denominations have not usually covered the same amount of textual material; however, they are often better equipped for the dealing with congregational matters and pastoral duties.) Why should Orthodox women who can pass the test for ordination be denied the title?

One possible contender is Haviva Ner-David, who has taken steps to become officially ordained and is adamant that she is not a

> man-wannabe. I do not perform *mitzvot* that are usually done only by men only because I want to prove a point . . . my love for Judaism and Hashem [God] is the driving force . . . The title 'rabbi' means something. It carries with it connotations of authority, morality, commitment to Judaism and a certain mastery of texts. These are all things which a woman who studies at Drisha would not get. Nothing is comparable to a rabbinical

---

[41] comments made by these rabbis in their lectures at the International Conference on Feminism and Orthodoxy, 16–17 March 1997, New York City

degree if you want to teach *Torah* and be involved in the *halachic* process. When I submitted a well-researched article on why women should take upon themselves the positive time-bound *mitzvot* (such as *tefillin* and *tallit*) to a number of *halachic* journals, it was rejected. If the same article had been written by a rabbi, I am certain it would have been more seriously considered.[42]

Four years later, she has taken an alternative route and hopes to be ordained privately by an Orthodox rabbi in Israel.[43] Even if Krasner-Davidson (who has renamed herself Ner-David) does not find an Orthodox community willing to accept her authority, she is questioning the control and power of the male establishment.

Was Greenberg indulging in a pipe-dream when she suggested that the ordination of Orthodox women is 'close at hand'?

The cumulative impact – of a critical mass of students of *Talmud* and *halachah*, a plethora of rising-star teachers, the support of educational institutions and the presence of respected women rabbis in the liberal denominations – will be to transform the expectations of Orthodox women. This will be a powerful agent for change.[44]

And what of the change? What would the Orthodox world look like if there were female rabbis? After all, a religious leader should be a source of comfort in times of sorrow, and a source of hope in times of joy. It is their role to ask questions and to answer questions; to teach and to be taught; to love all those you come near, and be loved by them. A rabbi asks of a community to engage themselves with *Torah* and the commandments, to come closer to God and to welcome others into their community with acts of kindness and compassion. I have been wondering how my experience of Judaism would have been different with an Orthodox woman rabbi as an influential person in my life.

[42] Krasner-Davidson, H., 'Why I'm Applying to Yeshiva U', *Moment*, December 1993, p. 55
[43] Gross, N., 'Breaking Down the Rabbinate Walls', *Jerusalem Report*, 20 February 1997
[44] Greenberg, B , op. cit., *Moment*, December 1993, pp. 51–2

At the time of my *bat mitzvah*, she might have given me inspiration to participate more meaningfully. I might have been able to look up to her as a role model. I could have asked her my questions about boys, about suffering and all those other meaning-of-life questions I was obsessed with. In about ten years' time, it will be Avigayil's *bat mitzvah*. If there are Orthodox women rabbis, her whole experience of reaching Jewish adulthood will be so different – she will have her own role model to identify with, and she might even think about becoming a rabbi herself.

When my parents died, an Orthodox woman rabbi might have been able to empathise in a constructive way. She would have given me the option to say the *Kaddish* and would have taught me the right pronunciation had I decided to say it. She would have held my hand and told me not to be embarrassed that the words were foreign to me. When I die, what will the rabbi tell my daughters?

When I got married, she would have been more sympathetic to a request that the name of my mother be included in my *ketubah*, and she would have calmed my nerves before going to the *mikveh* on the night before my wedding. She might even have come with me. What will the Orthodox world look like by the time my daughters are ready to get married? Will the rabbi be wearing taffeta too?

When I had my daughters, she would have helped me to develop an appropriate service to herald their births. She might have popped in to see how I was managing, and offered insights from her own experience. I could have talked to her about the pain of my Caesarean deliveries, and asked about prayers of thanksgiving, for there were times I literally thought I was going to expire on the operating table. It would never occur to me to discuss this with a male rabbi. She would also be sensitive to the needs of infertile couples and the issues around adoption. A woman might feel more comfortable talking to her about her concerns, just as a man might feel more comfortable talking to an Orthodox male rabbi. [45]

At the synagogue, she would tell me of the prayers written by

<hr>

45 A fine example of a sensitive male rabbi, who adopted children and discusses the issues compassionately, is seen in Gold, M., *And Hannah Wept: Infertility, Adoption and the Jewish Couple*, Jewish Publication Society, Philadelphia, 1988.

women hundreds of years ago, prayers that I could say in today's world at times of joy and at times of sadness. She might suggest that we tell others of these long-forgotten prayers which evoke the concerns that a woman has for her family, her livelihood and her community.

In the synagogue on a *Shabbat* morning, her head would be covered, not necessarily with a skullcap, but rather with a stylish woman's hat or beret. Her prayer shawl might be like that used by the men, or she may have bought a more decorated prayer shawl from one of the entrepreneurial Jewish women artists who have been designing a range of religious artefacts for women. And what about wearing *tefillin*, the phylacteries which are generally the preserve of men? Raising the issue of Orthodox women rabbis is not just about a title, but about the nature of obligation. As an Orthodox woman is not obligated to wear *tefillin* during prayer, how can an Orthodox woman rabbi encourage her community to do so? Can some of these contradictions be resolved?

She would deliver a learned sermon during the Saturday morning service drawing on biblical sources, rabbinic literature and contemporary Jewish thought.

And she might not lead the congregation in prayer on a Sabbath morning because the congregation has listened to their beloved male cantor for the last ten years, but that is OK. This is such a small part of her job, that she would be happy to sit back and enjoy the cantor's voice.

She would be particularly concerned about the problems of *agunot*. Obviously there are male rabbis who are very concerned about this issue and have been struggling to find a way to resolve it, but the concerted efforts and insights of women rabbis could pave the way to solutions. Excluding women from the legislative process has denied *halachah* the benefit of a woman's perspective, particularly in areas that directly impinge on her marital status. The effect of women's exclusion is 'the control of female subjects through maintaining them in virtual ignorance of the practices that enable ritual decision-making'.[46]

46 Boyarin, D., op. cit., p. 154

There are other legal issues where her 'touch' would have a great influence – for example, in the use of the *mikveh* and the area of sexual relations. I am sure that many women who are interested in the idea of the *mikveh* and want a more detailed exposition of what is involved are too shy to approach their local male rabbi. Women who are particularly uncomfortable about having to consult about intimate details of their body with a male rabbi, may consider it much more appropriate to talk to a woman. I know I would, and I currently send Jonathan away to do the asking. Like the sensitive *mikveh* lady, the female rabbi could encourage the use of the *mikveh* for symbolic healing after a rape, abortion or miscarriage.

She would not close her eyes to the social problems which beset a community, particularly those that threaten the health and safety of women and children, such as domestic violence and child abuse. There are many well-intentioned, empathic male rabbis, but there have also been complaints of incompetence and inappropriate comments made by male rabbis. Comments such as, 'Go home and make him [the abusive husband] chicken soup.' Women do not want to go and talk to their male rabbi because they do not always believe he will understand, nor do they feel he will be effective.

She would be a teacher, like the male rabbi, but she would include the wisdom and literature of women in her teaching. She would highlight the practices of women in the past which could inform our practices of today. She would inspire other educators to think about the role of women in the development of Jewish thought and lifestyle.

The private life of the female rabbi would be as varied as that of her male colleague. Some male rabbis are single, most are married, some have wives at home with children, some have wives who work outside the home. Some female rabbis would be single, others married, some would have children with husbands amenable to sharing childcare or contributing to nanny expenses. Jewish family structures are changing all the time due to factors such as the delayed childbearing age of professional women, availability of workplace childcare, increased incidence of divorce, the dependency of elderly parents, unemployment, reduced working hours and other changes in the workplace. The advent of the Orthodox female rabbi would be just one more variable that would influence the diversity of Jewish families in the future.

The question of Orthodox women rabbis is largely irrelevant in the world of my friend with ten children who has the time to be *davenning mincha*. However, her community has been affected by many of the changes in the lives of Orthodox women, and they do not pass unnoticed. As we were chatting, I explained that I was in New York to attend a conference on feminism and Orthodoxy, and I spoke briefly about the way the conference was looking at expanding opportunities for Orthodox women.

'How fascinating!' she said. 'I would have loved to come!'

That was not the response I was expecting as I assumed feminism was a dirty word in her neighbourhood.

'Really?' I asked

'Of course.'

And then we spoke about bringing up children and the way we shape and mould their characters and influence their moral development. It became clear that this woman did not view feminism as the enemy, but rather was interested in exploring what it means in the context of the ultra-Orthodox world and the challenges for its girls.

Part of the problem has been the image of feminism and the lack of clarity about its meaning for the Orthodox community. While many of the activities of Orthodox feminists, let alone Orthodox women rabbis, are irrelevant, and would certainly be considered heretical in the ultra-Orthodox enclaves of Williamsburg, Stamford Hill and Bnei Brak, their leaders are worried.

The front-cover article of the *Jewish Observer*, a widely read and 'approved' magazine in the ultra-Orthodox community, featured the 'Feminism and Orthodoxy' conference in its April 1997 edition and its lead article reported on the conference. It was most amusing to read these authors describe the conference as a conclave – a cardinals' meeting place for papal election – and it was predictable that they would focus on the more contentious issues of women rabbis, prayer groups and women's education. They virtually ignored the range of study sessions on non-'controversial' issues, the sense of collegiality and the genuine respect shown by women to each other and to the rabbis who attended. It was unclear if the two men who wrote the article actually attended the conference, because most of the article relied on second-hand accounts and other newspaper reports of the proceedings.

Worse still, the article fed into the widespread false perception that Orthodox feminists don't like motherhood and deride the role of the homemaker. This is completely untrue: it is precisely because they love their children that they want to make sure Orthodoxy can respond to the modern world which their children will encounter. As to home-making, some women stay at home, some work outside the home, but all juggle responsibilities and tasks according to their unique family demands. In a case of 'she doth protest too much' it seems to me that if the ultra-Orthodox establishment were not so concerned about the issues of women's participation, they would not have given such prominence to the conference, nor presented some arguments in a way that may have (unintentionally) caused its female readership to question their own status.[47]

In the Orthodox world I belong to, the issue of women's participation cannot be ignored any longer. It has contributed to the fragmentation of the Orthodox world as those modern Orthodox communities that permit women's prayer groups and encourage women to study *Talmud* are already regarded suspiciously. Should they lend even a sliver of credence to the idea of women rabbis, they would face hostile opposition from the ultra-Orthodox and Chassidic communities which would eventually lead to an irreparable split that modern Orthodox leaders feel they cannot afford to risk.

Symbolically, the issue of women rabbis is high on the Orthodox feminist agenda and there are women ready to take on the mantle of rabbinical leadership, but the real question is whether we as a community are ready to accept them. Personally, I think the other 'subversive' activities of Orthodox women, such as getting a good education and enhancing the level of their ritual

[47] *Jewish Observer*, April 1997, 8–15

participation, are strategically more urgent and achievable. Educated and spiritually committed women can only enhance
Orthodox Judaism and give the community the confidence to
embrace the idea of women rabbis. As we have relied on men for
all our decisions, now the greatest obstacle is our own resistance
to accepting women as being equally competent in matters of
Jewish law. The hardest thing will be to convince ourselves to rely
on the authority of learned women and to ask questions of these
women leaders.

At the same time, the modern Orthodox establishment is not
monolithic, and there are women who oppose women's prayer
groups and who do not seek a greater role in ritual life. Those
choices must also be respected and maintained. Orthodox activists
must not alienate those women, nor develop an élitist attitude
which excludes those women who choose not to participate.
However, I would suggest that all Orthodox women want to see an
end to discriminatory practices in the area of divorce, and the vast
majority want their daughters to have access to the education they
deserve in order to be able to make their own choices.

The initiatives of Orthodox feminists give me some hope that
Orthodox Judaism could still be relevant in your lives, responsive
to contemporary dilemmas and respectful of the minds of half its
population. Religious feminists are symbolic of the struggle
between modernity and tradition, and religious leaders trying to
silence our voices are symbolically, and in practice, rejecting
modernity.

Professor Sylvia Barack Fishman likens the attempt to silence
women to a 'symbolic exorcism'.[48] Although there are rabbis who
have gone to tremendous lengths and personal sacrifice to support
Orthodox women's innovations, there are many more seeking to
create a more restrictive environment for women. In their rhetoric
and decisions, these rabbis are asking women to symbolise the
rejection of modernity. Rabbis across the globe have publicly

---

[48] 'Sociological Analysis of Orthodox Jewish Women', lecture presented at
the International Conference on Feminism and Orthodoxy, 16 March 1997,
New York City, USA

UNDER MY HAT 241

denounced the activities of Orthodox feminists, accusing them of destroying the fabric of Jewish family life.

Rather, I would argue that it is 'the *Torah* of the mother' (Proverbs 1:8), combined with the faith and loyalty of educated and devoted Orthodox women, that is enhancing Judaism for all its children. It is the rabbis in refusing to address the pain of my exclusion and the male leaders in failing to welcome both of you, who are jeopardising the future of the Jewish community.

Every day of the week you see me reading and studying, you hear me praying, you watch me working. (You also see me loading and unloading the washing machine, chopping the onions and collecting up all the nappies – but for the sake of this point, let's put all that to one side for now.) The burden of being your role model is tremendous, but I feel a responsibility to show you that every aspect of my life is just as Jewishly-important for me as it is for your father. I want you to know that you have options. The charted path is safe and worn: you can take it, it is yours. But there is an uncharted path being carved out as I write these words, by women far braver than your mother. It is also yours for the taking. Whatever you decide, I just never want you to think that the only option you ever had was to dish out the crisps or make jam doughnuts.

Epilogue

I talked to my mother as I wrote this book. I asked her questions about her life, her thoughts, her hopes for the future. I talked to both of you as I wrote this book. I asked you both about the way you see things, your thoughts and the life you want. No one answered. My mother is dead. Avigayil struggles to compose a grammatically correct sentence and Elisheva has just discovered the joy of being vertical. So I talked to myself. It is a habit I have been perfecting.

Anyone eavesdropping on this conversation would have realised that I have more questions than answers, more contradictory positions than convenient resolutions. That's life. I helped to create a contradictory life by choosing conflicting values, but is that such a bad thing? Of course, there are times when I wished there was more intellectual coherence. Emotionally, it would be so convenient to believe in God without any reservations about the merits of such an Omnipresent's actions. How satisfying to believe that when I perform a *mitzvah*, whether it be to visit a sick person or to light the *Shabbat* candles, I am really making a difference to the world.

It can be all that simple, or it can be fraught with the sort of questioning I bring into the equation. Perhaps that's why I like being Orthodox: there's room for cynicism, debate and dilemmas. What fun would there be for me if it was all neatly resolved?

But sometimes, I feel like this life your father and I have created for you is ahistorical: devoid of grandparents, disconnected from our own childhood experiences and caught in a timewarp as Orthodoxy fails to address the changing roles of its daughters and sons. Because of that, it would be much easier to say Orthodoxy doesn't 'speak' to me, but I feel that I have the responsibility to 'speak' to Orthodoxy.

I appreciate what Judaism offers me, and the contribution it makes to the rest of the world. Ultimately, I do believe that observing the laws, bringing the tradition into every aspect of our daily rhythmn and actively studying the classic, and more modern, Jewish texts is the only way to ensure the survival of Judaism. However, admitting to conflict when I cannot always reconcile Jewish law and practices with the modern world, does not make me any less of a committed Jew. Rather, this forces me actively to engage with the teachings of tradition and locate myself within a vast spectrum of ideas and opinions.

The rabbis say that a woman earns merit by sending her husband and sons to learn. This paragon of selfless virtue puts the needs of others before her own, and she is embodied in the self-sacrificing wife of Rabbi Akiva. Her wealthy father Kalba Savua, did not approve of their marriage and disinherited her. Nevertheless, she lived in dire poverty and encouraged this illiterate forty-year-old peasant to spend twenty-four years away from home getting an education.[1] Her munificent act gave the Jewish world one of its rabbinical heroes.

Well, call me selfish, but I want to develop to my own intellectual and spiritual potential. As a community, can we afford to ignore the religious yearnings of modern women who want to share the spiritual quest with men in a partnership characterised by equal access to study and increased opportunities within ritual life? Can we expect women to regard themselves as serious and fully obligated members of the community if we do not provide a range of role models they can aspire to and seek counsel from?

It would be easier to say that 'nothing changes in Orthodoxy' but if one looks at the tremendous changes in the last twenty-five years, regarding the education of women, women's involvement in ritual life and consciousness raising about the impact of feminism on Orthodoxy, we have certainly created a social movement that is making a serious impression on the nature of contemporary Orthodoxy. Since the Enlightenment, questions of science, the nature of knowledge and the issue of personal autonomy have all

[1] Babylonian Talmud, Nedarim 50a

challenged the defined boundaries of Orthodox thought. In the 1990s the nature of women's participation in Orthodox life is the most immediate and inevitable outcome of this process of challenging Orthodoxy. It is clear that the fragmentation of Orthodoxy is largely centred on the debates concerning the status of women. Challenges from women to read from the *Sefer Torah*, resolve the problem of *agunot*, study *Talmud* on a par with men and participate to a greater extent in ritual life are some of the demands which have divided rabbis and their communities.

While some regard these challenges as an affront to tradition, others welcome them as a positive sign of women's commitment to preserving Orthodoxy. I argue that women are the *defenders of the faith* and not the destroyers of the tradition. It is because women care so much that they are trying to find ways to accommodate their needs within Orthodoxy. It would be so much simpler to walk away. But we stay. We stay because we care too much. Why doesn't anyone seem to recognise this?

For me, two daughters later, I have realised the obvious: women have the power to determine the future of Orthodoxy. If we continue to feel excluded by it, we will simply leave. It is in our control, and the rabbinical establishment are ignoring our concerns at their peril. If I take you to baby-naming ceremonies for girls, *bat mitzvah* celebrations, *Rosh Hodesh* groups and prayer groups, if you see women saying *Kaddish* and women studying *Talmud*, there is a much greater chance you will feel that Orthodoxy has a place for you.

But women cannot bring about this revolution alone. Perhaps women with sons have an even harder task ahead. It is their responsibility to raise young men who are going to help young women of the future to shape Orthodoxy in the twenty-first century. Jewish men must be involved and Women's Issues must be owned by the whole community. Many women's concerns have been marginalised and trivialised by the male establishment: a strategy that has separated women's issues from communal concerns and defined them as the private domain of angry, discontented women who do not understand their 'true' role as Jewish women and homemakers. However, men should be encouraged to think about issues from the 'other side': they cannot expect women to have fulfilling lives as professional women in the secular world and be content with a secondary and submissive role in their religious life. It doesn't mean we don't care about our families: in fact, we care so much about family life and raising children that we are urging the community to take these issues seriously. Women have to talk to their rabbis, and the rabbis have to listen, really listen. Don't men worry that their daughters might be seriously disadvantaged by inequities in religious law and custom?

Orthodox feminists also have an important role to play in bridging the growing divide between secularism and religion in Israel: they have a social responsibility to model tolerant behaviour and respect for the tradition while at the same time challenging inequities that are incompatible with the end of the twentieth century.

Orthodox women should also be talking to women from other orthodoxies. The *shaytel*, the nun's wimple and the veil are all variations on the same theme. As a community, we may not be ready for Orthodox women rabbis, but it is no coincidence that their rabbinical ordination has emerged at the same time as the ordination of women priests and the rise in Muslim feminist consciousness in some circles. It seems that for many religions Women's Issues are at the heart of the struggle between modernity and tradition. Women pressing for change within their own religious tradition can learn from the experiences of other women – be it in terms of strategy, theological argument or handling the social fallout which comes from agitating for change.

Institutions where women may seriously study and interpret texts, including the *Talmud*, have changed the educational land-scape. For too long, rabbis have been handing down decisions about women which are not grounded in *halachah* but, as a group of rabbis in New York demonstrated in the case of the *bat mitzvah* that they wanted to stop, on a sociological premise that it is *poretz geder bemesorat Yisrael*, breaking the fences of Jewish tradition. They cling to their version of acceptable social norms and desired behaviour. But as Professor Kenneth Kitchen observed about the available archaeological evidence for the events described in the

Bible, 'The absence of evidence is not evidence of absence.' As long as rabbis and men can use their greater knowledge to intimidate women into a position of ignorant submission, the ground rules are unfair.

However, as women scholars begin to interpret the law and act as *poskot* on issues affecting the community, the standing of the rabbis will be affected. It is beginning to happen: in Israel women are trained in aspects of Jewish divorce law and act for women in the rabbinical courts, and in New York women will be trained in lab procedures and Jewish law relating to the collection of semen at a clinic for infertile Orthodox families.[2] This scenario was unimaginable ten years ago!

As we begin to articulate a theology of Orthodox feminism, as more women begin to acquire the same amount of knowledge as men and write *responsa* to complex questions, the community will start to defer to its women scholars, thus gradually sharing the power between men and women. Won't we all be better off?

When I started to write this book and watched incredulously as the words flew out of my fingertips on to the computer screen, I started to panic that the process might make me lose my faith and conviction. I worried that the process of critiquing the Orthodox world, and my place in it as a mother of two young daughters, might make me feel that I was short-changing both of you.

As I started to talk to people about some of the ideas in this book, virtual strangers kept asking me, 'Why are you still Orthodox?' 'What is the attraction?' Apparently, what I was saying seemed incongruous with the way I live my daily life. At first I internalised these questions, and began a defensive strategy of convoluted explanation which bordered on apologetics. I was apologising for believing that it is important to continue the unfolding drama of a three-thousand-year-old history because I want Jewish culture and tradition to survive. Then I started to wonder what made them ask the question: what negative messages had they internalised about an Orthodox lifestyle which compelled them to make me justify my position?

2 Jolkovsky, B., op. cit., *Forward*, 13 June 1997

Of course, no system is perfect and I can see the problems. I make no apologies for the dishonest and corrupt members of the religious establishment and I can't defend their actions. Of course, we live in a world different from that in which the religion was conceived, and some of its arguments are at odds with modern sensibilities. But that is the challenge, and sometimes I get annoyed when Orthodox communities are portrayed as colonies of an outlandish species to be regarded with patronising interest. We are not curiosities of the late twentieth century, but rather people trying to reconcile ourselves to the inherent dilemmas of being religious people in a largely secular world.

Sometimes I worry that my own ambivalences will deter both of you and give you several windows of opportunity to reject the lifestyle your father and I have chosen. But I hope this makes my relationship with you more honest, and I want you to realise that your Jewish heritage is much deeper because of the oft-neglected, but rich tradition of women's experiences, even if these experiences are fraught with conflict and unresolved questions. At least, let me make a plea for women and men to engage more honestly with the tradition so that women are not denied what rightfully belongs to them.

As I finish this book, I have accepted that the contradictory Orthodox life I have written about is who I am. It's the good and the bad. It's me, it's your foremothers and your forefathers, and I want you to have it. I want it to be a way of life that both of you, as fully-fledged women, can treasure, rejoice with, grow old with and seek comfort from.

So that's it, kids. I wanted you to have a memory. I wanted to tell you about your mother, because I wanted to understand my own mother. And now, I can't wait for you to grow up.

Bibliography

NEWSPAPERS AND MAGAZINES REFERRED TO:

Forward

Generation: A Journal of Australian Jewish Life, Thought and Community

International Committee for Women of the Wall, Inc. Newsletter

Israel Women's Network Newsletter

Jerusalem Report

Jewish Chronicle

Jewish Observer

Jewish Press

Jewish Tradition: National Publication of the Union of Orthodox Synagogues of South Africa

Lilith magazine

Moment magazine

New Moon magazine

Prooftexts: A Journal of Jewish Literary Theory

Women's Tefillah Network Newsletter

BOOKS REFERRED TO:

Adelman, P., *Miriam's Well: Rituals for Jewish Women Around the Year*, Biblio Press, New York, 1990

Alderman, G., *Modern British Jewry*, Clarendon Press, Oxford, 1992

Alpert, R., *Like Bread on the Seder Plate: Jewish Lesbians and the Transformation of Tradition*, Columbia University Press, New York, 1997

Amram, D., *The Makers of Hebrew Books in Italy*, The Holland Press, London, 1963, 1988

Armstrong, K., *Through the Narrow Gate: A Nun's Story*, Macmillan, London, 1981

Aschkenasy, N., *Eve's Journey: Feminine Images in Hebraic Literary Tradition*, Wayne State University Press, Detroit, 1986

Aviad, J., *Return to Judaism: Religious Renewal in Israel*, University of Chicago Press, Illinois, 1983

Baskin, J. and Tenenbaum, S. (eds), *Gender and Jewish Studies: A Curriculum Guide*, Biblio Press, New York, 1994

Baskin, J., *Women of the Word: Jewish Women and Jewish Writing*, Wayne State University, Detroit, 1994

Baskin, J., *Jewish Women in Historical Perspective*, Wayne State University, Detroit, 1991

Berkovits, E., *Jewish Women in Time and Torah*, KTAV, Hoboken, NJ, 1990

Berkovits, E., *Not in Heaven: The Nature and Function of Halakha*, KTAV, New York, 1983

Berrin, S. (ed.), *Celebrating the New Moon: A* Rosh Chodesh *Sourcebook*, Jason Aronson, Northvale, NJ, 1995

Boyarin, D., *Unheroic Conduct: The Rise of Heterosexuality and the Invention of the Jewish Man*, California University Press, Berkeley, 1997

Brayer, M., *The Jewish Woman in Rabbinic Literature, Volume 2: A Psychohistorical Perspective*, KTAV, Hoboken, NJ, 1986

Brewer, J. Scherer, *Sex and the Modern Jewish Woman: An Annotated Bibliography*, Biblio Press, Fresh Meadows, 1986

Bristow, Edward, *Prostitution and Prejudice: The Jewish Fight against White Slavery, 1870–1939*, Oxford University Press, Oxford, 1982

Broner, E., *Mornings and Mourning: A Kaddish Journal*, Harper San Francisco, San Francisco, 1994

Brooks, G., *Nine Parts of Desire: The Hidden World of Islamic Women*, Hamish Hamilton, London, 1995

Cantor, A., *The Jewish Woman, 1900–1985: A Bibliography*, Biblio Press New York, 1987

Cantor, A., *Jewish Women, Jewish Men: The Legacy of Patriarchy in Jewish Life*, Harper, San Francisco, 1995

Cardin, Rabbi N. (ed & trans.), *Out of the Depths I Call to You: A Book of Prayers for the Married Jewish Woman*, Jason Aronson, Northvale, NJ, 1992

Commentary magazine (editors), *The Condition of Jewish Belief*, American Jewish Committee, New York, 1966 (reprinted 1989, Jason Aronson, Northvale, NJ)

Danziger, M. H., *Returning to Tradition: The Contemporary Revival of Orthodox Judaism*, Yale University Press, New Haven, 1989

Davidman, L., *Tradition in a Rootless World: Women Turn to Orthodox Judaism*, University of California Press, California, 1991

Dawidowicz, L. (ed.), *The Golden Tradition: Jewish Life and Thought in Eastern Europe*, Schocken Books, New York, 1967

Edinger, D., *Bertha Pappenheim: Freud's Anna O.*, Congregation Solel, Chicago, 1968

Eichenbaum, L. and Orbach, S., *Outside In, Inside Out: Women's Psychology: A Feminist Psychoanalytic Approach*, Penguin, 1982

Eilberg-Schwartz, Howard, and Doniger, Wendy (eds), *Off With Her Head: The Denial of Women's Identity in Myth, Religion and Culture*, University of California Press, Berkeley, 1995

Eilberg-Schwartz, H. (ed.). *People of the Body: Jews and Judaism from an Embodied Perspective*, State University of New York Press, Albany, 1992

El-Or, T., *Educated and Ignorant: Ultra-Orthodox Jewish Women and Their World*, Lynne Rienner, Boulder and London, 1994

Elon, M., *The Principles of Jewish Law*, Keter Publishing, Jerusalem, 1975

Feldman, A., *The River, The Kettle, The Bird: The Torah Guide to Successful Marriage*, CSB Publications, Jerusalem, 1987

Fineman, I., *A Woman of Valour: The Life of Henrietta Szold*, Simon and Schuster, New York, 1961

Fishman, S., *A Breath of Life: Feminism in the American Jewish Community*, Free Press, New York, 1993

Forman, F. *et al.* (eds), *Found Treasures: Stories by Yiddish Women Writers*, Second Story Press, Toronto, 1994

Frankiel, T., *The Voice of Sarah: Feminine Spirituality and Traditional Judaism*, HarperCollins, New York, 1990

Freeman, L., *The Story of Anna O.*, Paragon House, New York, 1972

Freidan, B., *The Feminine Mystique*, Penguin, New York, 1963

Frymer-Kensky, T., *In the Wake of the Goddesses: Women, Culture and the Biblical Transformation of Pagan Myth*, Fawcett Columbine, New York, 1992

Gold, M., *And Hannah Wept: Infertility, Adoption and the Jewish Couple*, Jewish Publication Society, Philadelphia, 1988

Goldman, A., *The Search for God at Harvard*, Random House, New York, 1991

Goldstein, R., *The Mind-Body Problem*, Random House, 1983, Penguin, New York, 1993

Goodkin, J. and Citron, J., *Women in the Jewish Community: Review and Recommendations*, Women in the Community, London, 1994

Greenberg, B., *On Women and Judaism*, Jewish Publication Society, Philadelphia, 1981

Greenberg, M., *There is Hope for Children: Youth Aliyah, Henrietta Szold and Hadassah*, Hadassah Organization, New York, 1986

Greenberg, S. (ed.), *On the Ordination of Women as Rabbis: Studies and Responsa*, Jewish Theological Seminary of America, New York, 1988

Grossman, S. and Haut R. (eds), *Daughters of the King: Women and the Synagogue*, Jewish Publication Society, Philadelphia, 1992

Hamelsdorf, O. and Adelsberg, S., *Jewish Women and Jewish Law Bibliography*, Biblio Press, Fresh Meadows, 1980

Hecht, N. S., Jackson, B. S., Passamaneck, S. M., Piattelli, D. and Rabello, A. M. (eds), *An Introduction to the History and Sources of Jewish Law*, Oxford University Press, 1996

Henry, S. and Taitz, E., *Written Out of History*, Biblio Press, New York, 1990

Heschel, S., *On Being a Jewish Feminist*, Schocken Books, New York, 1983, 1995

Joselit, J., *The Wonders of America: Reinventing Jewish Culture, 1880–1950*, Hill and Wang, New York, 1994

Jung, L. (ed.), *Jewish Leaders, 1750–1940*, Boys Town Jerusalem Publishers, Jerusalem, 1964

Kaplan, M., *The Jewish Feminist Movement in Germany: The Campaigns of the Judischer Frauenbund, 1904–1938*, Greenwood Press, Connecticut 1979

Kardish, S., *A History of Mikvaot in Britain*, Vallentine Mitchell, London, 1996

Kaufman, D., *Rachel's Daughters: Newly Orthodox Jewish Women*, Rutgers University Press, New Brunswick, 1991

Kaufman, M., *The Woman in Jewish Law and Tradition*, Jason Aronson, Northvale, NJ, 1993

Klaperman,G., *The Story of Yeshiva University, the First Jewish University in America*, Collier-Macmillan, London, 1969

Klirs, T. (compiled and introduced by), *The Merit of Our Mothers: A Bilingual Anthology of Jewish Women's Prayers*, Hebrew Union College Press, Cincinnati, 1992

Koltun, E. (ed.), *The Jewish Woman*, Schocken Books, New York, 1976

Kranzler, G., *Hasidic Williamsburg: A Contemporary American Hasidic Community*, Jason Aronson, Northvale, NJ, 1995

Kuzmack, Linda, *Woman's Cause: The Jewish Women's Movement in England and the United States, 1881–1933*, Ohio State University, Columbus, Ohio, 1990

Lamm, M., *The Jewish Way in Death and Mourning*, Jonathan David Publishing, New York, 1969

Lamm, M., *The Jewish Way in Love and Marriage*, Harper and Row, New York, 1980

Las, N., *Jewish Women in a Changing World: A History of the International Council of Jewish Women, 1899–1995*, The Avraham Harman Institute of Contemporary Jewry, Jerusalem, 1996

Lowenthal, M. (ed.), *Henrietta Szold: Her Life and Letters*, Greenwood Press, Connecticut, 1975

Malmgreen, G., *Religion in the Lives of English Women, 1760–1930*, Indiana University Press, 1986

Marcus, J., *The American Jewish Woman, 1654–1980*, KTAV, New York, 1981

Marcus, J., *The American Jewish Woman: A Documentary History*, KTAV/American Jewish Archives, 1981

Masnik, A., *The Jewish Woman: An Annotated Selected Bibliography, 1986–1993*, Biblio Press, New York, 1996

McBride, J., *The Color of Water*, Riverhead Books, New York, 1996

Memoirs of Glückel of Hameln, Schocken, New York, 1977

Miller, Y., *In Search of the Jewish Woman*, Feldheim, New York, 1984

Mintz, J., *Legends of the Hasidim*, University of Chicago Press, Chicago, 1986

Ochs, V., *Words on Fire: One Woman's Journey into the Sacred*, Harcourt Brace Jovanovich, San Diego, 1990

Patai, R., *On Jewish Folklore*, Wayne State University Press, Detroit, 1983

Pogrebin, L., *Deborah, Golda and Me*, Crown, New York, 1992

Porter, J. (ed.), *Women in Chains: A Sourcebook of the Agunah*, Jason Aronson, Northvale, NJ, 1995

Priesand, S., *Judaism and the Modern Woman*, Behrman House, New York, 1975

Rabinowicz, H., *A World Apart: The Story of the Chassidim in Britain*, Vallentine Mitchell, London, 1997

Riskin, S., *Women and Jewish Divorce: The Rebellious Wife, the* Agunah *and the Right of Women to Initiate Divorce in Jewish Law: A* Halakhic *Solution*, KTAV, Hoboken, NJ, 1989

Rittner, C. and Roth, J. (eds), *Different Voices: Women and the Holocaust*, Paragon, New York, 1993

Roiphe, A., *Lovingkindness*, Summitt Books, New York, 1987

Rubin, D., *Daughters of Destiny: Women Who Revolutionized Jewish Life and* Torah *Education*, Mesorah Publications, New York, 1988

Sabar, Y. (trans. and ed.), *The Folk Literature of the Kurdistani Jews: An Anthology*, Yale University Press, New Haven, 1982

Schneider, S. Weidman, *Jewish and Female*, Simon and Schuster, New York, 1984

Scult, M., *A Biography of Mordechai M. Kaplan*, Wayne State University Press, Detroit, 1994

Seidman, N., *A Marriage Made in Heaven: The Sexual Politics of Hebrew and Yiddish*, University of California Press, Berkeley, 1997

Sefer Hasidim, Marguiles edition, Mossad Harav Kook, 1973

Sered, S. Starr, *Women as Ritual Experts: The Religious Lives of Elderly Jewish Women in Jerusalem*, Oxford University Press, New York, 1992

Shargel, D., *Lost Love: The Untold Story of Henrietta Szold: from her Journal and Letters*, Jewish Publication Society, Philadelphia, 1997

Shepherd, N., *A Price Below Rubies: Jewish Women as Rebels and Radicals*, Weidenfeld and Nicolson, London, 1993

Sheridan, S. (ed.), *Hear Our Voice: Women Rabbis Tell Their Story*, SCM Press, London, 1994

Solotaroff, T. and Rapoport, N. (ed.), *The Schocken Book of Contemporary Jewish Fiction*, Schocken Books, New York, 1992

Strassfield, S. and Strassfield, M., *The Second Jewish Catalogue*, Jewish Publication Society, Philadelphia, 1976

Summers A., *Damned Whores and God's Police*, Penguin, London, 1975

Swirski, B. and Safir, M., *Calling the Equality Bluff: Women in Israel*, Pergamon Press, New York, 1991

Tarnor, N., *A Book of Jewish Women's Prayers: Translations from the Yiddish*, Jason Aronson, Northvale, NJ, 1992

Umansky, E. & Ashton, D., *Four Centuries of Jewish Women's Spirituality*, Beacon Press, Boston, 1991

Wagenknecht, E., *Daughters of the Covenant: Portraits of Six Jewish Women*, University of Massachusetts Press, Amherst, 1983

Waxman, M., *A History of Jewish Literature, Volume 2: From the Twelfth Century to the Middle of the Eighteenth Century*, Bloch Publishing, New York, 1933

Weiss, A., *Women and Prayer: A* Halachic *Analysis of Women's Prayer Groups*, KTAV, Hoboken, NJ, 1991

Weiss Halivni, D., *The Sword and The Book*, Farrar Strauss & Giroux, New York, 1996

Winkler, G., *They Called Her Rebbe*, Judaica Press, New York, 1990

Wolowelsky, J., *Women, Jewish Law and Modernity: New Opportunities in a Post-Feminist Age*, KTAV, Hoboken, NJ, 1997

Yalom, I., *When Nietzsche Wept: A Novel of Obsession*, HarperCollins, New York, 1992

Yamani, M. (ed.), *Feminism and Islam*, Ithaca Press, Reading, 1996

Young, S., *An Anthology of Sacred Texts by and about Women*, Pandora HarperCollins, London, 1993

Zemon Davis, N., *Women on the Margins: Three Seventeenth-Century Lives*, Harvard University Press, Cambridge, 1996

Zinberg, I., *History of Jewish Literature, Volume 7: Old Yiddish Literature from its Origins to the Haskalah Period*, KTAV, New York, 1975

Zolty, S., *And All Your Children Shall be Learned: Women and the Study of Torah in Jewish Law and History*, Jason Aronson, Northvale, NJ, 1993